PROMISED LANDS

PROMISED LANDS

*Hadassah Kaplan and the Legacy of
American Jewish Women in Early
Twentieth-Century Palestine*

Sharon Ann Musher

NEW YORK UNIVERSITY PRESS
New York

NEW YORK UNIVERSITY PRESS
New York
www.nyupress.org

© 2025 by New York University
All rights reserved

Please contact the Library of Congress for Cataloging-in-Publication data.

ISBN: 9781479832743 (hardback)
ISBN: 9781479832798 (library ebook)
ISBN: 9781479832781 (consumer ebook)

This book is printed on acid-free paper, and its binding materials are chosen for strength and durability. We strive to use environmentally responsible suppliers and materials to the greatest extent possible in publishing our books.

Manufactured in the United States of America

10 9 8 7 6 5 4 3 2 1

Also available as an ebook

*To my daughters,
Elena, Ariella, and Rachel,
with love and admiration*

CONTENTS

Cast of Characters   ix

Introduction: Reconstructing Hadassah   1

1. Choosing to Go   15

2. The Attraction   41

3. The Journey   64

4. Getting Settled   90

5. Finding Her Way   118

6. Returning Home   152

Conclusion: Israel on My List   181

Acknowledgments   197

Notes   201

Bibliography   231

Index   247

About the Author   263

CAST OF CHARACTERS

HADASSAH KAPLAN'S FAMILY

Albert Addelston: A lawyer and born-and-bred New Yorker whom Mordecai Kaplan's eldest daughter, Judith, briefly married in the summer of 1932. They divorced the following summer.

Ira Eisenstein: A rabbi, a scholar, a disciple of Mordecai Kaplan, and Judith's second husband (they married in 1934). Ira shared the pulpit of the Society for the Advancement of Judaism (SAJ) with Mordecai for more than twenty years. In 1968, he founded the Reconstructionist Rabbinical College in Philadelphia.

Miriam Eisenstein: The eldest daughter of Judith and Ira Eisenstein's three children, Ethan, Miriam, and Ann. Miriam served as an attorney in the Civil Rights Division of the Department of Justice from 1969 to 1999.

Hadassah Kaplan (Musher): The second daughter of Mordecai and Lena Kaplan. She was a teacher, a lay leader, and a philanthropist, contributing especially to her father's synagogue, the SAJ, the Reconstructionist Foundation and Rabbinical College, and Hebrew University. She married Sidney Musher, and they had three sons.

Judith Kaplan (Eisenstein): The eldest daughter of Mordecai and Lena Kaplan. At twelve and a half years old, she became the first bat mitzvah. She was a teacher and composer of Jewish songs, who earned a PhD in musicology when she was in her fifties.

Mordecai Kaplan: A Lithuanian-born, New York–educated rabbi who founded an American form of Judaism, known as Reconstructionism, and a synagogue devoted to that approach: the SAJ. He married Lena Rubin, and they had four daughters: Judith, Hadassah, Naomi, and Selma.

Lena (Rubin) Kaplan: One of nine siblings who migrated to New York, she was a two-year-old when they made the journey from Mishitz, Germany. Lena married Mordecai Kaplan, raised their daughters, and served as a Jewish lay leader who was especially active at her husband's synagogue, the SAJ, and with the Jewish Zionist organization Hadassah.

Naomi Kaplan (Wenner): The third daughter of Mordecai and Lena Kaplan. During the 1930s, she attended medical school at the American University of Beirut. She became a psychiatrist, psychoanalyst, sculptor, and—along with her husband, Seymour Wenner—parent to two sons.

Selma Kaplan (Goldman): Named after Solomon Schechter, Selma was the youngest of the Kaplans' daughters. She taught, raised two children, and—with her first husband, the entertainment lawyer Saul Jaffe—produced a TV version of Thornton Wilder's *Our Town*.

HADASSAH KAPLAN'S FRIENDS

Esther "Sis" Callner: A twenty-nine-year-old Jewish woman from Chicago whom Hadassah met on the ship to Palestine. One of Sis's brothers married a sister of Rose Gell Jacobs, who chaperoned both Hadassah and Sis.

Zadoc Chelouche: A married, thirty-five-year-old Sephardic man who was born in North Carolina but migrated to Palestine as a child with his family. Hadassah befriended him while traveling back to New York through Europe. The two spent time together in Tripoli, Beirut, and London.

Sylva Gelber: A Canadian Jew who attended Camp Modin with Hadassah and traveled to Palestine shortly after Hadassah arrived. She remained there for fifteen years, working as a social worker, before returning in 1947 to Canada, where she became a leading women's rights advocate.

Simon and Minnie Halkin: Simon was a Russian-born poet. He and his wife, Minnie, who was from the Bronx, spent considerable time with Hadassah on the beaches of Tel Aviv in the spring of 1933. Simon, who eventually chaired Hebrew University's Hebrew Literature program, was also the brother of Abe, Hadassah's Hebrew tutor in New York before her travels.

Reba Isaacson: A contemporary of Hadassah's who attended the SAJ, Hebrew school, Camp Modin, and Hunter College with her. Reba became a musician and a visual artist.

Miriam Kronick: A Canadian friend of Hadassah's whom she knew from Camp Modin. Miriam, known as "Kronick," was living in Tel Aviv with her mother when Hadassah arrived.

Joel Lipsky: Another friend of Hadassah's, Joel—who later changed his name to Carmichael—was the third son of Louis Lipsky, a writer, translator, and American Zionist leader.

Ted Lurie: This friend of Hadassah's was born in New York and educated at Cornell University before moving to Palestine, where he worked as

Gershon Agronsky's assistant at the *Palestine Post*. He eventually became editor of the by then renamed *Jerusalem Post*.

Helen Schwartz: Another Canadian friend of Hadassah's from Camp Modin. She was already in Palestine when Hadassah arrived, and the two frequently traveled together, including their journey home through Europe chaperoned by Helen's mother.

Van W. Knox: A non-Jewish architect whom Hadassah and her compatriot Reba befriended on the *Exochorda*, the ship they sailed to Palestine.

HADASSAH KAPLAN'S BEAUS

Al Ginsberg: A Jewish lawyer originally from St. Paul, Minnesota, who lived in New York, where he attended the SAJ before traveling abroad. Hadassah spent time with him in Haifa, Paris, and London.

Alvan "Read" Henry: A non-Jewish, American son of an international judge whom Hadassah became acquainted with on the boat to Palestine. "Read" was heading to Alexandria, Egypt, to spend a year with his parents before returning to Yale University to finish his studies.

Harry Joffe: A boyfriend of Hadassah's living in Tel Aviv. He was born in South Africa.

Ralph Lieberman: The older brother of Hadassah's friend Rose Lieberman. Ralph and Hadassah dated in New York before she went to Palestine.

David Magnes: The son of the Zionist, Reform rabbi, and founder of Hebrew University Judah Magnes and Beatrice Lowenstein Magnes, a founder of the Jewish Zionist women's organization Hadassah.

Sidney Musher: An inventor and philanthropist who grew up in Washington, DC, and attended Johns Hopkins University on a scholarship. His achievements include the creation of synthetic baby formulas and identifying the healing properties in Aveeno bath soaps. He retired at the age of sixty and devoted himself full-time for the next twenty-five years to managing and directing the Palestine Endowment Fund. In 1935, Sidney and Hadassah married. They had three sons, including my father, David.

Jacob "Jack" Simon: Hadassah befriended Jack at the end of her journey to Palestine. He was a United Press correspondent and the American council general.

John "Jack" Wilner Sundelson: A PhD student in public finance at Columbia University who dated Hadassah, whom he called "Elsa," before she went to Palestine.

FRIENDS AND COLLEAGUES OF HADASSAH KAPLAN'S PARENTS

Gershon Agronsky (Agron): A journalist who founded an English daily newspaper, the *Palestine Post*, which, in 1950, became the *Jerusalem Post*. Agron, as he later became known, also served as mayor of Jerusalem from 1955 until his death in 1959.

Libbie Suchoff Berkson: A Jewish educator trained by Mordecai Kaplan and also a colleague of his at Teachers' Institute. "Aunt Libbie," as she was known, ran Camp Modin along with her husband, Isaac B. Berkson. She was one of Hadassah's chaperones during her year abroad.

Sam Dinin: A Jewish educator and student of Mordecai Kaplan who played a key role in building foundational institutions of American Jewish education, including the Board of Jewish Education, the University of Judaism, and Camp Ramah in Ojai. Hadassah traveled through Europe with him on her way back to New York.

Julia Aronson and Alexander Dushkin: Julia trained as a nutritionist at Cornell University, was part of the inner circle of Henrietta Szold (founder of the organization Hadassah), and acted as one of Hadassah's chaperones. Alexander was a student of Mordecai Kaplan's and an influential Jewish educator who built Chicago's Board of Jewish Education, the School of Education at Hebrew University, and Camp Modin.

Sarah (Baum) and Edward Epstein: Sarah was an active member of the organization Hadassah. Her husband, Edward, was a wholesaler of men's sportswear. The couple, who were the Kaplans' friends and the parents of three children, were initially to have chaperoned Hadassah. They, however, left New York for Palestine after she did.

Lillian Ruth Bentwich Friedlander: A widowed friend and colleague of the Kaplans who, with her children, moved from New York City to Palestine after the murder, in 1920, of her husband, Israel Friedlander, a biblical scholar at Kaplan's Teachers' Institute, on an American Jewish Joint Distribution Committee relief mission in the Ukraine. Lillian served as one of Hadassah's mentors in Jerusalem.

Anna Grossman Sherman: A Palestinian-born Jewish educator raised in New York City who studied and then taught with Mordecai Kaplan at Teachers' Institute. Anna moved to Palestine with her husband, Earl, and had her first of three children in Jerusalem the year that Hadassah visited. Anna also functioned as an adviser to Hadassah.

Abe Halkin: A colleague of Mordecai Kaplan's at the Jewish Theological Seminary and a professor of Semitics. Abe was also Hadassah's Hebrew teacher in New York City and the brother of one of her friends in Palestine, Simon Halkin.

Rose Gell Jacobs: Part of Henrietta Szold's original study circle in New York City, Rose served as a national president of the organization Hadassah, worked on Youth Aliya, and was instrumental in establishing Hadassah Hospital on Mt. Scopus. Rose chaperoned Hadassah Kaplan, traveling with her on the boat to Palestine.

Joseph Klausner: A professor of Hebrew literature and history at Hebrew University whom Mordecai Kaplan and the SAJ supported in his work as editor of a Hebrew monthly magazine *Hashiloach* and with whom Hadassah aspired to study when she was in Palestine.

Esther Lamport: A friend and congregant of the Kaplans whose daughter Felicia in 1928 shared a bat mitzvah at the SAJ with the youngest Kaplan daughter, Selma. Esther lived in a pension in Tel Aviv when Hadassah was in Palestine and frequently hosted her.

Joseph and Esther Levy: Joseph was raised in Palestine and educated at the American University in Beirut. Fluent in both Hebrew and Arabic, he was the Palestine correspondent for the *New York Times* from 1929 to 1939. His wife, Esther, was a New Yorker and a congregant of Mordecai Kaplan's SAJ.

Irma Lindheim: A fund-raiser, educator, and president of the organization Hadassah who migrated to Palestine in 1933 as a forty-seven-year-old widow and mother of five. She returned to the US in the mid-1960s and designed family-centered educational programs.

Judah Magnes: A San Francisco–born Reform rabbi who was both a pulpit rabbi and a Jewish communal leader before moving in 1922 to Palestine, where he built and led Hebrew University as chancellor and then president. Judah also was a leading binationalist, founding Brit Shalom and the Ihud Association, which advocated for the creation of an Arab-Jewish state and reconciliation between the two peoples.

Jessie Sampter: A queer, disabled, Jewish female educator of German descent who grew up in New York City, where she studied with Mordecai Kaplan, before migrating to Palestine. She eventually settled in Kibbutz Givat Brenner.

Bertha and Albert Schoolman: Both Bertha and Albert were students of Mordecai Kaplan's, members of his congregation, Jewish educators, and founders of Camps Cejwin and Modin. Bertha was active in the organization Hadassah and Youth Aliya. She was one of Hadassah's chaperones on the ship to Palestine and continued to advise her during the year.

Henrietta Szold: Founded and directed Hadassah, an American Jewish women's organization dedicated to providing social and especially health services to women and children in Palestine regardless of their religion or ethnicity. Henrietta was also a graduate-school classmate of Mordecai Kaplan's and a close friend.

Frieda Schiff Warburg: A Jewish philanthropist married to the German American banker Felix Warburg. Felix and Frieda were patrons of Mordecai Kaplan's synagogue, the SAJ. Frieda was active in the Jewish Theological Seminary, the American Jewish Joint Distribution Committee, Hadassah, and the Henry Street Settlement.

David Yellin: A linguist born in Jerusalem who led the movement for Hebrew speaking and education in Palestine. Toward that end, David trained educators to teach Hebrew at his Hebrew Teachers' Seminary in Jerusalem.

Introduction

Reconstructing Hadassah

In the spring of 2013, just after the funeral of my 101-year-old grandmother, Hadassah, I found myself pulling open the small drawers of her elegant, wooden-nook desk looking to recover traces of the vivacious woman she had been before dementia overshadowed her final years. Tucked inside a mail-order catalogue between the sections on sweatshirts and bras, I came across a letter dated April 6, 1925, from her father, Mordecai Kaplan. My great-grandfather was the founder of a modern, American-based Jewish ideology called Reconstructionism. He was best known for pioneering the idea of a Jewish community center and initiating—with his eldest daughter, Judith—the bat mitzvah, a now-more-than-century-old Jewish right of passage for girls. In his note written in English and sent from Jerusalem, Mordecai apologized to his wife, Lena, for not corresponding more but explained that existing between two languages—English and Hebrew—made him inarticulate. He told her that he had just delivered a Hebrew lecture on "the nature of the Jewish self consciousness" at the opening ceremony for Hebrew University and promised, when he returned to New York, to translate a detailed account from his Hebrew diary, which he had recorded five days earlier.[1]

I wondered what other gems were squirreled away among my grandmother's papers. I knew that her father's papers, including the diaries he kept for sixty-two years, had been preserved in the archives of the Reconstructionist Rabbinical College (RRC) and the Jewish Theological Seminary (JTS).[2] It was unclear what personal correspondence remained in Hadassah's possession, how much she herself had written, and if that material would interest anyone beyond my family. Still, I asked my parents, as they sorted through her records, to keep an eye out for her datebooks from the year she spent in Palestine in the early 1930s as a nineteen-year-old New Yorker.

Grandma first talked to me about that year in 1994. We spent a lot of time together that summer in her log cabin in Fairfield, Connecticut. I had just finished college and was heading to graduate school to study history. At eighty-two, she still stayed up late, drove fast, beat me at tennis, skinny-dipped regularly (her friends knew never to show up unannounced), and could distinguish a blue jay from a northern cardinal by their songs. Sitting on her screened porch, listening to classical music and working through a stack of newspapers, journals, and books, we read and talked late into many nights. In my green leather journal, I recorded some of our conversations, especially about her life when she was just a few years younger than I was at the time.

Like many young, Jewish women of her generation, Hadassah wanted to be a teacher. When she was fifteen and a half, she entered Hunter College, a tuition-free, public secondary and teacher-training school known as the "Jewish Girls' Radcliffe," the female counterpart to Harvard University. After three years, Hadassah graduated with a teaching certificate. Shortly before she was to begin her second year of teaching, in the middle of August 1932, her supervisor informed her that the school would not rehire her. Hadassah's prospects for finding work were slim. For the next two years, school officials banned all new hiring. They also furloughed teachers, slashed wages, instituted loyalty oaths, and spread out the remaining work among substitutes, offering such positions to unemployed men before even considering the plethora of trained women.[3]

Without a job or a life partner, Hadassah decided that it would be a "grand thing" to go to Palestine. Her cousins Dorothy and Naomi Rubin laughed at her; nevertheless, she recalled her parents similarly resolving, during a Sabbath walk, that she should spend the year abroad.[4] Over the next ten days, Hadassah bought a one-way ticket, found chaperones and a friend to travel with, packed her bag, and boarded the *Exochorda* bound for Jaffa. She spent nine months living in Jerusalem, studying Hebrew, and traveling through mandatory Palestine and then two months returning through the Middle East and Europe.

When Grandma described her year abroad to me, I assumed that she had documented it as she continued to chronicle her comings and goings throughout her life. I was familiar with her minuscule handwriting in tiny, hardcover datebooks issued by Jewish institutions connected to her father, first the Society for the Advancement of Judaism (SAJ) and later the Jewish Reconstructionist Federation.[5] I wondered what—if any—insights the presumably sparse records she had kept would provide into her travels and their meaning. I expected them to hold facts about her daily life—where she had gone, with whom, and what she had done—rather than introspection.

Women's history and the history of those who did not hold significant public positions is often dismissed and quite literally discarded. When the task of sorting through the fragments of a life fall to an overextended younger generation, it is rare that such papers are preserved. Organizing them takes time, valuable space is required for storage, and, even then, flooding or other natural disasters often destroy them. Social and oral historians have long endeavored to record, preserve, and make accessible a range of records and, through them, experiences. Digitization and a renewed movement to draw attention to the histories of the underrepresented have furthered such efforts. Nevertheless, traditional archives—especially national ones—have tended to conserve political records that highlight the deeds and actions of those (often white men) who held major power and influence.[6]

Searching for the voices of women and underrepresented people in archives often entails reading documents against the grain. Mordecai's diaries, for example, rarely comment on his family life; instead, they record his ideas and events connected to Judaism, synagogue life, professional meetings, and his career.[7] His youngest daughter, Selma, described herself as having been "born in the margins."[8] I would later find that the brief entry marking her birth and explaining that she was named after Solomon Schechter was, indeed, in the body of the journal's text, but generally the diaries focus on Mordecai's intellectual and political more than personal struggles.[9] In contrast, I imagined that Grandma's cryptic datebooks might provide a window into the private realm, insights into the operations of a house full of strong women, including the ways that they influenced their father's thinking. Reading between the lines, as the historian Laurel Thatcher Ulrich had done with the much-rarer diary of an eighteenth-century midwife, Martha Ballard, I aspired to uncover and make accessible to contemporary readers an intimate portrait of Hadassah's world, her family, and the women with whom she traveled.[10]

The young woman who emerges from both my memory and the record eventually uncovered was strikingly beautiful, a blue-eyed brunette

Figure I.1. Hadassah Kaplan, Beirut, Lebanon, June 1933. (Personal collection)

with a dazzling smile whose exuberance was magnetic. On Hadassah's 1932 passport, she listed herself as five foot six, but her substantial heels made her appear taller before age began to erode her physical stature and sneakers became her staple footwear. Although she was the daughter of immigrants, she was a born-and-bred New Yorker without an easily discernable accent. She was an athlete, a social dancer, a lover of theater, art, and movies, and an extrovert. She was also a letter writer throughout her life, intermittently, a keeper of diaries, and an archivist of family records.[11] She maintained particularly thick documentation of her year abroad. In addition to terse datebooks, she saved her correspondence with her three sisters and parents as well as their responses to her, meticulously labeled photographs, a composition book in Hebrew and English, a detailed budget, and even receipts.

Such records provide a window into the role that a Jewish homeland played in the imagination of American Jewish women in the early twentieth century, before such connections became normative. In traveling to Palestine, Hadassah joined a cohort of risk-taking young women in challenging cultural conventions, including an emphasis on domesticity, while simultaneously reinforcing their connections to family and community. For women with the means to travel, spending time in Palestine could serve as an agent of change. It provided an informal education that enhanced knowledge, skills, and a sense of autonomy, helping them to modernize and perform new types of Jewish identities. Such women might pursue adventure, learning, and meaningful work (both paid and voluntary). They might challenge barriers based on race, class, and religion, experiment with alternative gender roles, and explore unconventional and subversive ideological commitments. At the same time, they could maintain and develop Jewish connections by contributing to the revival of the Hebrew language, the upbuilding of a Jewish homeland, and the development of a creative Jewish culture, including music, art, and dance. Furthermore, since few of them would settle permanently in Palestine, most of them would return to the United States with a strengthened connection to Palestine and later Israel that for many shaped the rest of their personal lives, as well as their families, synagogues, and communities. In short, spending time in Palestine helped individuals like Hadassah to become a new type of American Jewish woman: a sophisticated individual who adeptly negotiated between old and new worlds. It also provided a language—both literally and metaphorically—to make Jewish life vibrant personally and for the next generation. Travel and time spent abroad empowered American Jewish women to share their love of learning, language, and the arts and to draw attention to what would become Israeli culture as they endeavored to build lives of meaning for themselves, their families, and their community. It enabled them to use what is sometimes dismissed as "women's work"—teaching, event organizing, and other forms of volunteering—to shape American Jewish institutions and communities as well as to forge an American Judaism that would become increasingly recognizable in the aftermath of World War II: one connecting American Jews with Israel.

Before the founding of the State of Israel in 1948, Zionism meant a range of different things to those, like Hadassah, who identified with it. Some people—both Jews and Christians—were drawn to the notion of a Jewish homeland in Palestine; others advocated for one elsewhere.[12] Those who were influenced by the Austrian journalist and organizer Theodor Herzl saw a Jewish state as a political solution to the "Jewish Problem": the persistence of antisemitism. Ongoing persecution was evident in pogroms, organized mass violence targeting Jewish men, women, and children, which emerged in the 1880s and intensified in the early twentieth century with attacks in Kishinev (1903), Odessa (1905), and Ukraine (1918 and 1919). In addition to brutality, anti-Jewish sentiment endured even in liberal democracies. In a nationalist era, Zionism appeared to counter aggression and exclusion by offering Jews a redemptive narrative of personal and communal emancipation. With their own land, government, and language, political Zionists rejected the diaspora, exile, and victimization for newly liberated Jewish culture, society, and selves.[13]

In contrast to those who turned to Palestine to combat the "Jewish Problem" of persistent antisemitism, Hadassah and her family looked to it to solve the "Problem of Judaism": Why should emancipated Jews, especially those who lived in liberal democracies like the United States, retain their Jewish identity as they embraced a national one? Many Jews influenced by the Enlightenment (Haskalah), civic emancipation, and participation in US democracy chose to assimilate into the majority culture. By the early twentieth century, few who had the freedom to identify as they wished decided to embrace the Jewish traditions they inherited. To them, Judaism did not provide a path for living fulfilling lives in a modern world. Instead, they turned to the country where they dwelt and its Christian mores to find personal growth and communal engagement. Assuming that integration and assimilation were possible for American Jews, Hadassah's father feared the challenges offered by freedom, more than those resulting from discrimination. Mordecai assumed that American Jews would reconcile their twoness, as both Americans and Jews, by rejecting Jewish practice for twentieth-century American Protestantism.

To counter such assimilation and remain salient, Mordecai argued that Judaism needed a cultural and spiritual renaissance. As a pulpit rabbi, he strove to revive Judaism by turning the synagogues he served into community centers where people would dance, sing (preferably in Hebrew), make and appreciate Jewish art, and even swim and play basketball together. But he wanted those communities to do more than provide cultural sustenance. Mordecai was deeply committed to the fostering of a spiritual renaissance. For fifty years, he taught homiletics, Bible, and interpretation to Jewish educators at the Teachers' Institute of the Conservative movement's Jewish Theological Seminary. Mordecai trained generations of Jewish teachers within an experiential, student-centered, and communitarian pedagogy that used language, art, music, dance, and literature to shape and sustain Jewish creativity and consciousness.[14] Part of his approach was to amend traditional laws to counter gender-based religious, legal, and civic inequities. Mordecai's initiation of egalitarian rituals, including the bat mitzvah, fit into the mission of recognizing Judaism as a "living social process, in which the right to ... legislate anew is accepted as organic to the very life of the Jewish people and as the guarantee of its future."[15]

Mordecai's reconstructionist vision, however, required more than synagogues, Hebrew schools, and community centers in New York City to thrive. Influenced by the Russian-born, spiritual Zionist Ahad Ha'am, Mordecai believed that an evolving Jewish civilization needed a homeland in Palestine to remake the Jewish people and forge a new type of Jewish nation. He envisioned that physical center as a source of cultural, ethical, and religious values.[16] Rather than serving as a marker of difference and an impediment to happiness, Judaism physically grounded in a homeland, he contended, would forge ethical beings and inspire self-realization. Mordecai understood a Jewish homeland as a source of spiritual and cultural revitalization that could help Jews live meaningful lives not only in Palestine but throughout the diaspora.[17] According to his biographer Mel Scult, Mordecai was so devoted to Zionism that he nearly called his approach "Zionist Judaism" rather than Reconstructionism.[18]

Reviving Hebrew as a modern language represented an important vehicle for reinvigorating the evolving Jewish civilization that Mordecai described. For more than two thousand years, Hebrew had served as a language for prayer, literature, and study but not a spoken tongue. In the early twentieth century, Jews tended to communicate in their local vernacular or a dialect based on the area from which they came. In Mordecai's home on the Upper West Side of Manhattan, Hadassah and her sisters grew up speaking English, but most New York Jews from eastern Europe, Ashkenazim, spoke Yiddish, a German dialect incorporating many languages. In contrast, Sephardim, descendants of Iberian Jews who either converted to Catholicism or left Spain after the expulsion of 1492, generally spoke Ladino, a Judeo-Spanish language, or Arabic. Jews living in Palestine, like those in the diaspora, were polyglots. In 1912, 43 percent of Tel Aviv residents reported that they spoke Hebrew,

35 percent Yiddish, 11 percent Russian, and the remainder a combination of French, English, Ladino, Arabic, and German. After World War I, the Allies divided the territory, including Palestine, that the defeated Ottoman Empire had controlled since the early sixteenth century. In 1922, the Council of the League of Nations approved Great Britain's Mandate over Palestine. That same year, the British recognized Hebrew alongside English and Arabic as the Mandate's official languages. Nevertheless, a survey by the World Zionist Organization found that Yiddish was spoken in more Palestinian Jewish households than Hebrew was. A Tower of Babel could be found in British Mandate Palestine, where linguistic chaos predominated between Jewish diasporic complexity and an overwhelming majority of Arabic speakers.[19]

Reclaiming Hebrew as a spoken language within this multilingual reality had required deliberate efforts, such as those engaged in by the Kaplans. Beginning in the 1880s, the Lithuanian-born lexicologist Eliezer Ben-Yehuda developed a modern Hebrew vocabulary in partnership with his family, reviving a language that had not been the vernacular since biblical times. Ben-Yehuda oversaw a Hebrew Language Committee, which sought to regulate and spread Hebrew usage and recruited teachers to train a younger generation in the emerging language. This cohort worked to make Hebrew into Palestine's vernacular. They understood the revived ancient tongue as a cultural tool to unite multilingual Jews, tie them to the biblical land of Israel, and foster their sense of nationhood.[20] By the 1920s, learning Hebrew by only speaking it—Ivrit b'Ivrit—had become the norm at Mordecai's Teachers' Institute, even as both teachers and students struggled to master the language. The Kaplan girls studied Hebrew at Hebrew school, at camp, and with tutors. But attitudes toward Hebrew's revival—and how such revitalization should occur—were not uniform. Some Hebraists, such as the Jewish scholar Simon Rawidowicz, disconnected the language from Zionism, viewing its restoration, even more than the formation of a Jewish homeland, as facilitating collective identity and creativity.[21] Others, particularly refugees living in Palestine who struggled to acclimate to a new land they had not necessarily chosen, saw efforts to make them speak only in Hebrew as a negation of their past.[22]

Like Ben-Yehuda, Kaplan and his family were unusual in their attitude toward Hebrew and Palestine. During the interwar period, few

Americans identified as Zionists, much less studied modern Hebrew. Many Orthodox Jews viewed Zionism as a pseudomessianic and heretical effort to end exile and hasten redemption.[23] Reform Jews insisted that the United States was "our Zion." Socialists understood Zionism to be bourgeois, and Yiddishists objected to it for invalidating the diaspora. Anti-Zionism also reigned outside the Jewish world among State Department officials, missionaries, educators, Arab Americans, and communists. Christian writers charged American Zionists with "dual nationality, allegiance, and hyphenism."[24] And liberal antisemites "railed against Zionism, . . . label[ling it] racist, separatist, un-American, communistic, anti-gentile, exploitative, and a creature of world Jewish money."[25]

But Hadassah, influenced by her father, teachers, and mentors, envisioned spending time in Palestine, studying Hebrew, traveling, and reporting on her experiences as a vehicle for engaging in meaningful work and contributing to her father's mission. From an early age, Judith, Hadassah's older sister, had assumed the psychological mantle of her father's eldest son and protégé. Even Judith's career as a Jewish composer and music teacher, which she began at age fifteen, aligned with her father's goals of reconstructing Judaism. Hadassah, in contrast, was more social and less cerebral than her older sister was. Her younger sisters, Naomi and Selma, were still in college, where each exhibited significant talents and determination and where they would continue to find guidance from committed teachers and advisers. But as an unemployed Hunter College graduate with a teaching certificate, Hadassah had less established mentorship in place as she tried to figure out her next step.

Traveling to Palestine offered a productive way for an adventurous young woman like Hadassah to explore the world. Hadassah was part of a relatively small but influential group of somewhat unconventional American Jewish women who studied, worked, volunteered, traveled, and occasionally settled permanently in Palestine. By contributing to the development of a living Judaism, such women could challenge cultural norms while remaining so-called good Jewish daughters, wives, and mothers. They played a disproportionately large role both in Palestine's evolution and also in shaping the next generation's attitude toward a Jewish homeland, by making Zionism central to American Jewish education, institutions, and identity. This book traces what motivated

Hadassah to go to Palestine, her transatlantic journey, her adjustment to life in Jerusalem, and her efforts to remain a devoted daughter while experimenting with collective living and testing the boundaries of socially permissible behavior and political ideologies, including socialism and feminism. The story unfolds largely through Hadassah's archive— the letters, diaries, and photos she kept. Framing her choices are the perspectives of her parents, sisters, peers, and contemporaries.

The Palestine found in Hadassah's archive is a world of relative quiet despite tumultuous times. In the newspapers, she follows news of Hitler becoming chancellor of Germany that January. When she travels through Europe, she occasionally reports having heard about book burnings. Unlike her contemporary Ruth Gruber, the soon-to-be foreign correspondent who studied in 1931 in Germany, where she was acutely aware of rising antisemitism, Hadassah appears to have remained largely blind to the looming trauma.[26] She does not discuss family or close friends who are trying to escape Nazi Germany, nor does she appear to interact with new European refugees in Palestine. Additionally, she is not particularly attuned to growing Arab nationalism. When she uses the term "Palestinians," she refers only to Jews living in the land. And she rarely encounters British officers, much less comments on their inability to resolve dual claims by Jews and Arabs for national self-determination.

Hadassah's travels reveal less about the lived experiences of people in British Mandate Palestine and Europe in the buildup to World War II than they do about a perceived role that Jewish women and Zionism might play in reviving American Jewry. Her archive offers a peek into the options available for venturesome, young, American Jewish women in New York City coming of age following women's suffrage. It suggests that—for those who were able—visiting Palestine and traveling more generally offered a vehicle for personal autonomy and self-expression within socially acceptable parameters. Hadassah's story also contributes to literature gendering Zionism and examining the lives and legacies of previously little-remembered women travelers.[27]

The connection between American Jewish women and Palestine— like my grandmother herself—was not without controversy. Palestine during the interwar period was not an empty land waiting for Jewish settlement and a Hebrew cultural renaissance. Although a small, indigenous Jewish population had long lived in Palestine, the majority of the land's inhabitants were non-Jewish Arabs. One year before Hadassah's travels, the 1931 Census of Palestine recorded that nearly 85 percent of Palestinians were Muslim or Christian, whereas only 17 percent, or 174,610 people, were Jewish. The majority of Arab Palestinians were rural inhabitants and subsistence farmers struggling with a global depression, poor agricultural yields, a growing Jewish population, and strong incentives for small Arab landowners to sell their property to Jews. Indeed, despite efforts by the mandatory government to limit Jewish immigration and prohibit land transfer to Jews, the Jewish population in Palestine more than doubled, from 164,000 in 1930 to 370,000 in 1936. That same decade, Jews acquired 300,000 dunam, or more than 74,000 acres, in Palestine. The Mandate's demographics made a roadmap to a Jewish state nearly inconceivable the year Hadassah spent in Palestine. Although Arab Palestinians remained in the majority, they, nevertheless, objected to the growing Jewish presence in Palestine, seeing it as a threat to their own national self-determination.[28]

Hadassah's archive, like Mordecai's diaries, is limited by her worldview. Similar to most travelogues created by Westerners at the time, she drew on Orientalist stereotypes to describe Arabs in simplistic, and at times denigrating, ways that justified colonial hierarchy.[29] Wary that studying only one perspective can reproduce power dynamics, I endeavor to supplement Hadassah's story with alternative points of view.[30] I do not wish to whitewash or excuse her flaws or to build a monument to the travels of American Jewish women. Hadassah was a complex person, not a heroine, and her actions, along with those of her peers, had both intended and unintended consequences. This book aims to illuminate how Hadassah forged her life in the context of the constraints she faced and the opportunities she found and what lessons might be derived from such choices. I use Hadassah as a case study to explore what she and her peers expected, saw, and failed to register in Palestine, how their journey affected them, and how they impacted Palestine, the US, and the broader diaspora.

Hadassah's archive not only provides insight into the emerging relationship between American Jewish women and Palestine but also deepens our knowledge of Mordecai Kaplan and Reconstructionism. Few scholars have explored how Mordecai's family, including his wife and four bright, talented, and headstrong daughters, shaped his conception of the role of women in Judaism.[31] In particular, the struggles of Mordecai's daughters to articulate themselves and attain self-awareness informed his egalitarianism. Hadassah's experiences in Palestine also contributed to her father's thinking about Zionism, commitment to a Hebraist cultural renaissance, and desire to spend time in Palestine.

In discussing various members of the Kaplan family, I have frequently chosen to use first names. To some readers, it may appear jarring or disrespectful to refer to Rabbi Mordecai Menachem Kaplan, for example, simply as Mordecai, but I do not intend it in that way. If, like many books and archives, I used the name "Kaplan" to refer to Mordecai alone, then his wife, Lena, and four daughters—Judith, Hadassah, Naomi, and Selma—would become subsumed under their famous husband and father.[32] Relying on last names can also be confusing, given that many women of the generation I am describing chose to change their names after marriage. Instead, this story draws on first names to distinguish individuals from one another. Yet, occasionally, for stylistic purposes or if I am writing about only one individual within a family, I deploy last names or honorifics, such as "Rabbi," "Mr.," or "Mrs.," in telling the story.

* * *

When I first began thinking about this book, I was just a little older than my grandmother had been when she went to Palestine. I was drawn to Hadassah's story of her journey because I too was a young American Jewish woman who was about to travel and study abroad. It was also an optimistic moment, shortly after the signing of the Oslo Accords between Israel and the Palestine Liberation Organization (PLO), when the prospects of a two-state solution for Jews and Palestinians seemed viable and the assassination of Israeli Prime Minister Yitzhak Rabin unthinkable. I am now roughly the age that my great-grandmother Lena was when she encouraged her daughter to travel. I too have seen my eldest of three daughters, Elena, spend a post-COVID-19 gap year between high school and college traveling and working abroad, including two months on a kibbutz in Israel. Elena was born in the early 2000s during the Second Intifada, meaning Palestinian uprising or literally "shaking off," when disillusionment with the reality of life for Palestinians in the West Bank and Gaza Strip and the failures of Oslo led young Palestinian militants violently to resist occupation and the Israeli Defense Force (IDF) and Israeli settlers forcefully to suppress such unrest.

Elena and her sisters have witnessed the normalization of anti-Israel sentiment and the popularization of a settler-colonial discourse, which describes Zionism as a racist enterprise led by Jewish Europeans to eliminate native Palestinians and claim the land for themselves. Such critiques grew shriller—particularly across college campuses—as the Palestinian death toll rose exorbitantly in Israel's war in Gaza following the Palestinian militant group Hamas's horrific October 7, 2023, attack on Israeli communities along the border with Gaza, when it committed sex crimes, abducted nearly 250 hostages, and killed roughly 1,200 Israeli men, women, and children. In the current climate, criticism of Israel has moved far beyond college campuses. South Africa brought Israel to the United Nation's International Court of Justice (ICJ) on charges of having committed genocide, on the basis, in part, of racist statements by far-right Israeli politicians. Although the ICJ ruled against the claim, it, nevertheless, warned Israel that it needed to take measures to prevent genocide.

On the other hand, many American Jewish institutions, including synagogues, camps, Hebrew schools, and day schools, offer counternarratives that often romanticize Israel's foundational story and place much of the blame for the failure of peace negotiations on Palestinians. Their accounts typically ignore—or minimize—Palestinian perception of the founding of the State of Israel, which they consider a Nakba (catastrophe), and experiences of Israeli occupation. They also downplay the extremism of right-wing Israeli governments, which have incentivized the development of settlements, threatened permanently to occupy land Israel conquered in the Six-Day War of 1967, and often turned a blind eye to settler violence against Palestinians in the West Bank. Instead, American Jewish institutions tend to focus on growing antisemitism both on the right and on the left. Meanwhile, competing definitions of antisemitism and disagreements regarding the relationship between Zionism and antisemitism further complicate the situation.[33]

Much has changed for American Jews, women, and Israel since Hadassah's journey. Today, the American Jewish community is markedly more diverse, women have significantly more personal and professional opportunities, and American Jews have become increasingly divided over the notion and reality of a Jewish state. Some see Israel—and Jews more generally—in an existential crisis for survival in the context of growing antisemitism. Others view Jewish power and religious and ethnic nationalism as creating inherent problems for ethical and democratic decision-making protective of minority rights. Even before the October 7, 2023, attack and the war in Gaza, Israel appeared to be on the verge of a virtual civil war, with activists regularly taking to the streets to protest judicial reforms that would weaken the ability of the Supreme Court to check the power of right-wing governments.

Within this contentious environment, I offer Hadassah's story as an intergenerational bridge. I want my daughters, their peers, and all those interested in learning about the relationship between American Jews and Israel to understand how and why Zionism became such an important vehicle for their ancestors and for American Jewish women more generally. Recovering the experiences of Hadassah and her cohort reminds readers of what the idea of a Jewish homeland meant to a generation aspiring to create a religiously and ethically meaningful world. As struggles with the complicated realities of Jewish nationhood, continuity, and the failures of peaceful negotiations persist, remembering an earlier generation's dreams and lacuna might reveal "roads not taken" and help to forge future directions.[34] Hadassah's story further provides insight into the complicated relationships among four dynamic sisters and their ambitious and influential parents as they reflected on what role gender, marriage, work, and a Jewish homeland might play in living fulfilling Jewish lives.

1

Choosing to Go

The Kaplans were among the many New Yorkers who saw their city at the turn of the last century as a "promised land." After all, it provided work, housing, food, clothing, and free public education from kindergarten through college.[1] On the eve of World War II, the family lived in New York City among close to two million Jews, who represented more than one quarter of all New Yorkers and the city's largest ethnic minority.[2] To put the size of New York's Jewish community in context, the total Jewish population in Europe was nine and a half million in 1933. Thus, New York's Jewish population was more than one-fifth as large as all of Europe's, which held more than 60 percent of the world's Jews before World War II.[3]

The Kaplan family settled into New York's "city of renters," where they joined their peers in frequently transplanting themselves to accommodate changes in family size, jobs, and income.[4] Taking advantage of developing public transportation to leave behind crowded streets, overflowing pushcarts, unsanitary sweatshops, and deteriorating tenements on the Lower East Side, many Jews moved to the broader and more tree-lined streets of Brooklyn and the Bronx. Before the Great Depression, more Jews had moved to those boroughs than lived in Manhattan.[5] The Kaplans, however, took a slightly less common route, moving up the East Side in stages and then to the Upper West Side. Although they were not among the city's wealthiest Jews, manufacturers, professionals, and businesspeople, the family's geography gave them the moniker assigned to the same cohort: "uptown Jews." As teachers and spiritual leaders for those who could afford to move uptown, the Kaplans lived among an elite set of New York Jews who found their homes in elegant, elevator-operated apartment buildings near Central Park, where they might shop at local department stores, frequent soda fountains at corner drugstores, and occasionally attend stately synagogues, such as Temple Emanu-El or Congregation Shearith Israel, the Spanish-Portuguese synagogue. Like

15

most Jewish New Yorkers, whether uptown or in the outer boroughs, the Kaplans continued to live in ethnic enclaves, where they would regularly encounter relatives and friends both on the streets and within synagogues, local public schools, supplementary religious schools, kosher bakers, butcher shops, and delicatessens.[6]

In 1889, eight-year-old Mordecai, born Mottel in Svencionys, Lithuania, traveled to New York with his mother and older sister following a year in Paris. There, the family joined their father, Israel, who had arrived a year earlier. Israel was part of an entourage of younger rabbis assisting Rabbi Jacob Joseph, a renowned scholar, whom businessmen brought from Vilna to New York to serve as the city's chief rabbi. Under the auspices of the recently formed Association of American Orthodox Hebrew Congregations, Joseph sought to unify Orthodox Jews and preserve their religious commitments, despite countervailing pressures of democracy and city living. Rather than solidifying Orthodoxy, however, the association caused an uproar when its rabbis imposed a half-penny tax on chickens to raise money to ensure that meat sold in New York met the Orthodox community's standard of kashrut, religious laws preparing food for consumption. Local authorities wanted to control the criteria themselves, uptown Jews thought the rabbis were profiteering, and radical ones mocked the very notion of religious guidelines for food. Disgusted by the process, Mordecai's father left the group shortly after arriving in New York, choosing instead to work independently as a ritual slaughterer.[7] After a few years, the family moved from the Lower East Side—32 Suffolk Street—to midtown, near where the Conservative movement's rabbinical school, the Jewish Theological Seminary, then stood. Unlike many of the industrialists the Kaplans lived among, Jewish learning and prayer remained central to them. JTS, where Mordecai studied, sought both to maintain and to update traditional Judaism. How Jews could both be modern Americans and remain authentically Jewish would long animate Mordecai's thinking.

As a child, Mordecai divided his days between public education in the morning and Hebrew and Jewish studies in the afternoons, including regularly learning with his father. At fourteen, he enrolled in both JTS and City College, which was then located in Harlem and known as the "Harvard of the Proletariat." He would go on to pursue a PhD in philosophy from Columbia University, to teach at JTS, and to play leadership roles in New York's synagogues, beginning at the Upper East Side's Orthodox Kehillat Jeshurun (KJ).

It was through KJ that Mordecai met Lena Rubin. When she was two years old, Lena had migrated from Mishitz, Germany, along with her widowed mother and seven siblings, including one who was younger than she.[8] They joined their eldest brother, who had established himself on New York's Lower East Side in the clothing industry. By the time Lena and Mordecai met, the Rubin brothers had moved to the Upper East Side, started families of their own, and achieved prominence both in clothing manufacturing and as lay leaders at KJ. According to one version of their first encounter, the Hebrew school principal crossed paths with the beautiful and modish young woman just as she was leaving the apartment with one of her many suitors. Mordecai was making a house call to complain about the misbehavior of one of her nephews. Unsurprisingly, the younger generation of nieces and nephews was not as pleased as were their parents and grandmother when the short courtship ended in marriage. Nevertheless, as family lore dictates, Lena's brothers not only provided her with a trousseau but brought their fashion-conscious sister a wedding dress from Paris.[9]

As a married couple, the Kaplans lived on the Upper East Side, just outside of Yorkville, a block away from the Ninety-Second Street Y, a community center developed by German Jews, and about a half a mile away from KJ. A resourceful woman, who, like her husband, sought meaningful ways to practice Judaism and contribute to the community, Lena joined an informal study group consisting of the daughters and wives of JTS faculty. The Hadassah Study Circle, which the Zionist organizer Henrietta Szold led, gathered in one another's homes to debate the ideas of Zionist leaders and to discuss Jewish history. In the fall of 1911, with a toddler at home and pregnant with her second daughter, twenty-seven-year-old Lena hosted the group in her apartment. The story—perhaps apocryphal—is that the Kaplans so much liked the collective's name that they gave it to their second daughter when she was born that January. The following month, Szold officially founded *Hadassah*, the national Zionist women's organization that focused on improving the health and hygiene of women and children in Palestine.[10] Grandma used to joke that they named it after her.

Hadassah means "myrtle." In Hebrew, it refers to the Persian Queen Esther, whose bravery in approaching King Ahasuerus about a planned Jewish genocide encouraged their self-defense—along with the annihilation of their attackers. The Kaplans' naming their daughter Hadassah indicated their commitments to Jewish peoplehood, social reform, and the idea that women should play a key role in both efforts. Like the motto of the emerging *Hadassah* organization, Jeremiah 8:22, the Kaplans hoped that their daughter's actions might create a balm to heal the collective people of Palestine while ensuring a Jewish homeland.[11]

Hadassah's name and her family's connections with the women's organization begin to explain her interest in Palestine. But clarifying why Hadassah went to Palestine with her parents' support in the summer of 1932 requires a closer look at the constraints faced by American Jewish women during the Depression and the paths available to them. The summer before Franklin Delano Roosevelt's election, most people—young and old—were struggling just to make ends meet. How did Hadassah have the means to travel? Hadassah's decision to go reflected tangible limits faced by young, Jewish, single women in New York as well as the perception that Palestine provided those with the capacity to travel a chance for personal, communal, and professional development.

All of a Kind Family Moves Uptown

Even as Mordecai traversed the city to teach and preach, Hadassah spent much of her childhood attending public school, synagogue, and Hebrew school within a few-block radius of her home. Just as the Kaplans had welcomed their first daughter, Judith, Mordecai left his pulpit position at the Upper East Side's KJ. In the fall of 1909, he became principal of the Jewish Theological Center's Teachers' Institute, which met both uptown (on East 111th Street) and downtown (on East Houston and Stuyvesant Streets).[12] It would be nine more years before the family—which by then included Judith (nine), Hadassah (six), and two younger girls, Naomi (three) and Selma (two)—would move to Central Park West on Manhattan's Upper West Side, a neighborhood of "distinctive skylines" and "respectable calm."[13] In addition to putting them near Teachers' Institute's uptown premises, their relocation would leave them proximate to their father's new synagogue, which would eventually become the ten-story building called the Jewish Center. While continuing to work at Teachers' Institute, Mordecai served as the Jewish Center's founding rabbi.[14] The family of six moved into 1 West Eighty-Ninth Street, a red-brick- and white-limestone-trimmed seven-story apartment building three blocks from the Center. Then it was known as the Catherine, but today the edifice is better known for housing the Dwight School. The family's new apartment had enough room to put two people in each of three bedrooms. The eldest two—Judith and Hadassah—would room together, as would the youngest two, Naomi and Selma.

The daughters' domestic arrangements reflected affinities in their personalities and upbringings. The eldest girls, Judith and Hadassah, experienced some of the same pressures and intensities. Both attended public schools, where they were expected to excel academically, function in diverse communities, and also study Hebrew, Jewish studies, and music on the side. Hadassah was a bright and good student. While she played the violin and piano and sang—which she loved well into her senior years—she was neither a musical nor a linguistic prodigy. In contrast, Judith learned to read English when she was two and a half and began to study Hebrew with a tutor at four. By the time she was ten, she was studying *Chumash* with her father—the first five books of the Hebrew Bible—including Rashi's commentary, biblical explanations written in the unique script of a medieval French rabbi, Shlomo Yitzhaki, known by the acronym "Rashi."[15] That her father took Judith on long walks around the reservoir (1.6 miles) beginning when she was three years old and expressed frustration over not studying with her daily, as he had done with his own father, indicates some of Mordecai's intensity.[16] Meanwhile, in addition to secular and Jewish learning, Judith studied at the Institute of Musical Art (now the Juilliard School) from the time she was seven to eighteen.[17] Hadassah could easily beat her older sister in tennis or a swimming race, but when it came to those intellectual and artistic pursuits that she believed her parents most prized, there was not much of a competition. Furthermore, Hadassah was sensitive to her parents' judgment and jealous of her more intellectual sister. In a partially blacked-out section of her diary, the fourteen-year-old Hadassah accused her parents of not talking to her seriously and just seeing her as a flapper. Employing what was presumably adolescent hyperbole, she insisted, "They hate me!"[18] Despite Hadassah's many talents, she felt deficient compared to Judith.

While the youngest Kaplan daughters felt pressure from their older sisters, Naomi and Selma also operated in a significantly different world. The younger set of girls, who were between three and seven years apart from their older siblings, came of age in a more secluded realm than did their sisters. In addition to having tutors, Naomi and Selma mostly attended private schools from nursery through graduate school. They also shared a closeness evident in both their joking and their life choices. As children, they put on airs as they walked to school speaking gibberish to each other, which they pretended was French.[19] In their final years, Selma would move to the assisted living facility in Maryland where Naomi had lived, although it would remove her from an apartment in New York City where she and Hadassah had lived two blocks away from each other for much of their adult lives. Selma, who would write lyrics for family songs and poems throughout her long life, composed a special book of limericks for Naomi, titled *When We Were Very Young . . . and a Little Later, Too.*[20]

If the eldest and youngest Kaplan sisters had certain similarities, the daughters aligned differently physically and socially. Hadassah's beauty and Selma's glamour set them apart from their more studious counterparts. Indeed, Selma, with her blond hair and blue eyes, would come to resemble a Hollywood star. Hadassah, the second-to-oldest daughter, and Selma, the baby, shared a sense of style and even, especially as Selma matured, clothing. As young women, they were sharp-tongued and witty in addition to being regularly coiffed, wearing at least lipstick, and frequently being surrounded by a bevy of interested young men. In contrast, both Judith and Naomi were much more focused on their work than on their external form or social life. Judith would earn a PhD in musicology when she was in her fifties. Meanwhile, Naomi rarely went out and studied incessantly. She graduated medical school despite both her father's concern and the open hostility of her peers due to her gender. She went on to become a psychiatrist, a psychoanalyst, and later a sculptor. Notwithstanding Naomi's many accomplishments, she maintained a negative self-image throughout her life. As one of her sons recalled, she saw herself as too tall, too skinny, and with teeth "sticking straight out."[21]

When the sisters were young children, however, beyond Judith's uncanny language and musical talents, it was hard to know how each might develop and relate to one another and to the broader Jewish community. Mordecai hoped that the Jewish Center, with its pool and school, would provide a community where they—alongside other Jews on the Upper West Side—might both play and pray.[22] Toward that end, the Kaplans enrolled their youngest two daughters in the Jewish Center's progressive Jewish Day School, which, like his Teachers Institute, included art, music, and dancing. The older two went to public school and the Jewish Center for Hebrew school.

But the Kaplans' time at the Jewish Center was short-lived. Like KJ, the Center was Orthodox, meaning that it adhered to traditional Jewish beliefs and practices. After three years, Mordecai resigned over both political and religious disputes. Labeling him a Bolshevik, many of his congregants—businesspeople themselves—objected to his economic sermonizing, including his lecturing against the "moral bankruptcy of the competitive system" and his advocacy for the minimum wage, health insurance, and the five-day workweek. Even more than their opposition to his politics, Mordecai's congregants protested his open criticism of Orthodoxy, as he reinterpreted traditions, fostered Jewish solidarity, and formulated a new ritual code.[23]

While Mordecai's departure from the Jewish Center led the family to pull their daughters from its schools, it did not mark the end of his pulpit work.[24] A year later, Mordecai took half of the Center's congregation with him a block away to a newly formed institution that was neither Reform nor Orthodox: the Society for the Advancement of Judaism. Temporarily opening in an apartment owned by the singer and songwriter George M. Cohen, who composed "I'm a Yankee Doodle Dandy" and "You're a Grand Old Flag," the SAJ would later move across the street, where it remains to this day in a building designed by the architect Albert Goldhammer.[25] With its carved wooden doors and façade of sculptured stone, the SAJ endeavored to become a modest Jewish center in its own right, incorporating art, music, adult and children's education, Zionist activities, and publications.

As Mordecai watched his daughters grow and followed political changes—particularly the passage of the Nineteenth Amendment granting women, at least in the North, the right to vote—he looked to create a ceremony that would mark a girl's maturation. He was not a radical feminist and believed that women would need to claim religious equality for themselves. Nevertheless, as the father of four talented girls and as someone committed to Jewish continuity, Mordecai recognized that only if women developed strong Jewish identities would they pass them on to their children.[26] Shortly after establishing the SAJ in 1922, he asked the Board of Trustees' approval to initiate the bat mitzvah, marking a Jewish girl's right of passage, and requested that the first honor go to his eldest daughter, twelve-and-a-half-year-old Judith.[27]

Unlike today, when preparations for b'nei mitzvah often take months or even years, Hadassah's older sister only learned about the event the day before. On March 17, Mordecai brought Judith into his office and asked her to practice the blessings before and after reading Torah (the Pentateuch) and to recite a supplemental Torah portion in Hebrew and English. Judith recalled her father "severely" correcting her diction. Like most teenage girls, she was nervous, not so much about causing discomfort to her disapproving grandmothers but more seriously about how her friends would respond. She explained,

> It would be less than the whole truth to say that I was as full of ardor about the subject as my father was. Oh, to be sure, I passionately espoused the cause of women's rights. Let us say that I was ambivalent (a word that had not entered the common vocabulary at that time), being perfectly willing to defy the standards of my grandmothers, pleased to have a somewhat flattering attention paid me, and yet perturbed about the possible effect this might have on the attitude of my peers—the early teenagers (that word, too, was not yet in the vocabulary), who even then could be remarkably cruel to the "exception," to the non-conformist.[28]

The next morning, after Mordecai concluded reading from the Torah scrolls, Judith left the comfort of the women's section, where her disapproving grandmothers remained to stand a "very respectable distance" from the bimah, the synagogue's podium. She read from her *Chumash*, both in Hebrew and in English, the section her father had selected. Afterward, she recalled, "no thunder sounded, no lightening struck. The institution of the bat mitzvah had been born without incident, and the rest of the day was all rejoicing."[29]

Most accounts of Judith's bat mitzvah concur that it created relatively little havoc. Mordecai only recorded two sentences in his diary on March 28, 1922: "Last Sabbath a week ago (March 18) I inaugurated the ceremony of the Bat Mitzvah at the S.A.J. Meeting House (41 West 86th St.) about which more details later. My daughter Judith was the first one to have her Bat Mitzvah celebrated there." Despite his promise, he never returned to the subject in his diary.[30]

Scholarship about the ceremony has emphasized its centrality for Mordecai's evolving ideology. According to the historian Deborah Dash Moore, for example, Mordecai's invention of the bat mitzvah symbolized his reconceptualization of Jewish commandments (*mitzvot* and, specifically in this case, the male rite of passage or bar mitzvah) not as requirements but instead as folkways or daily customs that people may freely chose, without fear of divine sanctions or communal sanctions. In this case, the bat mitzvah represented a creative Jewish practice reflective of an evolving Jewish civilization and responsive to modern society, specifically the suffrage movement and growing, but ever incomplete, gender equality. Such a novel ritual symbolized "religious poetry in action" and manifested how daily customs, such as the equal treatment and education of boys and girls and the development of equitable rituals and leadership opportunities, had the potential to create a more egalitarian Jewish society—one that contemporary Jewish women might actively choose to join and pursue.[31]

Two years after Judith became a bat mitzvah, when Hadassah turned twelve, she too participated in the young women's rite of passage. In 1924, even as ready-to-wear, mass-produced clothing had grown common, Lena sewed her second daughter's bat mitzvah dress, adding a beige silk trim, tiny pleats to the collar and skirt, and a dark-red ribbon.[32] Signing what had by then become the standard SAJ oath for a girl's coming of age, Hadassah vowed, "I pledge my allegiance to the people and faith of Israel, and solemnly promise to fulfil, to the best of my abilities, the moral and religious duties incumbent upon me as a Jewess. As an earnest [*sic*] of my sincere desire to remain ever a true daughter of Israel," she continued, "I further pledge myself to devote some time each week during the next seven years to Jewish study."[33] Hadassah would keep this commitment through her continued attendance at the SAJ's Hebrew school and Hebrew tutoring. Even at the SAJ, however, becoming a bat mitzvah marked the height of a girl's ritual participation in the service rather than its beginning. It was not until the mid-1940s that women at the SAJ, including those who had previously become bat mitzvah, would be able to play leadership roles in the service that had earlier been reserved for men, such as saying the blessing (an aliyah, meaning "going up") before reading from or holding the Torah and counting for a prayer quorum, minyan.[34]

"I was Bas Mitzvah," Hadassah recorded in her diary using the Ashkenazi pronunciation common at the time, "+ only made one ^small mistake. In afternoon we had Seudah [celebration; sic]."[35] Given her parents' proclivities, the celebration would have been a modest one. Following her sister Judith's bat mitzvah, the family had sponsored a kiddush for the congregation and then thrown a birthday party that evening at the house with her sisters and a few female friends from Hebrew school. "Papa," the youngest daughter, Selma, recounted, "didn't approve of large parties in the night." He refused to attend elaborate affairs and insisted that parties following such events should be for family only.[36] Mordecai shared his disdain for the materialistic and showy coming-out parties that had come to characterize bar mitzvah parties at the turn of the century with many of his colleagues. They hoped that the more subdued bat mitzvah celebrations would rub off on their brothers and reestablish the ritual as a meaningful religious practice.[37]

At the time, Hadassah attended Wadleigh High School for Girls in Harlem, where she and Judith had transferred after a short stint at another magnet girls' school: Hunter, on the Upper East Side. Believing it to be New York's best public school, Lena had wanted her girls to attend the feeder school for the renowned Hunter College. Despite Hunter's prized standing, thirteen-year-old Judith was not impressed. At the beginning of eighth grade, roughly six months after she had become a bat mitzvah, the precocious girl lobbied her parents to switch schools. She criticized Hunter for "liv[ing] on its 'rep'" and offering no course selections, except for a choice between French and German.[38] Both Hunter and Wadleigh were connected by initial leadership. New York City's first public high school for girls was named after Lydia Wadleigh, an American educator who was also instrumental in establishing the Female Normal and High School that would eventually become Hunter College.

Mordecai, persuaded by his eldest daughter, agreed to transfer the girls to Wadleigh a few weeks into the fall semester, shortly before the Jewish High Holidays began. At the time of Wadleigh's founding at the turn of the twentieth century, the recently constructed Third Avenue elevated train, better known as the "El," had brought many aspiring middle- to upper-class, ethnic immigrants—Germans, Jews, and Italians among them—from the Lower East Side to Harlem. By the time Judith convinced her father to let her attend the school (accompanied by Hadassah), the neighborhood had changed racially, as the Great Migration brought African Americans from the South to Harlem. Judith and Hadassah began at Wadleigh in 1922, just as the school was beginning to enroll Black students and hire Black faculty. Although the thirteen-year-old Judith did not comment in her diary on friendships—across color lines or otherwise—she did make a point of describing a classmate as a "daughter of Africa."[39] Her note suggested both that she found her classmate's race noteworthy and also worthy of linguistic respect. By 1945, nearly two decades after the Kaplan girls graduated from Wadleigh, the institution had become predominantly Black.[40]

Judith gushed about her new school. Besides her German instructor, whom she accused of overworking and being condescending to the students, she praised her teachers for mentoring, challenging, and even befriending them. The students, in turn, called their instructors by their first names. "Strange though it may seem," Judith confided in her diary, "when I went to Hunter, with all my old friends, I felt less comfortable and happy than I did today, all alone, with no one to talk to!" She continued, "I have promised myself that starting my thirteenth year in such splendid surroundings, I will try as hard as I can, to live up to what I know Papa and Mamma expect of me."[41]

Mordecai's expectations of Judith were especially high. Until she married his assistant rabbi Ira Eisenstein, Mordecai treated his firstborn like an intellectual companion and an eldest son. She regularly challenged him by asking questions. When she was in her sixties, Judith recollected a particularly momentous conversation between the two. "I remember," she recalled, "I was about 12, not even 12, before my bat mitzvah. I decided I did not believe in God. I thought this was really calamitous, but I faced him with it, expecting the heavens to fall. . . . All he did was question me and say God??? And it began right then and there, and there was never a time when I couldn't go to him and talk things out."[42] By the time Judith was fifteen, she was teaching Jewish music at summer camp. She would receive a bachelor's and then a master's degree from a joint program she pioneered between her father's Teachers' Institute and Columbia University's Teachers College. Between 1929 and 1954, she would serve as an educator in her father's Teachers' Institute, only leaving to move to Chicago for her husband's job.[43] Although father and daughter had their differences, Judith's place as her father's intellectual companion, if not disciple, was clear.

Interestingly, one year before an eighteen-year-old Judith had completed her undergraduate degree and two years before the stock market crashed, she would ask her parents if she might spend a year in Palestine. Believing that she was motivated by difficulties in finding male companionship, Mordecai discouraged her. Instead, he suggested that she join social and intellectual organizations for young people. "This [engagement with peers through New York–based social clubs]," he recorded in his diary, "is certainly a better way of solving her problems than to go away to Palestine for a year where she thought she would escape from the surroundings in which she moves at present."[44] The Kaplans, especially Mordecai, however, responded differently to their second daughter five years later, perhaps because of birth order, Judith's clearer professional and musical aspirations, Hadassah's personality, or the changing times.

Hadassah's trajectory was not nearly as evident as Judith's. She too sought her parents' approval, but she was significantly less interested in school and intellectual debate than her older sister was. "I couldn't argue with him," Hadassah retrospectively recalled of her father. "I wasn't interested in those things."[45] Instead, she was driven by typical teenage pursuits: friends, sports, and boys. At fifteen and a half, Hadassah replaced her trek north along Central Park West to Wadleigh on 115th Street with a crosstown walk or bus ride to Hunter College's Upper East Side campus. Her new commute to the red-brick Gothic structure would take her across Central Park, whose playgrounds and ballfields Robert Moses would not redevelop until the 1930s.[46] In three years, she would earn a bachelor's degree and teacher's certification. Hadassah joined many of her peers in going to the public women's college, which continued to train teachers in pedagogy and curriculum, even as it diversified the courses offered. Especially for upwardly mobile Jewish women, attending Hunter College was a popular option. During the 1930s, more than half of the women enrolled in New York City's public colleges were Jewish, and Jewish women were two to three times more likely than their non-Jewish peers to attend college. Like Hadassah, many of them were drawn to Hunter because it was predominantly Jewish and the largest women's college in the US.[47] Hunter attracted academically advanced students who could pass highly selective academic exams. It particularly appealed to pupils who found themselves excluded from more elite schools either because of prohibitive costs or restrictive clauses, which barred or limited women and minorities, including Jews, Catholics, and African Americans.[48] Although scholars have assumed that Hunter, like Brooklyn and City College, was 80 to 90 percent Jewish, the 1931 yearbook from Hadassah's senior year suggests a more diverse student body and environment. Using estimates based on names, phenotypes, and activities (for example, the Catholic Newman and Lutheran Clubs versus the Jewish Menorah Society), it seems more likely that three-quarters of Hadassah's graduating class was Jewish, with the remainder including Italian, German, Irish, and African American students. Culturally, however, like most institutions of its time, Hunter remained Christian. Major social events revolved around Halloween, Christmas, and St. Valentine's Day. The 1931 yearbook's write-up of the Jewish and Zionist Menorah Society, for example, somewhat ironically described the group as having held "an exhibition and sale of Palestinian exports . . . just before the Christmas vacation."[49]

Hunter's location allowed many young Jewish women like Hadassah to pursue an education while remaining at home and often working. The proximity of its Upper East Side location to subway lines from the Lower East Side, the Bronx, Brooklyn, and Queens, and the opening of a satellite campus in the Bronx the year Hadassah graduated, made the institution particularly accessible to immigrants and their children and those from working- and middle-class backgrounds. A 1938 "College Report" illustrated the commitment to education particularly by students coming from the Lower East Side and the outer boroughs, describing them as "spend[ing] more than half as much time in their underground campus—the subways—as they do in classes, lectures, or laboratories."[50] At a moment when private schools, colleges, and professional schools regularly set quotas or rejected students on the basis of religion, a Hunter education and, for many of its graduates, training to teach in the world's biggest public school system offered entry into a field that was relatively welcoming.[51]

Herman Wouk's novel *Marjorie Morningstar*, written in 1955 but set in the 1930s, provides some insight into the types of dreams animating Hunter students like Hadassah. The fictional Marjorie Morgenstern, for example, came from an upper-middle-class background and took the same route that Hadassah did from her family's apartment on Central Park West to Hunter College. But rather than being drawn toward teaching as Hadassah was, Marjorie sought a less traditional path, pursuing a career as an actress and falling in love with an assimilated Jewish actor and playwright, personified in the film version by the decidedly non-Jewish Gene Kelly. The bulk of the novel traces Marjorie's explorations as a young, single woman who insists that she is more than just a so-called "Shirley" seeking social conformity, marriage to a self-styled "Sidney," and a life focused on domesticity. Critics then and now have complained that the novel's abrupt ending—with Marjorie marrying a lawyer, having four children, and settling into suburban, postwar-style life in Westchester—unfairly curtailed her dreams.[52]

Hadassah was not quite as rebellious as the fictional Marjorie. Still, she was daring. She began to smoke her first year in college to fit in with friends who were older than she. She also was not a particularly serious student. Retrospectively, she claimed that she "didn't learn anything" at Hunter until she returned to study there when she was older. As a young woman, Hadassah was known to enjoy parties. She described herself staying out until 3:00 a.m. while substitute teaching in a public school on Twenty-First Street, where lessons were regularly punctuated by the sound of Ninth Avenue's elevated train. Hadassah recalled the school dentist, in the context of Prohibition, checking her breath before teaching.[53] Such behavior might have contributed to her job insecurity, though it is difficult to imagine her regularly carousing when she would have had to return to a house where her father and sisters competed to see who could stay up studying later—and where their father generally won.[54] Still, in the middle of August 1932, shortly before the next school year was to begin, Hadassah received a letter from her school's superintendent letting her know that the school would not renew her teaching position.[55]

Weighing Options

Hadassah, unlike many of her contemporaries, was in the privileged position of not needing to fear for her livelihood. After all, she was a nineteen-year-old, single woman, living at home with her parents. Her father's income, as a dean at Teachers' Institute as well as a pulpit rabbi, was relatively secure, despite the financial challenges faced by both JTS and the SAJ. In 1931, after graduating from Hunter College, Hadassah even managed to buy a used car for $85. It was a Willy's Knight, which according to the manufacturers' suggested retail price in 1929 went for $1,145, more than half of what the average family needed to survive for a year, according to a Brookings Institute study.[56]

Financial pressures aside, Hadassah loved her job as a substitute teacher. More than sixty years later, she still fondly recalled the second graders she taught. They included six-year-old William Woodruff, who proposed to her in a letter: "If you do not marry with another man, will you marry with me?"[57] Despite her enthusiasm, limited professional opportunities existed in education for young, Jewish women in the early 1930s.[58] Only substitute instructors would find work, and that was for minimal compensation. Hadassah recalled teachers receiving only six dollars every other day, with school officials justifying such policies on the grounds that it was "better to employ two people for half a salary than one."[59]

Despite such conditions, a glut of young women, most of them Jewish like Hadassah, still wanted to teach. In June 1931, Hadassah was one of seven hundred Hunter College graduates to take the teaching license exam, even as the school—mindful of limited positions—encouraged its students to expand their aspirations. Administrators at other schools were more explicit in redirecting their Jewish women students away from the teaching profession. Although New Jersey needed teachers, Dean Mabel Smith Douglass of New Jersey College of Women advised Jewish students, particularly those whose "Jewishness is markedly apparent in face or name," not to major in education.[60] Nevertheless, Jewish women of Hadassah's background were more likely to go into teaching than into other similar professions, such as nursing, librarianship, and social work.[61] In Hadassah's own family, all but one of her three sisters became educators.[62] In the late nineteenth and early twentieth centuries,

American Jewish women pursued teaching as a field in unprecedented numbers. Their attraction to the profession represented a new trend, since prior to migrating to the United States, few Jewish women received a formal education.[63] Even after such migration, economic and cultural barriers in the early twentieth century compelled many American Jewish girls to leave the classroom for the factory before eighth grade, often to support the study of an older brother. Nevertheless, the daughters of parents like the Kaplans, who recognized the cultural value of education and could afford to keep their girls in school, increasingly pursued their longing to learn and to teach.[64]

Hadassah acquired her teaching certification just as the process to become a teacher was growing more competitive. In 1930, New York City's Board of Examiners passed 22 percent (1,423) of all applicants for teaching licenses for elementary school. The following year—the year Hadassah graduated—that number decreased dramatically. Only 376 candidates, or 11 percent, of the 3,300 passed. An article from the *New York Sun* that Hadassah clipped and tucked into her Hunter College yearbook labeled it "the worst mortality ever," particularly since 18 to 20 percent of applicants generally earned licensure. "With a waiting list of more than 4,000 candidates," the *Sun* reported, "the examiners are making the test so stiff that relatively few can hope to pass. The examiners contend it would be useless to license more, since the candidates would merely lose their licenses through failure of appointment within the statutory three-year period."[65] If Hadassah thought things could not get worse for aspiring teachers like herself, she was wrong. In 1933, two years after Hadassah's graduation when she set sail for Palestine, New York's Board of Examiners closed three out of six teacher training colleges to counter the oversupply of teachers. The following year, it accredited only 5 percent, or 194, of prospective teachers. Later that year, the board stopped licensing teachers altogether and did not restart certification until 1940, six years later.[66]

Hadassah's ability to earn her license a year after graduating reflected a shift from an earlier patronage system to competitive civil service exams, making teaching more accessible than it had previously been. Nevertheless, discrimination persisted. The supplemental assessments for prospective teachers, for example, limited placements.[67] While Jewish applicants like Hadassah tended to do well in their written exams, few of them had the social capital—or the "right" accent—to pass the more subjective parts of the qualifying process, including classroom assessment, evaluation of performance, and an interview. A 1937 investigation of job discrimination by the American Jewish Congress's (AJC's) Commission on Economic Problems indicated that only 6 out of 165 Jewish applicants for teaching certification in New York qualified, even though they passed the written exam at rates equivalent to the 55 non-Jewish candidates. The AJC report further found overt bigotry among teacher placement agencies, where forms asked applicants to teach in public schools to attest to their church attendance and membership.[68] Such biases persisted despite civil rights legislation in New York prohibiting discrimination based on race, color, or religion. Although teaching placement agencies added a footnote specifying that questions regarding church were "not to be answered by candidates for positions in public schools of New York State," the AJC recounted instances—ones that it contested in court—when applicants were asked their religion and had positions rescinded because of their Judaism. The study also described as "depressing" the obstacles prospective Jewish teachers faced to employment in New York's private schools. "One [hiring] agency," the AJC attested, "recalled having placed *one Jewish teacher in eight years.*"[69]

As a Jewish woman, Hadassah found that her prospects for finding work as a teacher were slimmer than those of her male counterparts. Discriminatory admissions policies at professional schools and hiring practices in industry, commerce, finance, and the professions, including medicine, law, and dentistry, encouraged Jewish men to pursue careers in secondary education. Despite biases, they still were more likely to find work as teachers than their female equivalents were.[70] The hiring of teachers off annual rankings of exam scores illustrates such disparities. Although women dominated these lists ten to one, jobs and their listings were sex segregated. More men both applied for and received teaching jobs. Whereas all the men from the 1930s list of aspiring teachers were hired into permanent positions within seven years of licensing, not a single female educator was employed as a teacher in that time.[71] Clearly, Hadassah was not the only Jewish, female teacher to be unemployed.

Hadassah also was disadvantaged in finding work by her youth. According to the Russell Sage Foundation, half of all Americans who were younger than twenty-five were out of work in 1934. No matter how hard former students had studied and even if they had obtained professional degrees, full-time or stable jobs were difficult to acquire. In New York, Jewish young people like Hadassah were twice as likely to find themselves unemployed as were adults overall. Even before the Depression, Mordecai bemoaned the plight of hiring discrimination for youth. "The difficulties," he confided to his diary, "experienced by Jewish young people who try to find employment are indescribable. At every agency the applicant is expected to state his religion. As soon as they state that they are Jewish they are told that no position can be gotten for them. In some agencies, they actually tear up the application as soon as it is filled out by a Jew."[72] Young Jewish women like Hadassah were at a triple disadvantage in their efforts to find employment.

The employment restrictions that Hadassah and her peers faced concerned parents, social workers, and communal leaders. Families like the Kaplans who could afford it and could work around quotas kept their children in school. But that option was much more available to better-off young Jewish men than to women like Hadassah. Despite restrictions in higher education, Jewish men were ten times more likely than Jewish women to attend graduate or professional school, according to a 1935 study.[73] With opportunities for school and work limited, parents and civic authorities alike fretted that common forms of entertainment, such as movies and public beaches, would deteriorate young people's bodies and minds, turning them into juvenile delinquents.[74] Even more so, they feared the psychological consequences of the next generation's failure to obtain employment despite personal striving.[75] The AJC warned that "shame and deep resentment plagued this generation. "Jewishness," the Commission on Economic Problem attested,

> throws one into a lower caste, regardless of all personal qualities[. It] is a sadly recurrent and established phenomenon among thousands of American Jews. In an effort to traverse the vicious barrier many consciously and systematically drop Jewish associations. Those who have "passed" live as twentieth-century Marranos [a Spanish or Portuguese Jew who converted to Christianity in the Middle Ages to avoid persecution but still secretly practiced Judaism], in dread of discovery. Unless the Jewish community comes to the aid of its youth in their frantic efforts toward economic adjustment, moral and social consequences of catastrophic scope may ensue.[76]

Evidence of a Jewish tendency to "pass," as AJC warned, can be seen in the growing numbers of American Jews petitioning the civil court to change their ethnic-sounding names into something more American, so that they might attain work, secure middle-class status, and avoid social ridicule.[77] Growing antisemitism both domestically and abroad raised American Jewish anxiety about the prospect of attaining future employment, income, and well-being, much less living Jewish lives. It, furthermore, challenged their faith in the American dream and conception of the US as a "Golden Land" and New York as a "Promised" one.[78] As Hadassah's sister Judith put it, "There isn't a soul in NY who knows what he'll be doing the next day. The good old days of planning for the future are gone!"[79]

Hadassah's lack of employment would not have been as problematic if she had been ready to marry. Her friends and family reported an anecdotal avalanche of weddings and babies—including twins—the year Hadassah went to Palestine.[80] The Kaplans experienced their own wedding with Hadassah's eldest sister, Judith, shortly before Hadassah set sail. That June, the eldest Kaplan daughter married a handsome, New York attorney, named Albert Addelston, whom the family had known for years. Al had even taken Judith's younger sister, the socially awkward Naomi, to a speakeasy on her sixteenth birthday.[81]

While adjusting to married life and giving private music lessons, Judith taught music and a history course on Jewish music at her father's Teachers' Institute. Judith's efforts to balance work and family resonated with New York's liberal attitude toward the employment of married teachers.[82] Many school boards elsewhere required married women to resign, but New York allowed them to continue working. Still, a norm discriminating against married women's employment existed during the 1930s, which was reinforced by federal government policy (Section 213 of the 1932 Economy Act) preventing married couples from both working for the government. Marriage bars on working women exemplified the gendered assumption during the Depression that jobs should be reserved for married men to provide for their families and that married women did not actually need to work. Such conventions, of course, ignored women whose husbands could not work, did not earn enough to support a family, or had deserted them. The bans on married women working were not new: many firms, including General Electric and Ford, consistently fired married women. Only about 15 percent of married women in 1930 held jobs, a rate that basically matched Americans' opposition to married women working as measured in opinion polls. One survey, for example, found that 89 percent of the public thought married women like Judith should not work.[83]

In the summer of 1932, Hadassah had neither viable work prospects nor a breadwinner in sight. Still, a beautiful and animated woman, she was not without beaus. The year before she left for Palestine, Hadassah turned down at least two marriage proposals: one from John "Jack" Sundelsohn, a graduate student at Columbia University pursuing a doctorate in public finance, examining the economics of public works, and a second from her wealthy friend Virginia Lieberman's brother, Ralph.[84] Both Jack and Ralph continued to pursue Hadassah, sending her flowers before her trip and writing letters on elegant stationery to her in Palestine.[85] Ralph, as well as a third admirer, Milton Kail, saw her off on the boat.[86] Milton handed her a "beautiful cigarette case" before she left, wrote her long letters, and even phoned her younger sister Selma to "inquire after the patriate [sic]."[87] Most significantly, roughly a year before her journey, Hadassah met Sidney Musher, the man she would eventually marry. But at the time, the relationship did not proceed beyond a few dates.

Sidney recalled having been caught up in the economic crisis of the day. In 1932, the food-processing company he had worked for, Van Camp Co., was involved in a Ponzi scheme, fired him, and went bankrupt. Nevertheless, Sidney, a graduate of Johns Hopkins University, which he attended on a $300 scholarship, continued to work in Van Camp's Baltimore lab, developing and applying for patents for oxidation and rancidity. He had already discovered a way to modify cow's milk to make it closer to breast milk and would go on to determine the cleaning and healing properties in Aveeno colloidal oatmeal. He would sell both patents to manufacturers, the latter to General Mills, which would name the resulting product after its main ingredient: Aveeno. Despite such longer-term successes, in the early 1930s, Sidney found himself living with his parents in New York, traveling weekly to experiment in Van Camp's lab in Baltimore, without a regular paycheck, and incapable of seriously thinking about enduring relationships.[88]

Sidney and Hadassah were not alone. Many of their peers felt unable to pursue marriage in their current context. As the recently married Judith explained, "The days of people getting married and planning to wait and save for two years before having a baby are over because this year has been one of constant surprises—each one (and I'm not talking personally only)—taking away with it a little remaining safety and courage."[89] The national marriage rate dropped precipitously from roughly ten marriages per thousand in 1929 to just under eight per thousand in 1932. The rates were even lower among Jews.[90] The majority of Jews younger than twenty-five, like Hadassah, made ends meet by living with their parents into young adulthood. "Whatever their aspirations for the future, most maintained an obligation to the household," helping to support one another.[91] Indeed, the relative absence of Jewish homeless shelters in New York City—there was only one—reflected the expectation (if not the reality) that such families would largely care for their own.[92]

Affording Palestine

Although Hadassah was part of a broader cohort, her story nevertheless remains exceptional. Few Americans had the financial means to travel abroad during the Depression. According to a 1929 Brookings Institute study, the average family needed $2,000 per year to survive, but nearly 60 percent of them earned less.[93] The estimated median family incomes of Jewish neighborhoods in New York City were somewhat higher, at roughly $3,000, but still not nearly enough to afford the luxury of international travel. But the story was somewhat different on the Upper West Side of Manhattan, where Hadassah and her family lived. At a median income of $8,700 per year, Jewish families on the Upper West Side earned almost seven times that of those living in older areas, nearly three times as much as Jewish communities generally in New York, and more than four times the survival rate.[94] While roughly 35 percent of New York's Jews continued to work in the garment industry, growing numbers had entered white-collared and skilled occupations by the 1930s. Such workers experienced less economic displacement than other groups did. Families like the Kaplans, who managed to maintain a "civil service job, a relatively stable business, or steady white-color employment," were able to keep their children in school, hire occasional household help, afford intermittent recreation, and even take summer vacations to the Catskills or Jersey Shore. Thus, despite the Depression, relative prosperity persisted in Hadassah's "gilded ghetto."[95]

Mordecai's congregants might not have felt the Depression's squeeze as much as other New Yorkers, but many of them nevertheless cut back on what they considered to be discretionary spending, including the payment of synagogue membership fees. By 1931, the SAJ, like many of its religious peers, had accumulated significant debt ($60,000) and owed its staff "thousands of dollars in back salaries."[96] Mordecai's board was particularly aggrieved when, in 1930, without consulting it, he hired an executive director for an annual salary of $2,500. Perhaps he thought his recent appointment to dean at the Jewish Theological Seminary entitled him to more assistance at the SAJ. Mordecai selected Ira Eisenstein, a newly minted graduate of the school, to assist him. Ira would later become Mordecai's son-in-law and protégé.[97] Lena was embarrassed when she realized that the synagogue's teachers and office staff had not been paid between the summer of 1932 and the following winter. To begin to fill the deficit, she organized a fund-raising concert.[98] Ira recalled having to visit the offices of synagogue members who refused to pay their dues in order to collect his salary.[99] "It seems funny," one of Hadassah's cousins commented perhaps a bit ironically, "that people who owe us [the synagogue] money find it so easy to purchase commodities of luxury and pleasure tickets and yet refuse to pay their just debts to the Institution on the plea of depression and hard times."[100] Although the Kaplans were not refusing to pay expenses they owed personally, they would find the funds to support their daughters' travels even as the SAJ's staff had to haggle for compensation.

Mordecai's salary was substantially more secure than that of his peers at the SAJ because he circumvented synagogue budgets and membership. Although he worked at multiple organizations, Mordecai did not draw a salary for his pulpit work and only took payment from the Teachers' Institute. In 1918, he explained his refusal to accept an annual salary of $7,500 from the Jewish Center because he wanted to maintain his freedom to preach. He did not, he rationalized in his diary, want to become "the slave of a higher standard of living." "I am convinced," he continued, "that unless those at the helm of Jewish life display something of the spirit of sacrifice that now permeates the nations of the world, the Jewish people have no chance for survival."[101] When he accepted pastoral salaries, he either donated them back to the synagogues where he worked or gave the funds to the Teachers' Institute. Still JTS's donors and contributions suffered during the Depression, leaving Mordecai financially vulnerable to potential wage cuts.[102]

Mordecai's refusal to accept fees for his pulpit work and the financial troubles of the Teachers' Institute left the family with what his biographer Mel Scult described as "financial difficulties." It also created a distinction between the economic status of the Kaplans and the families Mordecai served. In an interview with Scult, Seymour Wenner, who married the second-to-youngest Kaplan daughter, Naomi, described the Jewish Center as "really a rich cookie." Interrupting her husband, Naomi interjected, "Excluding his [Mordecai's] family."[103] Lena found the monetary pressure to be constant. She had occasionally managed the accounts for her brothers' businesses before beginning her own family, and, once married, she assiduously handled the house, finances, and family expenses.[104] Hadassah recalled that to make ends meet during the Depression, her mother sold her diamonds, with the exception of two: a pin and an engagement ring.[105] She also cashed in early on insurance policies.[106] Throughout Lena's correspondence with Hadassah, she worried that the "money problem" would prevent them from sending enough cash for Hadassah to stay in Palestine until June.[107] Such concerns shaped the pragmatic advice she gave her daughter about how to spend her time and resources. Lena encouraged Hadassah to save money. She warned her not to travel to Tel Aviv on the weekends and to take the cheapest route back to New York. Lena also advised Hadassah to focus on preparing for her future. To Lena, that meant learning Hebrew so that she could teach Hebrew school, should she not be able to secure a public-school position when she returned.[108]

Hadassah, who remained financially careful throughout her long life, heeded many of her mother's warnings. She boasted about being the only one of her sisters to attend all public schools. "I never spent any money," she recalled of her time studying at Hunter College. "I'd have a muffin and coffee for lunch for 35 cents. Papa offered to give me $100 to gain 10 pounds. I weighed 104 in college."[109] Hadassah saved her money while teaching to cover many of the expenses of her travels.[110] She began her trip with $295 in cash and $451 in the bank, although it was unclear how much she had earned and how much her family gifted her.[111] That money carried her for six months, until February. Over the next three months, she spent only roughly $50 more. While journeying, Hadassah, who joined her high school math club and majored in economics at Hunter, kept a detailed budget of her journey. She logged $1,101.99 over the course of the year, with expenses ranging from developing film, renting a deck chair, and buying shampoo, candlesticks, and cigarettes to purchasing her passage and visa.[112] Although she did not consider returning early, Hadassah responded to her mother's financial admonitions, writing the day after FDR's Bank Holiday, "Can't you even collect $10 on my car?"[113]

Lena and Mordecai were both immigrants and came from limited financial means, but they traveled with social capital and, despite familial recollection, acquired substantial resources prior to the Depression. The Kaplans were among the one-fifth of New York's two million Jews whose savings were diminished—if not wiped out—by the failure of the Jewish-owned Bank of the United States on December 11, 1930.[114] "Today," Mordecai wrote in his journal, "the U.S. Bank of which stock we have ten shares closed down. The shares cost us $2,080. That we are bearing our losses with equanimity is probably due more to the realization that there are thousands of people who are infinitely worse off than we rather than to any native or acquired ability to remain unperturbed." Mordecai's reflections show his cognizance of his misfortune in losing nearly $21,000 of what he called "actual hard earned cash," as well as an equal amount of paper profit in the market. But Mordecai also illustrated awareness of his relative privilege in the context of the Depression's widespread suffering.[115]

Despite financial loses, the Kaplans nevertheless managed to send most of their children to private colleges, where tuition and school fees were roughly $450 per year.[116] As noted earlier, Judith attended the Institute of Musical Art, Teachers' Institute, and Columbia University's Teachers College. More than other private institutions of higher education at the time, Columbia University's Teachers College admitted Jews, Catholics, and African Americans.[117] In contrast, Columbia University was among the Ivy League schools instituting quotas to limit Jewish enrollment. From 1928 to 1936, the university even created Seth Low Junior College, an alternative, preprofessional, non-degree-granting community college in Brooklyn intended to reduce the number of New York public-school students—particularly Jewish ones—who applied to Columbia. Entry into some public universities was also restricted by psychological and other screening tests. Even when such institutions admitted Jewish applicants, they socially excluded them from student unions, sororities, student government, and housing.[118] Such prohibitions probably encouraged the Kaplans to invest in private schools for their younger two daughters. Selma and Naomi studied at the Jewish Center's school when their father worked there and then went to public school. But in junior high school, they transferred to the private school Ethical Culture, and they continued in that mold, attending its successor, Fieldston, for high school. One of Mordecai's influential professors from Columbia University, Felix Adler, had initiated the schools as an offshoot of his New York Society for Ethical Culture. Although Mordecai disdained his teacher's rejection of Judaism, he was sufficiently drawn to Adler's philosophy of ethics and universalism to send his younger daughters to the movement's schools.[119] Naomi did not recall philosophical or ethical reasons driving her move to private school. Instead, she understood the transition as having more to do with improving her chance of being admitted to Barnard College. "Judith," she explained, "had not been admitted.... Somebody in the family had to go to Barnard. And since the public schools didn't achieve this I was sent to private school."[120] Both younger daughters would, indeed, acquire undergraduate degrees from Barnard College. Selma spent a semester during her sophomore year studying abroad in England, overlapping briefly with Hadassah in Europe. Naomi, who had studied physics at Fieldston with Robert Oppenheimer, the "father of the atomic bomb," received a bachelor's degree from Barnard in science after a brief foray in design.[121]

It is probable that some portion of the money for this level of travel and education came from Lena's family, which included leaders in the clothing industry and medical field. Six of Lena's brothers became financially successful businessmen. The seventh, Isadore Rubin, achieved prominence as an obstetrician gynecologist, developing a test named after him to check the fallopian tubes for blockages that could cause sterility. With regard to contributions toward Hadassah's travels, some documentation of what friends and family gave her exists. At the beginning of her trip, Israel Unterberg, the philanthropist and director of JTS who donated the building that housed Mordecai's Teachers' Institute, enclosed a check as a token of support in a letter to Hadassah expressing his pleasure that she was going to study at Hebrew University.[122] But even Lena did not know how much "the folks" had given Hadassah before her trip.[123] Nevertheless, she hoped that it would be enough and trusted that they would find a way to send her funds to make it through the year and then come home.

* * * *

In many respects, ideas mattered as much as, if not more than, means in explaining Hadassah's journey. Although she was unusual in her capacity to travel, the aspiration to visit Palestine grew more attractive to a cohort of American Jews during the Depression. They were drawn by the economic boom in mandatory Palestine, combined with a pioneering ideology and the desire to build a Jewish homeland, all of which contrasted with financial struggle and rising antisemitism in the US and abroad.[124] As a labor Zionist poem sung to the Yiddish tune "Zum Gali Gali" promised,

> Goodbye, America
> Goodbye, Yankee fashion
> I'm going to Palestine
> To hell with the Depression.[125]

Traveling to Palestine offered an escape from an Upper West Side where Hadassah, despite her talents and enthusiasm, would have been unlikely in the fall of 1932 to find either a job as a teacher or a life partner. Rather than competing against a glut of underemployed, young, Jewish, single women in New York, Hadassah looked to Palestine, where she could participate in her father's efforts to revitalize Judaism even as she retrained to teach Hebrew and Jewish studies. This would allow her to develop personally and professionally while contributing to communal goals. Her parents hoped that, despite their recent losses, with scrimping—and perhaps some help from their wider family—they would be able to contribute to Hadassah's travels. In any case, she had sufficient funds to begin her travels. Thus, with little to lose, Hadassah and her family looked east for new opportunities.

2

The Attraction

Two summers before Hadassah left for Palestine, even before she was considering going, Mordecai lamented his family's resistance to Jewish observance and bemoaned what it suggested about his own failures to influence the broader American Jewish community. In his diary, he recalled a conversation among his daughters. Judith praised an excellent Saturday-morning music class she was taking while her fiancé worked. This led the youngest two daughters—who otherwise had been granted an abundance of intellectual experiences—to protest the prohibitions placed on them by Jewish law, since their parents would not allow them to work on the Jewish Sabbath. Naomi, with tears in her eyes, and Selma, with a bit of snark given her family's commitment to learning, objected that their parents were denying them "an educational opportunity." "Why," Mordecai Kaplan reflected, "am I so downhearted? I think it is due to the overwhelming sense of futility that overcomes me whenever I realize how irrelevant all my efforts to reconstruct Judaism are. If I do not succeed in my own home to make Judaism live, if it means so little to my own children, what can I expect of other homes and the children of other people?"[1]

Six months earlier, at a celebration for Mordecai's fiftieth birthday, his children perfectly captured their father's frustration in a Gilbert and Sullivan spoof. Impersonating Mordecai, Albert Addelston, who was soon to marry Judith Eisenstein in what would be a short-lived relationship, sang of his father-in-law-to-be's ascent from childhood to marriage and fatherhood. The final couplet mourned Mordecai's inability to influence his daughters:

> But try as I may, I can't compel
> Any one of them [his daughters] to worry about Israel.[2]

In his diary, Mordecai labeled these concluding lines a "gem" and reflected that he saw "no use in trying to compel" his daughters to share his interests and worries. "If," he continued, "they cannot manage to lead

Jewish lives with some degree of spontaneity and naturalness, if they have to keep on denying themselves legitimate freedom of action, if they have to be forever poignantly and painfully conscious of their Jewishness, what earthly or spiritual benefit can they get out of it? . . . I want my children," he wrote perhaps most touchingly, "to be absolutely and unqualifiedly happy. I don't want them to do anything for my sake which they would not also do for their own sake."[3] But how could he ensure both his children's happiness and also their desire to live Jewish lives?

Mordecai hoped that Zionism might offer a viable solution. Although his own evolving ideas about a Jewish state were more complicated, the rabbi and father turned to Palestine thinking that contributing to the upbuilding of the Jewish community there might persuade his daughters and especially other Jewish women to choose to live Jewishly. He did not mean by that Orthodox observance of Jewish law but rather creative engagement and reinterpretation of Jewish customs in ways that felt relevant to them. What did American Jewish women like Hadassah know about Palestine during the 1930s, and what did they think it offered them? How and why did Kaplan invest so heavily in Zionism? To what extent was he—and other Jewish educators—aware of the challenges posed by such an ideology and place?

Hadassah was part of a small but influential cohort of American Jewish women—including single women, mothers, wives, divorcées, and widows—who went to Palestine in the early twentieth century as a respectable way to adventure and test some of the limits confining American Jewish women while remaining within boundaries considered acceptable by their parents and community. Hadassah and her peers turned to Palestine to explore their Judaism while seeking companionship, life partners, knowledge, careers, and personal and professional development. Investigating Hadassah's journey reveals what drew a generation of venturesome women to Palestine, while contextualizing the freedoms they found there in relation to the experiences of others, including Palestinian Arabs.

Hadassah, Camp Modin, and Zionism

Camp was at the center of the adolescent Hadassah's world. Beginning the summer after Hadassah became a bat mitzvah in 1924, Lena packed up her four daughters, ages nine, ten, twelve, and fifteen, and sent them by overnight train to the newly formed girls' side of Camp Modin in Canaan, Maine. The sisters made up almost half of the nine female campers that summer. The Kaplans hoped that "the summer camp with a Jewish idea" would immerse their daughters in Jewish communal experiences in the outdoors.

Two summers before the Kaplans arrived at Modin, Alexander Dushkin and Albert Schoolman opened an all-boys camp on the other side of Lake George. The men were congregants and former students of Mordecai, and their families were friendly. Alexander and Albert were both originally from Suwalki, Poland, approximately 125 miles—or what then might have been a five-day journey—from Sventzian, Lithuania, where Mordecai was born. Like their mentor, the men also migrated to the US as children, grew up in New York City, attended City College of New York, and participated in the Menorah Society, a national Jewish intellectual and cultural group that met on college campuses.[4] Mordecai recruited them to study at the Teachers' Institute. Schoolman even went on to earn a doctorate from Columbia (Mordecai pursued one in philosophy but did not complete it). All three men devoted their lives to Jewish education: Albert became the "father of the American Jewish summer camp" experience, best known for founding Camp Cejwin in 1919, three summers before establishing Modin; Alexander built and developed Chicago's Board of Jewish Education and then Hebrew University's school of education; and, of course, Mordecai taught educators at the Teachers' Institute.

As a couple, the Kaplans were also close to the men's wives, the Polish-born "Aunt Julia" Dushkin and the native New Yorker Bertha Schoolman, who—along with Libbie Suchoff Berkson, originally from Minsk—ran Modin's girls' side. All three women were college educated (Julia at Cornell University and Bertha and Libbie at Hunter College) and active with *Hadassah* and other Zionist organizations. Bertha and Libbie were also educators. Bertha even trained and taught at Mordecai's Teachers' Institute. The three women would chaperone Hadassah on her journey to Palestine. Mordecai's sending his daughters to Modin marked his investment in Jewish camping. For those who could afford it, summer camp was an appealing prospect, especially given fears of disease, such as the Spanish flu and polio, and the virtual absence of vaccinations. Modin attracted wealthier campers than did Cejwin, which Albert Schoolman had previously established to educate the Americanized children of working-class Jews. At Modin, the Kaplan girls joined prominent American and Canadian families, including those who had previously sent their children to camps lacking Jewish content. The Dushkins and Schoolmans believed that summer camps presented vital pedagogical opportunities for Jewish learning and living.[5]

Zionism and the development of the Hebrew language played central roles both in the Kaplan girls' training and also in Modin's pedagogy. Alexander Dushkin explained in his memoir that before there were language-intensive camps, Modin encouraged modern Hebrew through Hebrew tables, study periods, and the translation of "new Palestine songs into English." "While in its Jewish outlook," Alexander wrote, "Camp Modin was not affiliated with any one ideological group. It was intensely Zionist and religiously Conservative, with leanings toward Liberal Reconstruction."[6] Donald Gribetz, a longtime camper and affiliate of Cejwin, recalled Judaism at camp as "parve." "The real religion of the Schoolmans and their camp," he contended, "was Zionism—*that* was their Judaism."[7]

The activities Hadassah described in her letters home suggested the camp's focus on Judaism and Zionism. There were daily lessons and singing in Hebrew and two language tables where the campers spoke "*nothing* but Hebrew."[8] Hadassah reported reading the Bible daily with her Canadian friend Sylva Gelber. She also notified her parents when Judith read haftorah, a portion from the Book of Prophets that is chanted on the Jewish Sabbath.

Hadassah was the primary correspondent among her sisters, who would scrawl a note or two at the end of Hadassah's detailed letters. Judith mostly insisted that she was too busy playing, teaching, and providing musical accompaniment to write. The younger girls penned messages about their swimming, diving, and sports competitions. Hadassah wrote home more extensively, discussing services and performances and what she learned about the collegiate system for Jews in Canada. In her letters, she described leading Hebrew songs, organizing campfires, and composing and performing skits. Once she avoided having to learn her lines on short notice by fixing cards with her parts into her costume—a cheese cloth and cotton scarf. Of course, Hadassah's letters home might have been influenced by her eagerness to impress her parents; nevertheless, they include evidence of both Jewish engagement and fun.

Camp complemented Hadassah's more formal training in Hebrew and Jewish studies during the school years. After public school, Hadassah attended supplemental programs first at the Jewish Center and then, when her father left the former and created the latter, at the Society for the Advancement of Judaism. The girls also had private tutoring. Hadassah studied Hebrew with Abraham Halkin, a professor of Semitics at the Jewish Theological Seminary.[9]

At camp, however, learning was combined with swimming, tennis, music making, acting, relationships, and pleasure. When Hadassah was twelve, she divulged to her diary about her camp crushes, including on a boy named Arnold. "I wish he'd write," she confessed during the school year. "I'd eat him up."[10] According to her camp friend Sylva, by the time Hadassah was fourteen, young men had "terribly violent" crushes on the teenager, who that summer qualified as a lifeguard and was also awarded "all-around athlete" at banquet.[11] "Some 'gentleman killer' you're turning out to be!" Sylva recalled. "Is that the way I brought you up??"[12] Hadassah did not write to her parents about her crushes, but she also did not shy away from somewhat-risqué stories. For example, she relayed discovering the joys of skinny-dipping with her girlfriends in "skin colored bathing suit[s]," followed by late-night snacks of saltines and pickles hidden in their bunks.[13]

Despite Mordecai's proclamations about wanting his daughters to be "unqualifiedly happy"–which Hadassah appears to have been at camp—he was unimpressed. While visiting Modin in 1927, when his daughters were twelve, thirteen, fifteen, and eighteen, he described both the services and the "mental life of the children" as "elementary," even more so because the campers—children he viewed as "rather pampered"—did not understand the Hebrew they used for prayers.[14] Mordecai did not soften his criticism or even acknowledge that, by that point, his eldest daughter, Judith, was one of the camp's key educators in charge of Jewish music and prayer. His disparaging tone exemplifies his dissatisfaction with American Judaism—and its ramifications for the people around him, including his own daughters.

Even if Mordecai was not excited by Modin, it had a significant impact on impressionable campers like Hadassah and her sisters. Camp served as a space where young women who had already become bat mitzvah could continue to lead services, even when they were prohibited from doing so in their synagogues, including the progressive SAJ.[15] Camp's idealized images of a Jewish homeland also served as a powerful impetus for Hadassah and her peers, particularly those "in search of a cause." "Our youthful passion," recalled Sylva, "was ignited by the image of the builders of that land, of the dreamers draining the swamps, of the exuberant youth singing and dancing the night away, the light of the Middle East moon, of the watchman with his rifle slung over his back."[16] Sylva's memory suggests that Modin succeeded in enlisting young Jews, as American Zionist groups encouraged.

Hadassah and her fellow campers might have been familiar with some of the visual representations of "the Orient" that a wide range of American Jewish organizations in the early twentieth century promoted.[17] Perhaps Hadassah read the Jewish Palestinian, anti-Zionist Myriam Harry's *A Springtide in Palestine* (1924).[18] Or maybe she was acquainted with the Zionist educator Irma Lindheim's documentation of her sabbatical in Palestine following eighteen years of married life with five children. Lindheim published her letters home in *The Immortal Adventure* (1928).[19] During the 1920s, when Hadassah was a camper, Zionist iconography in the US tended to represent Jewish Palestinians as American frontiersmen, rugged individuals, and *shomrim*, or guards. By the 1930s, the pioneer, or *halutz*, image prevailed, including representations of educated young idealists working collectively to reclaim swamps, deserts, and a Jewish folk culture of song and dance. Such representations idealized a Zionist narrative and "chronically underrepresented" Arab Palestinians.[20] Nevertheless, they suggested that aid to, and support of, Palestine could make American Jews both better Jews, by countering anti-Jewish stereotypes, and also better Americans, by giving them an aspirational and spiritual homeland that they, like other immigrants at the time, might imagine, long for, and occasionally visit.[21]

Hadassah, despite her father's left leanings, was not systematically exposed to labor Zionism. She and her sisters began at Modin's girls' camp five summers before Hashomer Hatzair (The Young Guard) opened its first summer camp in Highland Mills, New York. The Zionist, Socialist, youth-led movement would train young people to work the land, live collectively, and move to Palestine as a group as a sign of their broader rejection of bourgeois culture and institutions. Hashomer Hatzair would train its members to transform themselves personally and to forge a new, more collective, society. B'nei Akiva, the youth group of the religious Zionist Mizrachi movement, did not form in Palestine until 1929. It too built camps and youth programs promoting *Torah v' Avodah*, Jewish learning and labor or pioneering. The Zionism that Hadassah imbibed as a youth was more individualized and less movement based than what would emerge a decade later. Following World War II and the establishment of the State of Israel, the connection between Zionism and a range of Jewish camps, including Ramah, Young Judea, and Yavneh, would become more entrenched.[22]

Modin promoted Zionist iconography, like that which inspired Hadassah, because the camp's leaders saw Palestine as the center of a Jewish cultural renaissance. Influenced by Mordecai, but also by the Jewish educator and Hebraist Sansom Benderly, they were part of a cohort that sought to study, work, travel, and generally spend considerable time in Palestine by themselves, with their spouses, and/or with their children. They endeavored to participate in the reemergence of Hebrew as a living, modern language and the reinvigoration of Jewish creativity and consciousness through literature, song, dance, and folkways. Sojourns to Palestine engrossed this group in the world that Jewish educators were trying to create in progressive classrooms. They also promoted Ivrit b'Ivrit—learning Hebrew by only speaking it—which had become the norm at Mordecai's Teachers' Institute by the 1920s. Time spent in Palestine provided a living environment that merged the classroom with a broader community, taught through play and experience, and drew on Jewish art and culture to unite Jews around a cultural and creative community and identity.[23]

The Holy Land ideal, vicarious or armchair tourism, and actual journeys to Palestine had long inspired both Jews and Christians. By the mid-1920s, however, visiting Palestine had become a rite-of-passage and a formative experience for American Jewish educators and reformers like Mordecai and his peers.[24] Indeed, Rabbi Kaplan began to look for opportunities to work in, and experience, Palestine following passage of the Balfour Declaration in 1917, which conveyed British support for "the establishment in Palestine of a national home for Jewish people."[25] In December 1918, he emphasized the importance of such pilgrimages for Jewish revitalization. "Every Jew," he wrote in his diary, "should go to [visit] Palestine.... Every institution should consider a trip to Palestine as its most important course."[26] Despite his proclamations, Mordecai himself would not make it to Palestine for another six years.

Alexander Dushkin agreed with his mentor, viewing sojourns to Palestine as vital to both the education and vocation of Jewish professionals. "I went not as a tourist," he wrote of his time spent in Palestine during the 1920s and 1930s,

> but as a student, intent on completing my preparation for professional service in American Jewish education.... As an educator facing the prodigious tasks of Jewish life in America, I felt a deep need of immediate personal contact with the historic homeland, and of direct confrontation with those who were recreating there our Hebraic civilization. I needed the reassuring knowledge and the abiding faith to be derived from living experience in pioneering Palestine. I saw myself as the first of many such students who would be coming in future years to bring back to their communities sustaining strength from the creative spirit of the Land.[27]

By the time Hadassah found herself single and unemployed in the summer of 1932, she had already spent considerable formative time having been taught and influenced by a cohort of educators, including her own father and Alexander, who viewed time spent in Palestine not as a luxury but rather as essential "for every Jew," students and laypeople among them. According to this philosophy, firsthand experience in Palestine was vital training for active participation in American Jewish life.

Promised Land Tourism, Migration, and Jewish Women

Proclaiming travel to Palestine to be essential was one thing, but actually making it accessible was another. Changes in the travel industry, however, made such tours markedly more plausible for people like the Kaplans and Dushkins, even if they continued to fall short of ubiquity. In the 1890s, a second-class round-trip ticket from the US to Europe cost about $63, which was about as expensive as a modest bicycle. Although not cheap, bikes were affordable for many Americans.[28] The development of third-class steamship tickets, "tourist" accommodations, various levels of rail travel, and the guidebook industry made transatlantic journeys substantially more affordable than they had previously been for the middle and working classes.[29] When the US Congress limited immigration following the Russian Revolution and the Dillingham Immigration Restriction Action of 1921, European steamship companies pivoted from using steerage to carry immigrants one way to focus on a new class of tourists who would travel round-trip in Tourist Third Cabins.[30] The historian Daniel Soyer explains that, by the 1920s, "even former immigrants and others in modest circumstance by American standards had the resources to make a trip abroad."[31]

Tourism targeting Jews further swelled travel to Palestine. Enhancing such endeavors was the success of package tour operators, such as Thomas Cook & Son, the special attention they devoted to the "Jewish colonies in Palestine," an expansion in the number of "simple, but perfectly middle-class hotels" available in Palestine, and the opening, in December 1930, of the King David, the first luxury hotel there.[32] Shortly after Hadassah's trip, further infrastructure developed to facilitate travel. By 1933, the Zionist movement, including the organization *Hadassah*, allied with travel companies, such as Thomas Cook and the Cunard Line, to develop trips catering to Jewish tourists, facilitating the celebration of Jewish holidays, meeting political leaders, and seeing Zionist-inspired projects. Zionist organizations even partially subsidized tours to make them more affordable and established contests offering free trips as a reward for those who raised the most funds for their programs. Just as Dushkin had done, such organizations encouraged Western Jews to understand Palestine not as a tourist destination. Instead, they promoted it as a Jew's "most authentic home," with travel there representing a capstone to Zionist and educational engagement and an opportunity to "see their potential as a people and a nation."[33] "Nothing can so clarify one's outlook and stimulate one's interest," *Hadassah*'s newsletter explained, "as a vital and immediate contact with the Yishub [sic], no matter what the duration of one's stay."[34] The rate of tourism illustrates the success of this vision. In 1924, as many as seventy thousand Western tourists traveled to Palestine. Six years later, more than half that number (forty thousand) took the trip. Particularly in the context of the Depression, commentators were "amazed by how many Americans made the journey."[35]

Among those travelers were Jewish women like Hadassah, many of whom journeyed as wives, mothers, volunteers, social workers, nurses, and educators. The forces mobilizing women reformers to travel internationally also moved Jewish female activists. Their trips tended to include fact finding, recruitment toward causes, and the building of support networks. Scholars have long commented on the role that such travel played in liberating women from domestic obligations, heightening their agency, enhancing their control over time and money, and developing their writing voices.[36] Shortly before Hadassah's travels, in the spring and summer of 1932, Rebecca Aaronson Brickner, a Cleveland Jewish educator and a founding member of the *Hadassah* organization, journeyed to Palestine. A middle-class Jewish wife traveling elsewhere at the time without her husband, in this case a reform rabbi, but with her children might have seemed inappropriate. Brickner, however, could remain a so-called good wife while simultaneously pursuing her own interests in Palestine, working on her Hebrew, and studying Jewish history and modern Hebrew literature at Hebrew University. Women like Brickner found travel to Palestine liberating. "I feel that this trip has already done so much for me," she recalled. "It has opened new vistas for me and lifted me out of the rut I was falling into."[37] Although few of these travelers permanently settled in Palestine, many of them, like Brickner and Hadassah, would infuse active learning of Hebrew culture and nationalism into Hebrew schools (Talmud Torahs), suburban synagogue schools, children's literature, camps, youth groups, adult education, and cultural/art programs in the US.[38]

Traveling to Palestine would put Hadassah in league with a cohort of Jewish female reformers who, influenced by the Protestant Social Gospel movement, sought to forge a utopia in Palestine that would contain what they considered to be the best American values, including the principles of fighting injustice and equitable distribution of resources.[39] Some academics accuse such reformers of "altruistic imperialism": intending to help and uplift others while actually imposing a homogeneous Westernized moral framework onto those about whom they know little.[40] Other scholars, however, view them as engaging in maternalist activism, highlighting women's social reform. Such efforts encouraged an older generation of American women to import to Palestine ideals circulating in Progressive circles in the United States. That cohort included women, such as the founder of the *Hadassah* organization, Henrietta Szold, the social worker and *Hadassah* leader Alice Seligberg, and the poet and Zionist educator Jessie Sampter. Viewing as building blocks ideas rejected by many North Americans, such as social welfare, universal health care, and pluralism, they sought to forge a model society that would right the wrongs of capitalist society.[41] In that effort, they promoted and worked to improve the lives of women and children in Palestine regardless of their religion by reducing infant mortality, providing playgrounds, and employing John Dewey's educational style of directed living and learning through doing.[42]

Participating in such reform efforts created a vehicle for American Jewish women, such as the founders of Camp Modin and Hadassah's chaperones, to live Jewishly in a way that went beyond following a religious creed. This cohort would endeavor to popularize Zionism, which remained a contested and minority viewpoint within the Jewish community through the 1930s. Instead, they viewed Zionism as a tool for fighting assimilation in the United States and living spiritually, intellectually, and socially fulfilling and self-actualized lives.[43] Palestine, for them, provided a space where they could advance what they considered to be a progressive, Jewish civilization that would improve the lives of all and the world more broadly.[44]

The Kaplans believed that training with such reformers would prepare their daughter Hadassah to teach in the Jewish world and/or to join the ranks of Jewish female activists, particularly those engaged in the upbuilding of Jewish culture in Palestine and the US. In Lena's letters to her daughter, she repeatedly admonished her to cleave to *Hadassah*'s leaders, travel in their social circles, and learn about their work. "Will you get a chance to see what . . . Hadassah [the organization] is doing?" Lena wrote. "See that you do," she continued, "so that when you get back you can become an ardent Junior Hadassah + go out + do wonders."[45] If their daughter Hadassah spent time in Palestine among the idealistic *Hadassah* reformers and Jewish educators whom the Kaplans had long known, trusted, and trained, they hoped their somewhat-rebellious daughter might find a purposeful way to contribute to Jewish renewal.

Hadassah was not the only young American woman seeking to experience Palestine for herself and, at times, yoking herself to activists, reformers, and educators. In the ten days between when Hadassah decided to travel and when she actually boarded the *Exochorda*, she convinced Reba Isaacson, her friend from Hebrew school and Camp Modin, to travel with her. On the ship, they befriended the twenty-nine-year-old Chicagoan Esther Callner. Known as "Sis," Callner was a sister-in-law of one of Hadassah's chaperones, Rose Gell Jacobs, who had been part of Szold's original *Hadassah* Study Circle. A third camper from Modin, Hadassah's Canadian friend Sylva, arrived in Palestine shortly after the other three did.

Perhaps even more than Hadassah, Sylva was an adventurer, who loved music, stylish clothes, and "small sports cars," preferably red, which, when given the opportunity, "she drove 'like a bat out of hell.'" Her parents were relieved when she asked to go to Palestine after the Depression forced her to stop taking classes at Columbia and New York University. They were particularly concerned about their daughter's interest in theater. She had acted first in New York and then in Toronto, where she received positive reviews for producing an English version of the Yiddish classic *The Dybbuk*, about a young woman possessed by a demon representing a past love on the day of her wedding to another man.[46] Like the play's protagonist, Leah, Sylva also resisted a traditional path. "I was restless," she reflected in her memoir,

> a restlessness which was beyond my father's comprehension, but which sparked considerable sympathy and understanding in my mother. She had always imbued in me the ambition to be capable of standing on my own feet. . . . I cannot say what it was, other than his deep concern at the direction of my theatrical ambitions, that eventually persuaded my father to allow me to go to Palestine. . . . It may have been my father's hope that in that environment I would find a nice, clean-cut Jewish boy to marry. . . . Few if any of the Reform Jews, including some members of my own family, had any sympathy with the concept of a Jewish National Home.[47]

When Sylva and Hadassah went to Palestine in 1932, searching for a spouse was a considerably more socially acceptable pursuit for a young Jewish woman than supporting Zionism or pursuing a career in the arts. Until 1937, when the Reform Movement shifted its position on Jewish nationalism, those who were accustomed to abandoning traditional beliefs and practices to adapt to modernity viewed Judaism as a spiritual religion, not a political nation. They also rejected the idea of returning to an ancient homeland, believing overwhelmingly that they had found their Zion in the US.[48] Although some members of the movement came to identify with Zionism earlier, the sentiment did not shift officially until the movement issued the "Columbus Platform." The revised policy espoused Zionism and recognized the particularism inherent in observing the Jewish Sabbath and holidays.[49]

Tens of thousands of Western tourists, like Hadassah, Sylva, and Reba, visited Palestine as Holy Land tourists each year during the interwar period. It was much rarer, however, to find American Jews looking to settle in Palestine.[50] Such migration countered standard economic trends, bringing migrants from a high- to a mid- to low-income country. Religious or pioneering Zionism, bringing idealists to rural collective settlements, tended to drive such movement. Only approximately nine thousand Americans settled in Palestine during that period.[51] They constituted roughly 3 percent of the total population in Palestine and more than half of them (roughly 5,000) were female. Such migration increased almost tenfold between 1931 and 1935 (from 171 migrants per year to 1,602).[52]

Still, the significance of the group that Hadassah joined was markedly more qualitative than quantitative. Jews were not the only ones to be engaged in small ideological migrations at the time. Their movement could be likened to the Back-to-Africa migration led by the Jamaican political activist Marcus Garvey as well as the affinity of American Communists— women also prominent among them—for the Soviet Union.[53] According to the historian Joseph Glass, American migrants "played a significant role—far beyond their actual numbers—in shaping the landscape and society of Palestine."[54] And American Jewish women played a particularly significant role in that process. In 1931, almost twice as many American Jewish women between the ages of twenty-five and forty migrated to Palestine as men, and roughly 55 percent of Americans living in Palestine—approximately 1,670 girls and 3,300 women—identified as female in a 1931 census.[55] Like the majority of American Jews who migrated to Palestine, they tended to come from urban environments and settle into cities (they did so more than three to one). Like Hadassah, they were particularly attracted to Jerusalem and the newly founded "hill of spring," or Tel Aviv, a city of commerce, industry, and culture.[56] Mothers who lived in Jerusalem were predisposed to send their children to Deborah Kallen's progressive school. Sister of the social philosopher Horace M. Kallen, who promoted minority rights and rejected forced assimilation in the form of a melting pot, Deborah founded and ran a school in Jerusalem that implemented Dewey's pedagogy. When their children were in school, some women in this cohort attended Hebrew University and hired tutors to work on their Hebrew. Some of them also befriended Zionist intellectuals and Hebraicists, such as the Jewish poet Hayim Nahman Bialik; the physician, writer, and translator Shaul Tchernichovsky; the author of Hebrew literature Shmuel Agnon; the editor, writer, and Hebrew University professor of Hebrew literature and history Joseph Klausner; and the educators and major contributors to the development of Hebrew David and Itta Yellin.[57]

Mordecai Kaplan on "Judaism as a Civilization" and Zionism

Hadassah did not share the type of intellectual relationship with her father that her older sister, Judith, did. Hadassah's diaries and letters yield few clues as to how cognizant she was prior to her trip of her father and his colleagues' complicated ideas regarding Judaism and Jewish nationalism. Nevertheless, the ideas he communicated through his letters—in both Hebrew and English—influenced her thinking about Zionism, Judaism, and migration. Similarly, Hadassah's thoughts shaped her father's understanding of Palestine, Judaism, and women's status and experiences.

By the time Hadassah went to Palestine, Mordecai had written but not yet published a 522-page (minus endnotes) work that would become his magnus opus. *Judaism as a Civilization* argued that Judaism was in a state of crisis because it had lost its intellectual viability in a diverse, democratic United States where traditional Jewish concepts, including a personal and supernatural God, divine revelation, and the Jewish concept of chosenness, no longer made sense. Mordecai contended that American Jews felt alienated from a Jewish history and culture that seemed incompatible with modernity, yet they also experienced exclusion from a United States that prized homogeneity above hyphenated cultural, linguistic, and ethnic identities.[58] To counter such estrangement, Mordecai called for a "program of reconstruction" to redefine Judaism not as a religion based on theological truth claims and laws (halacha) but, instead, as a civilization premised on evolving social connections, cultural trends, and religious folkways and customs whose practice could forge ethical and spiritual lives. He argued, for example, that one ought to observe the Sabbath and the laws of kashrut not because of commandments from God or even sentimental memories of such customs but based on the sociological idea that observing such mores could help one to act justly.[59]

The development of communal consciousness was vital for Mordecai's notion of Judaism as a civilization. Judaism was not just a set of ideas, individual practices, or isolated spiritual quests but rather needed community for sustenance. Judaism represented a common collective identity based on shared social associations, including language, history, culture, practices, and moral values developed to help individuals attain perfection. Mordecai saw Jewish nationalism or peoplehood as key for salvation because it aided in establishing group experiences that could align individual perfection, that is, the things that individuals desire (wealth, personal happiness, etc.), with social cooperation, the things we say we want as a community (social justice, equality, etc.). He believed that group life was essential for solving the Jewish problem. He, furthermore, devoted himself to building Jewish communities—through the Kehillah, which organized New York's Jewish communal activities, and a series of cultural and religious community centers in New York: the secular Ninety-Second Street Y, the Orthodox Young Israel and Jewish Center, and Mordecai's synagogue, the SAJ.[60]

Given Mordecai's emphasis on peoplehood, it is unsurprising that a homeland was central to his notion of Judaism.[61] At a time when most American Jews were pre-, anti-, or non-Zionists, Mordecai promoted the movement in his sermons as a way of building group solidarity.[62] American Zionism grew in the aftermath of the Kishinev pogroms (1903) and the Russian Revolution (1905), but American Jewish leaders, such as Judah Magnes and Israel Friedlander, initially focused on building local Jewish communities, like New York's Kehillah, more than on Zionism.[63] American Jews who supported Zionism tended to do so financially rather than politically, concentrating on fund-raising and investment more than nation-state formation. Following the Balfour

Declaration, Zionism achieved a new level of legitimacy, with the themes of Jewish nationalism and peoplehood permeating "rabbinic sermons, cultural and social activities," including youth groups, and "school curricula." By 1930, one in five Jewish families had at least one member who belonged to a Zionist organization, even as Jewish affiliation with synagogues was declining.[64] But even so, by the peak of the Depression, only a little more than 1.5 percent of the total American Jewish population were dues-paying members of a Zionist organization, the majority of whom belonged to *Hadassah*.[65]

To Mordecai, however, Zionism provided a language, literature, code of laws, and communal life that would allow Judaism to reestablish itself as a civilization with ongoing relevance in modern times. Mordecai was introduced to Zionism at a young age by Isaac Jacob Reines, who in 1902 founded the global religious Zionist movement Mizrachi, a combination of *merkaz* and *ruhani*, meaning "religious center." Reines was Mordecai's rabbi and teacher in Lithuania and the one to whom he returned on his honeymoon, in 1909, for *smicha*, rabbinical ordination. Mordecai agreed with the Austrian founder of political Zionism, Theodor Herzl, that the ingathering of the Jewish people should not wait for divine intervention but rather was an end to which people should actively work.[66] But unlike Herzl, Mordecai was not primarily concerned with the creation of a political entity that would remedy antisemitism and the questions of dual loyalty by providing a haven for the homeless and objects of discrimination. Hadassah might have been aware of her father's disputes with her Hebrew tutor Abraham Halkin. Like his nephew, the American-born Israeli writer Hillel, Abraham insisted that Zionism necessitated migration to Palestine. In a talk Mordecai heard Abraham Halkin deliver after he returned from spending the summer of 1930 in Palestine, Halkin argued that "a Jew who really believed in Zionism must tear up his stakes and migrate to Palestine." Mordecai disagreed. "I am glad," he wrote in his diary, "I have formulated my conception of Judaism as a civilization. I feel that it is a satisfactory answer to the extremists who insist that Jews must give up all hopes of any kind of Jewish life outside of Palestine. The answer I try to give in the book [*Judaism as a Civilization*] is that if we really had enough energy to betake ourselves to Palestine, we could use that energy to work out a satisfactory modus vivendi as a Diaspora Nation with Palestine merely as the center."[67] Mordecai's refusal to dismiss the diaspora and to view universal Jewish migration to Palestine as an essential panacea would continue after the state's foundation. He would persist in arguing that to "salvage" and "regenerate" the spirit of Jewish peoplehood, there needed to be interaction and interdependence between the diaspora and Israel.[68]

More than Herzl, Ahad Ha'am influenced Mordecai. Like Ha'am, whom Mordecai first read as a teenager, Mordecai saw Zionism as a solution to the problem of Judaism (assimilation) rather than the problem of the Jews (antisemitism). But he was skeptical of Ha'am's emphasis on Jewish culture rather than religion and also found his ideas about Judaism to be "wanting in appreciation of indefinable religious longings and aspirations."[69] Mordecai also considered the American philanthropic mode of Zionism promoted by wealthy Americans, such as Louis Marshall and Felix Warburg, insufficient in responding to Judaism's crisis of modernity. Instead, he argued for a diasporic Judaism in which Palestine would operate as a center or engine for a cultural, spiritual renaissance of Judaism that would nurture Jewish life everywhere.[70] "The part to be played by Palestine," he explained, "is to be not that of a center radiating influence, but a central project eliciting the interest of the Jew in a common creative task."[71] Mordecai Americanized Ha'am's cultural ideas, imagining that American Jews—unlike European ones—could politically integrate themselves in the context of a liberal and democratic United States. He advocated the idea of "cultural hyphenism," that Jews could live simultaneously in—and equally embrace—two societies (or civilizations, to use his term), American and Jewish. Furthermore, Mordecai believed that Jews might foster a collective culture that could serve as an ethical force in daily life, even for those who were otherwise not religiously oriented.[72]

Revitalizing Jewish communities, according to Mordecai, was vital for promoting meaningful forms of Judaism. In "Judaism and Nationality," a 1909 speech Mordecai delivered to JTS alumni, he argued that Jewish nationalism—defined broadly as peoplehood not specific to the Zionist enterprise—would inhibit assimilation more than Orthodoxy would.[73] Solomon Schechter, the seminary chancellor and former Cambridge don who discovered a trove of medieval documents in Cairo known as the Geniza, was impressed by the young rabbi. Mordecai's former JTS classmate Henrietta Szold had previously recommended him to Schechter as a possible principal of Teachers' Institute. After hearing Mordecai speak, Schechter invited Mordecai to speak to him in his study and, once there, asked him to serve as the institute's principal.[74]

For Mordecai, Zionism represented a conduit for women to play leadership roles in Jewish renewal.[75] Strong women surrounded Mordecai for the greater part of his life, from his educated older sister to his four daughters. Thus, it is not surprising that he imagined women playing a vital role in a reconstructed Judaism. Yet, even in the progressive Reform Movement at the time, a bureaucratic hierarchy constrained women working in the Jewish community. Men generally controlled "finances, policies, and plans," while women's activism was usually channeled through auxiliary organizations.[76] The fall that Hadassah went to Palestine, Mordecai published "What the American Jewish Woman Can Do for Jewish Education." The article, which Hadassah had originally typed for her father and which she read when it came out, argued that Zionism and especially the organization *Hadassah* provided a vehicle for Jewish women to apply their idealism and maternalist instincts to transform Judaism from obsolete religious beliefs and practices into a living civilization.[77] Mordecai further contended that emancipation had alienated more women than men, since women rarely received Jewish educations. He advocated Zionism, and specifically involvement in the organization *Hadassah*, to interest women in the "modern struggle for Jewish survival."[78] Mordecai hoped that working to improve the lives and health of mothers and children in Palestine "regardless of race or creed" would encourage Jewish learning through studying Hebrew, reading Jewish literature, and visiting Palestine. According to Mordecai, "The ideal of Palestine endows those who come under its influence with the courage to be different, when to be different is in the interests of justice and peace." Such meaningful experiences and knowledge, Mordecai furthermore concluded, would encourage women to seek personal fulfillment in Jewish homes, children, and synagogue attendance rather than through assimilation, conversion to Christianity, or the pursuit of materialism and upward mobility.[79]

But Mordecai was not unequivocal in his embrace of Jewish—or other types of—nationalism. Like his peers Horace Kallen and Randolph Bourne, who wrote for the Jewish intellectual English-language publication *Menorah* (founded in 1915), Mordecai criticized and warned against the creation of dominant national cultures from ethnonationalist, white, Anglo-Saxon uniformity to the American melting pot and European "Kultur." "Nationalism misapplied," Mordecai counseled in a sermon, "is dynamite."[80] More than Jewish statehood and security, he focused on rebuilding the nation of Israel and Jewish people to ensure the continuity of Judaism. Instead of racial nationalism, he embraced a concept of Jewish diasporic nationalism or peoplehood that surpassed political sovereignty and citizenship and instead brought together diverse peoples across religious, linguistic, cultural, racial, and ethnic boundaries within a pluralistic transnational community that preserved minority self-determination.[81] He viewed Jewish nationalism as a model for how minority groups could coexist in a pluralistic entity, particularly the United States.[82] In this instance, the emphasis by the organization *Hadassah* on providing health-care services to all regardless of their race, religion, or ethnicity illustrated how Jewish particularism could encourage universalist policies.

Mordecai was also mindful that an overemphasis on ethnonationalism could promote the type of bigotry among Jews that was increasingly becoming prominent among other nations. When he discussed the Mediterranean Sea on his first trip to Palestine in 1925 with Chaim Weizmann, Mordecai was offended that the man who would become the first president of Israel called the Mediterranean a "Jewish sea." "An imperialistic attitude like . . . [that]," Mordecai recorded in his journal, "grated on my ears. If the rabbis were imperialistic I understand, because it was only a psychological compensation for the inferior condition of the nation. But imperialism in the mouth of a Zionist has a hint of the chauvinism which reigns among modern nations."[83] Mordecai would go on to argue for the importance of creating an ethical nationhood based on universal and inclusive liberal values as opposed to a theocracy or ethnonationalist state.[84] Mordecai's diaries also reflect his concern about growing tensions between Jews and Arabs in Palestine. Particularly troubling is Mordecai's entry following disturbances in the summer of 1929, which he referred to as "Arab outrages."[85] For seven days, rioting, murder, and looting across Palestine, including desecrations of synagogues and cemeteries, represented a historical precedent to the more recent October 7, 2023, massacre by Hamas. In 1929, rumors spread by the Grand Mufti of Jerusalem, Haj Amin al-Husseini, triggered attacks across the country, particularly in Jerusalem, Hebron, Tiberias, and Safed, killing hundreds of Jews and Arabs but primarily targeting unarmed, non-Zionist, religious Jews in their homes. Recalling earlier destructions of the First and Second Temple, some Jews called the 1929 attack the "*dritter churban* (third destruction)."[86] The *Forverts*, the largest and most influential Yiddish newspaper of the time, labeled the violence "pogroms," recalling the anti-Jewish riots, or pogroms, prevalent in Russia and Poland and warning that a Jewish homeland would not prevent organized massacres of Jews.[87] Unsurprisingly, Jews were not unified in their conception of the violence. Pressured by the Communist Party, a Yiddish Communist newspaper, *Di Morgn Frayhayt*, shifted its initial position from condemning it to justifying it on Marxist grounds as "a revolt of the oppressed Arab masses" and an anticolonial response to British and Zionist imperialism.[88]

On August 30, just as the attacks were winding down, Mordecai joined a Zionist rally of twenty thousand at Madison Square Garden protesting the brutality against Jews. Reflecting in his diary, Mordecai used racist language to suggest that the recent events strengthened Jewish national self-determination while hindering the same among Arabs. "The actions of the Arabs during the last two weeks," he wrote in his journal, "will probably defer for a long time the granting of a representative assembly for Palestine. They have shown themselves unfit and incapable of self-government as any tribe of savages in the heart of Africa. This will give the Jews a chance to settle a sufficiently large number of their own people to be able to hold their own against the Arabs both politically and if need be also belligerently by the time Palestine will be ready to have a representative assembly."[89] In this entry, Kaplan, like many of his contemporaries, understood the destruction he read about as fitting into a narrative of Jewish victimhood and Arab savagery justifying a Jewish state and militarism. Rather than recognizing the anger of landless Arab Palestinians and their growing nationalism, Mordecai accepted a colonial and discriminatory hierarchy, suggesting that the disturbances of 1929 demonstrated the political incompetence of Arab Palestinians while justifying the expansion of Jewish economic, political, and military might.

But only three months later, Mordecai switched his stance, when he expressed support for Judah Magnes and binationalism in his diary. "At last I see the light," he wrote. "The Balfour Declaration has been like a foreign body in the system of Jewish revival, causing irritation and liable to set up a dangerous poison," he said, referring to the way the document legitimated a Jewish but not an Arab homeland, despite Arabs' demographic advantage. "I," Mordecai continued, "must have recourse once again to Ahad Ha'am to see to what extent he thought out clearly his program of Palestine as a cultural and not a political center."[90] Perhaps in that time he revisited Ha'am's "Truth from the Land of Israel," written in two installments in the early 1890s, in which he reminded Zionists of the Arabs living in Palestine and the importance of not dispossessing them.[91] When Mordecai returned to the subject again, writing in his diary a few days later, he both praised the spirit of those who were willing to sacrifice by settling in Palestine and also considered some of the tougher questions related to a Jewish national homeland. "Why," he asked his diary, "haven't we ever sat down to puzzle out the question 'How is it possible for the Jews ever to constitute a majority in Palestine? And not having a majority how can we have a national homeland in Palestine?' Why have we never asked, or why asking it have we dismissed all too easily the question 'Is it possible for the Arabs also to have a homeland in Palestine?'" Similarly, he insisted that serious consideration of the relationship between religion and state was needed. Fearing nationalism's potential to foster intolerance, he wondered if it would be possible to create an ethical-liberal Jewish nation even as he used now outdated language to racially other the culture and peoples east of Europe. "I do not yearn to live in Palestine," he concluded his journal entry. "I detest oriental life and manners.... A soil that is soaked with so much human blood will need long centuries of expiation by peace and security to atone for the cruel deeds that have been committed there." Instead of advocating for a nation-state, he argued that his Jewishness expressed itself intellectually in a lonely "desire to move mentally in the fields of Hebrew literature both ancient and modern."[92]

Camp Modin's director, Alexander Dushkin, similarly warned Jewish educators of the dangers inherent in representing Palestine as a cure-all and ignoring its complexities. In an article published in 1930 calling for "sanity in the teaching of Palestine," Alexander demanded a truthful pedagogy that would not represent "Palestine as paradise and America as exile" but would instead seek to develop "Jewish cultural activities" in both. At a moment when the American Jewish community was sharply reducing funding for Jewish education because of the Depression, Alexander argued that an escapist education centered on Palestine would estrange American Jews "who might otherwise support the upbuilding of Palestine" and alienate students "when they grow up." Furthermore, he warned that the idealization of Palestine exacerbated conflicts between Jews and Arabs, which were growing in the aftermath of the crisis in the summer of 1929.[93] "The great sin for which Palestine is expiating today," he advised,

> is *exaggeration*. It was exaggeration as to the power of that neglected land to absorb new settlers that caused our Zionist leaders to make grave mistakes in colonization—mistakes to which our enemies now gleefully point their finger. It was exaggerated statements regarding the political ambitions of the Jews that caused an avoidable suspicion on the part of Arab neighbors. It was exaggeration of their own powers and status that caused both the Yishub [*sic*] and the Zionist leaders scornfully to neglect the Arab problem, and to shut our eyes to the vagueness of British promise. We have become chastened somewhat, but we are not yet cured of exaggeration.[94]

Even as Alexander continued to urge Jewish educators and professionals to spend time in Palestine and promote Zionism to students and campers, he also warned against overstating Jewish ambition, claiming that it worsened otherwise-avoidable conflicts with Arab neighbors. Alexander, like Mordecai, was aware of the dangers inherent in ethno- and religious nationalism and the ways it threatened the possibility of pluralistic coexistence.

* * * *

Despite concerns about Zionism's impact on Arab Palestinians and the threat of rising ethnonationalism, Mordecai still saw its potential. As a father, he felt his own shortcomings in not being able to persuade even his own family of the beauty and meaning in Judaism. He hoped that Palestine and Zionism might reconstruct Judaism and educate, inspire, and provide professional opportunities for American Jewish women.

Traveling to Palestine offered Hadassah, a bright and rambunctious young woman, an opportunity to explore the world while still contributing to her father's vision of reconstructing Judaism. Hadassah retrospectively recalled that her decision to go to Palestine elevated her in her father's eyes. "He really relegated us to my mother when it came to anything important," she reflected. "I guess his mind wasn't really involved with children. . . . But he was most impressed that I went to Palestine. That really made it. By then I was a human being."[95]

Filled with dreams of purposeful autonomy and searching for adventure, Hadassah boarded the 450-foot long, eighty-two-hundred-ton American Export Liner *Flotilla* en route to Jaffa, Palestine, on September 20, 1932.[96] During a professionally and personally transitional moment, when she had few prospects for work in the United States and had completed her formal education, Hadassah imagined that the time she spent in Palestine would allow her to escape conventionality while still fulfilling cultural expectations for a so-called nice Jewish girl. Her parents trusted that their good friends would guide her in Palestine toward appropriate social circles and useful activities, such as work for the *Hadassah* organization. If she chose to become a Jewish educator, either because she failed to obtain a job in a public school or because she preferred such work, Hebrew knowledge and personal experience in Palestine would be vital for her professional development. Even if Hadassah did not formally pursue Jewish education, the Kaplans believed that her year in Palestine would help her to build a meaningful Jewish life. What exactly the year would bring and how it might impact Hadassah, however, remained unclear.

3

The Journey

During travel, passengers exist in limbo between the rituals of their old and new worlds. Photographs of Hadassah's send-off to Palestine exemplify this transition. Her father, Mordecai, his mother, Anna, and Hadassah's mother, Lena, dressed for the occasion, respectively wearing a three-piece suit with a timepiece and hats, pearls, gloves, and heels. They posed for a formal portrait on the deck of the SS *Exochorda* alongside Hadassah, whose chic outfit befitted both the formality of the moment and the elegance of the times. Despite the economic challenges many Americans faced during the Great Depression, the decade was also known as Hollywood's Golden Age, when the fashion conscious aspired to dress like their favorite movie stars even if it was a struggle to do so in reality.[1]

Clothes are important because they illustrate how people both see themselves and wish to be seen.[2] As Hadassah set sail, she was easily recognizable as her parents' daughter and her grandmother's granddaughter, but the tightrope she walked between grace and respectability, on the one hand, and adventure, on the other, was also evident in her appearance. A corsage adorned the young woman's neckline, and her contoured silhouette typified the style of the times. She wore a silk, figure-hugging day dress with a natural waistline and calf-length hemline that emphasized her curvaceous form. Over her short, styled bob, Hadassah fit a small, stylish cap, and she donned a single black glove, grasping its mate in the same hand along with a matching clutch. Black was the common color uniting her outfit, from her high-heeled shoes to her handbag, gloves, and medallion necklace and the felt trimming her hat. In Hadassah's social circle, hats, purses, necklaces, and gloves—short for daywear and long with evening attire—were still de rigueur even if they were not regular accessories.[3] The young women in Hadassah's Hunter yearbook, for example, only wore gloves occasionally, for the group portraits at their senior hop and junior prom. Generally, the students on campus

Figure 3.1. Hadassah, Mordecai, and Lena Kaplan (left to right) on the *Exochorda* docked in New York City, September 1932. (Personal collection)

were more likely to don sportswear, theatrical costumes, or academic robes than such evening—or even daytime—finery.[4] But Hadassah was taking special care as she embarked on her journey. Maintaining decorum, she would keep on her silk stockings and heels even while reclining on a deck chair.

Still, as Hadassah bid adieu to her well-wishers and the ship pulled out, the formalities of departure gave way to more casual gatherings of voyagers hoping to control their seasickness on deck. Hadassah's serendipitous encounters would lead to new friendships and the formation of spontaneous communities. Ocean travel put voyagers in a "world between worlds," where they confronted new people, foods, and customs in a setting that was neither entirely foreign nor quite familiar. For nearly a century, between the end of the American Civil War in 1865 and the growing popularity of air travel in the 1950s, ocean travel became what the historians Mark Rennella and Whitney Walton have called "an initiation or transition into another world, both imaginative and physical."[5] By 1935, the writer Thomas Wolfe suggested that ships had become "an important site of the imagination—a place that allowed people to think and act in ways that they might not allow themselves to do otherwise."[6] Travel brought a "sense of wonder, dislocation, excitement, and anticipation." By fostering a "history of possibility" as well as a global outlook, it encouraged wayfarers to question previously held beliefs and practices and to experiment with alternatives. In the best case, such a journey had the potential to "liberate the human imagination" and to cause a "dawn of consciousness."[7]

For young women like Hadassah, transatlantic travel—and writing about their experiences—held different possibilities than for male counterparts. When women had fewer personal freedoms and less professional autonomy than men, travel represented an alternative vehicle for self-determination and assertion—a space where a modern woman might pursue her own identity.[8] When people travel, they carry with them the additional baggage of how others perceive them, based, of course, not only on their expressed gender but also on their nationality, race, class, sexuality, and ability. Travel can heighten awareness of different aspects of one's identity, clarifying people's self-conceptions especially in contrast to those whom they encounter. It also has the capacity to convince itinerants to ignore identity-based constraints and differences and to forge a "geography of identity" depending on their own sensibilities.[9] Popular culture, including roughly contemporary films, such as *Now, Voyager* (1942), and more recent ones, for instance, *Titanic* (1997), portrayed transatlantic trips as liminal experiences where previously sheltered young women found entertainment and companionship onboard from those—including married men and those from differing social classes and races—whom they might not have otherwise encountered. Young, American, Jewish, female travelers like Hadassah pushed the boundaries of social, cultural, religious, and sexual norms, alternatively choosing to document or erase their actions from their journey's records. Such experiences encouraged self-expression beyond prescribed roles and limits.

When Hadassah boarded the *Exochorda*, she joined first-class travelers, including Jews, Arabs, Christian missionaries, Christian Scientists, businessmen, intellectuals, and single women, like herself, on a luxury cruise between New York and the Mediterranean. The ship was one of the American Export Lines' "Four Aces," identical vessels that carried both passengers and cargo. In 1929, the year the Great Depression hit, Lou Hoover, the president's wife, launched the first of the four ships, each of which was elegantly appointed with a smoking room, lounge, café, reception hall, and dining salon.¹⁰ Hadassah described the ship as "marvelous," with "all conveniences—bathtub, shower, hot + cold water—very good food + hospital, deck games, a bar, + comfortable beds, plenty of room to hang up + put away clothes; a victrola at meals; an orchestra (to which no-one listens, but which plays from about 9:00–11:00 P.M.); a newssheet containing abbreviated news from all over as heard over the radio," and, in addition to regular meals, servings on deck of bouillon and crackers at 11:00 a.m. and tea and cookies at 4:00 p.m.¹¹ According to a brochure issued in May 1932, the "Four Aces" provided "de luxe [sic] passenger service," for a forty-three-day, round-trip journey, costing $460 (just under $10 per day), or upward of $595 inclusive of shore trips.¹² Passengers, like Hadassah, landing before the *Exochorda*'s final disembarkation in New York, paid a discounted rate. As Hadassah's ledger indicates, she spent $222.40 for both her passage and visa, less than half of the total trip fee. Similarly, Hadassah's outbound journey lasted less than three weeks, bisecting the anticipated length of the round-trip voyage.¹³

With careful planning and attention to discounts, more frugal travel to Palestine was also possible. A few weeks after Hadassah sailed on the *Exochorda*, her Canadian camp friend Sylva Gelber traveled to Palestine for $175 on a discount line.¹⁴ Hadassah's mother, Lena, and older sister, Judith, saw Sylva off at the ship and were highly disparaging about the accommodations. They said the boat "was awful—the people horrible—+ her room still worse." Hadassah's younger sister Naomi queried Hadassah, "Did she survive?"¹⁵

During the low season (from mid-July through December), when Hadassah and Sylva set sail, rates were somewhat more moderate than in the winter.¹⁶ But even at high season, some of the luxury lines lowered prices to increase registration, which fell because of the Depression. In the winter of 1930, for example, the Holland America Line reduced its return tickets by 12 percent and eliminated its second-class status, replacing it with a tourist third cabin status for $25 less per passenger.¹⁷ By the winter of 1932, steamship agents across the country were engaged in rate cutting in response to public determination to "shop for bargains." Although cruise ship lines, such as Cunard, strove to standardize minimum rates and ensure that agents adhered to printed rates, their efforts were largely unsuccessful. In an allusion to the peddlers who sold their wares in the pushcart market on the Lower East Side, one *New York Times* correspondent insisted that steamship agents had become like the "Hester Street trader."[18]

If, like Sylva, you were flexible about the length of time you traveled, the quality of your accommodations, or the number of people with whom you traveled, you could reduce your costs more significantly. Some of the transatlantic ships, for example, carried more than one thousand passengers, providing differential pricing based on class.[19] And American Export Lines complemented its high-end cruises with "Vagabond Mediterranean Cruises." In a brochure published in 1934, the company bragged that its passengers could "roam . . . the Mediterranean at less than five dollars a day" or "for less than it costs you to live home."[20] Vagabond cruises put a few dozen passengers (thirty-seven) in cabins on the deck of cargo vessels. In 1929, this round-trip tour, without a clearly defined itinerary, charged $375 for seventy-five days.[21] Between 1934 and 1935, participation in such discounted trips increased 150 to 200 percent. "Passengers," reported Douglas Malcolm from the American Express travel service, "are showing a desire to travel as informally as possible at the minimum of cost, thus adding to the travel on vagabond freight ships."[22]

The passengers on the *Exochorda* with Hadassah represented a wide range of geographical areas, originally coming from the US, Poland, France, Greece, England, Egypt, and Palestine. Although the cruise was round-trip, only one of the 124 passengers—Arthur Dunning—intended to stay aboard throughout the journey and to return to New York. In contrast, traveling one way from New York, many travelers were returning home—either to their place of origin or to where they had been living for extended periods. More than half the passengers (seventy-seven) were headed to Alexandria. Hadassah was one of the twenty-three passengers traveling to Palestine (and one of nineteen going to Jaffa; another four were en route to Haifa). Sixteen others were on their way to Beirut, one to Tripoli, and two to Marseille. Some passengers, like Hadassah, intended their sojourn to be temporary. Others planned to remain at their destinations for the rest of their lives.

Hadassah's fellow travelers captivated her. "Of course," she wrote home, "the passengers are not the type you would find on a large ship in the tourist group during the summer. There are not gay young men, but the other people are so interesting + different from any I've come into contact with that I'm having a perfectly swell time + don't miss anything or anybody."[23] Although there was a history of homosexuality on cruise ships, Hadassah's reference to "gay young men" was probably colloquial rather than sexual.[24] She was meeting people whose life experiences differed from those she had previously encountered, even as she was chaperoned by those who had known her and her family throughout most of her life.

Based on the names and titles of the people boarding the *Exochorda* in New York alongside Hadassah, most passengers traveled as a family. There were nine husband-and-wife couples, counting the Egyptian Prince Said and Princess Nabila Toussoum. Eleven families included mothers, fathers, and between one and three children; among them were the Sephardic Jewish Hannaux family, who owned six department stores in Cairo and Alexandria modeled after Paris's Galeries Lafayette.[25] There were also the Tolkowskys, including the father, Samuel, his wife, Anne, and their three children. Samuel, who was born in Antwerp, eschewed the family business of diamond cutting to study agronomy and in 1911 settled in Palestine, where he used his skills as an agricultural engineer to develop the citrus industry. He was also a writer, documenting Jewish colonization, agriculture, and the history of Jaffa, where he and his family were heading.[26]

There were also nine mothers accompanying between one and four of their own children. One father, Chewfick Haddad, traveled with his two daughters, Emireh and Corrine. Some of the families journeying with a single parent left behind a spouse or planned to meet them at their destination. Others were recently divorced or widowed. There was a mother, daughter, and niece who, according to Hadassah, "amus[ed] the entire boat." Hadassah described the seventeen-year-old daughter as a heavyset alcoholic who explained that she drank so much because she "has so much to forget."[27] While trauma clearly haunted some passengers, others appeared to be using travel to reimagine their lives. Hadassah's recently widowed "deck chair neighbor" was heading to Naples. Similarly, the red-headed Lucy W. Pickford, whom Hadassah described as resembling a debutante, was looking to make a new start with her one-year-old baby. According to Hadassah, although Pickford still wore her wedding and engagement rings and used the last name of her husband, a Chicago surgeon, they had recently decided to divorce. With the assistance of all the "best doctors," Hadassah wrote home, Pickford's husband, who had suffered a nervous breakdown, decided that a "divorce . . . would free him of the responsibility of a wife + child, [and] would be the best thing for her."[28] Hadassah commented anecdotally in her letters on the proclivity toward divorce among the female passengers. "I can't tell you how many people are divorced. I was going to say it's peculiar, but I'm beginning to think it's a natural thing."[29]

Thirty-one passengers traveled without a spouse or child(ren). But to say this group sojourned alone would be inaccurate. At least three of them, Hadassah, Reba Isaacson (her friend from the Society for the Advancement of Judaism and Camp Modin), and Esther "Sis" Callner (a sister-in-law of Rose Gell Jacobs, one of Hadassah's escorts), journeyed with chaperones. Such mentors, who also traveled without male companions, combined advising young women with escorting their own children.

Some of the lone travelers were missionaries. Hadassah wrote home about several young men heading to Naples to study for the priesthood, whom she described, perhaps unsurprisingly, as having been "petrified" by her. The Reverend Martin Murray, on his way to Jaffa, was presumably among the less frightened ones since he treated Reba and Hadassah to drinks and dancing on the deck. Missionary families on the ship also included the Giffens, American midwestern-born missionaries who, with their son, were heading to Assuit, Egypt (via Alexandria), where they worked at a hospital. In addition, the Reverend William Miller was sailing with his wife and two daughters to Beirut, eventually proceeding to what was then known as Persia. Hadassah recalled that Miller's whole family was sick much of the journey, but he, nevertheless, "was perfectly marvelous to everybody and ran all over the boat helping people."[30]

The large-bag-toting, plume-pipe-smoking, Christian British missionary Miss Francis Newton was also on-board the *Exochorda* traveling to Haifa.[31] No documentation exists of Newton's interactions with Hadassah and her circle, but the relatively small nature of the ship makes it likely that they—and their ideas—met on deck in encounters that would have been interesting to observe. The women shared deep concerns regarding the well-being of women and children in Palestine. While Hadassah's chaperones worked through the philanthropic organization *Hadassah* to provide services for women and children from all backgrounds, Newton, who at sixty was a generation older than Hadassah's companions, primarily concentrated on the needs of Palestinian Arabs. Fluent in both written and spoken Arabic, Newton had, since 1888, used an inheritance from her mother to work and live intermittently in Palestine, administering a hospital in Jaffa and a series of girls' schools in Nazareth and Haifa. Her writing in the late 1930s and early 1940s would highlight British atrocities against Palestinian Arabs. She would also defend Muhammad Amin al-Husseini, the Grand Mufti of Jerusalem, for meeting with Hitler in 1941 and collaborating with the Nazis. Indeed, Newton's writings were so controversial in British Mandate Palestine that she would be deported in 1939 and not allowed to return until 1943.[32]

Although Hadassah was likely to—and did—encounter divergent views on the ship, her closest friend and roommate on the journey came from relatively similar circumstances to her own.[33] I knew Reba Isaacson (then Rottenberg) as one of the white-headed ladies in the audience listening to the Hunter College choir performances where my grandmother sang well into her nineties. She was also grandmother to Benjamin Shaykin, one of my Hebrew school classmates at the SAJ. Reba was born in New York on April 15, 1912, the day the *Titanic* sank. In an artist's blurb about her, Reba claimed that her Russian-born mother, Lena Isaacson, said Reba was "born to make up for all the lives lost that day" and that her mother's prediction motivated her "to live life to the fullest." One could argue that Reba's mother, Lena, had been deprived of such opportunities. Although she had won a scholarship to study opera at a conservatory in St. Petersburg, her father, who was an Orthodox rabbi, discouraged her from attending. Widowed as a young mother of four, when Reba was only eighteen months old, Lena went into the family's clothing manufacturing business (L. Isaacson & Sons, later renamed Donmoor-Donbrook) with her eldest son, thirteen-year-old Rueben Isaac. The business prospered, allowing Reba to enjoy many of the same privileges as Hadassah. Both girls were members of the SAJ, attended Camp Modin, and then went to Hunter College. They also both studied piano in musical and creative homes. In Palestine, Reba would rent a piano, sing in a Gilbert and Sullivan production (*Yeoman of the Guard*), and take watercolor classes with the American painter Minna Citron.[34]

One reason traveling to Palestine seemed particularly viable to Reba was that her older brother Fred had recently spent a year there. In 1929, while living in Palestine, he had met and married Claire Figatner, a British Jew. The two returned to New York the following year for Fred to work in the family business, but he remained profoundly connected to what would become the State of Israel, maintaining a residence there, in addition to New York, until his death in 1989.[35]

Hadassah had three chaperones on her journey: Rose Gell Jacobs, Julia Dushkin, and Bertha Schoolman. Each of these women knew her and her family well and shared many aspects of their values and background. The Schoolmans and Jacobses attended the SAJ. Bertha Schoolman was a Jewish educator who studied under Mordecai at Teachers' Institute, and both her husband and Julia Dushkin's were Mordecai's protégés. All three women were associated with Henrietta Szold and active members, if not leaders, of the organization *Hadassah*. Officially, Julia Dushkin was responsible for chaperoning Hadassah, Bertha Schoolman was to watch Reba, and Rose Gell Jacobs was to "look out for" her almost sister-in-law, twenty-nine-year-old Esther "Sis" Callner, whose brother's wife was Jacob's sister.[36] But the three matrons would collectively serve in loco parentis for Hadassah throughout her year abroad. She would spend Shabbats and holidays with them, travel with them domestically and regionally, and regularly consult them about how best to spend her time and with whom.

At forty-four, New York–born Rose Gell Jacobs was the eldest of Hadassah's mentors and the closest in age to her mother. Mordecai, in his diary, attributed his first trip to Palestine to Rose, who, after hearing his sermon on the pioneer movement in Palestine, allegedly suggested that he represent the Zionist Organization of America at the 1925 founding of Hebrew University.[37] In this respect, Mordecai's relationship with Rose was reminiscent of his connection to her close friend Henrietta Szold. Both women had helped him to advance professionally, with Szold bringing him to Solomon Schechter's attention, resulting in his appointment as principal for the Jewish Theological Seminary's Teachers' Institute.

When Rose boarded the *Exochorda*, she was in the last stretch of her first formal stint serving as national president of *Hadassah*, a position she would again hold from 1934 to 1937, but she had served as acting president since the early 1920s. Rose was one of Szold's closest associates, having been part of the *Hadassah* Study Circle from its earliest days. When the group met in the Kaplans' apartment just prior to Hadassah's birth, Jacobs (then Rose Gell) was a relatively new public-school teacher, with experience in the suffrage and progressive movements, who had completed a handful of graduate classes from Columbia's Teachers College.[38] In 1914, Jacobs traveled to Palestine on her honeymoon, the first of the *Hadassah* circle after Szold to do so. On her return, she transferred her professional energies and aspirations from teaching to Jewish communal work, building *Hadassah* chapters where she briefly lived in Tennessee and Georgia, attending international Zionist conventions, and serving in leadership positions in *Hadassah*. Jacobs would become indispensable in developing Youth Aliya—the resettlement of Jewish youth in Nazi-dominated areas to agricultural settlements in Palestine—and would initiate the building of Hadassah Hospital on Mt. Scopus. Furthermore, beginning in 1936, she would chair *Hadassah*'s Committee for the Study of Arab-Jewish relations, a research group that studied Arab culture and drafted proposals for American and world Zionist organizations to address the serious challenges Palestinian Arabs faced.[39] But *Hadassah* would disband the research committee in 1943, since the organization's supporters would increasingly embrace a Jewish state as opposed to binationalism.[40] Although the committee's work would continue under the auspices of the Emergency Committee for General Zionist Affairs, Jacobs would be disappointed by what she perceived as the abandonment of the effort to forge a rapprochement with Arab Palestinians. Her frustration with *Hadassah* ultimately would lead her to leave the institution that she had guided for more than three decades.[41]

Hadassah knew the Jacobses from the SAJ, where they were among the founders and regular attendees of services. Hadassah and her sisters were good friends with the Jacobses' eldest daughter, Ruth. Instead of accompanying her mother, the lively Ruth had been sent to her aunt in Vienna, where the young woman was to attend classes (she studied with Sigmund Freud) and, hopefully, to mature under the careful watch of her mother's sister. Instead, Ruth eloped a few months later with Wolfgang Emanuel Levy, a medical student and the son of a professor of Roman law.[42] Rose did, however, bring her twelve-year-old son, Joshua, with her to Palestine. The plan was for him to spend his bar mitzvah year as one of five hundred children attending a technical school for chemistry and physics in Haifa.

Even more than Rose Gell Jacobs, the Kaplans knew and trusted Julia Dushkin and Bertha Schoolman, the wives of Mordecai's students and protégés who most closely resembled him: Alexander Dushkin and Albert Schoolman. Like Rose, Julia and Bertha were traveling without their husbands but with their children. These mothers in their midthirties journeyed with well-matched daughters, including two six-year-olds, one who was nine, and a ten-year-old.

Julia Dushkin and her daughters were headed to Jerusalem, where she had lived when she last spent time in Palestine working for *Hadassah* as part of Szold's inner circle. Born in Poland and raised in New York, Julia Aronson (as she was then named) earned a degree in home economics from Cornell University, with a concentration in nutrition and family budgeting. Although it was less common for Jewish women, especially eastern European immigrants, to attend Cornell rather than Hunter College, Aronson would not have been the only Jewish student there. By 1919, there were about sixty-three Jewish women on campus, who accounted for nearly 2 percent of its overall student body and almost 20 percent of Cornell's Jewish student population. By the middle of the next decade, Cornell's administration had put into place a "system of scrutiny and selection" to limit the number of Jewish students at the school, particularly those like Aronson from eastern European backgrounds.[43]

After graduating, Aronson worked in social services in New York and Connecticut for two years. In 1919, she was about to travel to Belgium with the Hoover Commission when Szold, instead, convinced her to work in Palestine as a nutritionist. Aronson quickly became indispensable to Szold, eventually managing *Hadassah*'s headquarters. It was Szold who introduced Aronson to her future husband. At the time, Alexander Dushkin was serving as an inspector of Jewish schools and an educator in David Yellin's Hebrew Teachers' Seminary, which trained teachers in Jerusalem. The couple married in 1921 and remained in Palestine for another year, returning to the US in time for the birth of their first daughter, Esther.[44] The 1932 journey with Hadassah on the *Exochorda* was Julia Dushkin's first time returning to Palestine since then.

Hadassah's third chaperone, the native New Yorker Bertha Schoolman, had never visited Palestine before. As a Jewish educator who both trained and taught at Mordecai's Teachers' Institute she was eager to improve her Hebrew and familiarity with the place. She traveled with her two daughters to build her professional networks and improve both her Hebrew and that of her children. That January, her husband would join them, and they would return to New York in early summer. Schoolman's leadership roles with *Hadassah* and the Women's Zionist Organization encouraged her to continue to spend significant time in Palestine. Indeed, even as her family remained in New York, Schoolman's responsibilities as cochair of the Youth Aliya Management Committee led her to spend six months a year in Palestine and then the newly established Israel from 1947 through 1953.[45]

If the Kaplans, and especially Lena, were eager for their daughter to cleave to these *Hadassah* women, their daughter was somewhat less enthusiastic. The journey was quite rocky. Hadassah attributed feeling fine to her "heritage," but most of the passengers, including her mentors, suffered from seasickness. While she and Reba sat on the deck, wearing coats tailored to match their outfits, the Dushkins, Schoolmans, and Jacobses all stayed in their rooms, if not in their beds. "Gee it was funny," Hadassah wrote her family. "The deck was filled with people—all green—lying on deck chairs in misery. And occasionally—or rather every few minutes one would get up + lean over the rail. I never imagined it would be like that."[46] Hadassah and Reba rented deck chairs (two dollars each for the journey) near the newly installed pool, where, according to Hadassah's letters home, they read out loud Ahad Ha'am (an introduction and his essay on the "profane and sacred"), Jeremiah, Judges, and other biblical texts in Hebrew.[47] Hadassah also wrote that they discussed historical works in English, including a handbook of Palestine, a historical geography, and a history of Jews from biblical times to the British Mandate.

Conversations on deck often included others. When Reba tired of listening to Hadassah "summarize the highlights of Jewish history at the time of the Division of the Kingdom," she suggested that her friend tell it to nine-and-a-half-year-old Samuel Wagstaff, the son of a Christian Scientist divorcée from the "speakeasy neighborhood" in New York (Fifty-Fifth Street between Fifth and Sixth Avenues).[48] In addition to their lounging and reading, Hadassah and Reba played golf, tennis, and shuffleboard, with Hadassah chairing the golf tournaments.[49]

Figure 3.2. Hadassah Kaplan and Reba Isaacson on the *Exochorda* in the Atlantic Ocean, September 1932. (Personal collection)

Meanwhile, in New York, the Kaplans missed Hadassah, each sending separate notes to "The Steamer" at Port Jaffa as well as Federal Express in Tel Aviv and Jerusalem. "On the first Morning that you're on board ye honorable shippe—Exochordia," Hadassah's "Junior sister" Selma penned, "I am left with an empty house—or shall I say heart? . . . I spent this morning moving all your stuff into one drawer, and spreading my stuff into all the rest. But every other minute I pictured you sitting on that gorgeous promenade deck—or any other part of the boat with nothing but ocean around and do I get a wee bit jealous? Yes—but don't let that bother you. You just have a glorious time—and forget everyone and everything here—except every once in a while when it's time to write."[50]

The same day, Naomi teased, "I just bought two beautiful goldfish to adorn my room, and I named them Hadassah and Reba—aren't you honored. Hadassah is the bigger of the two—and eats a lot. Reba has been very lazy so far. But she (or he) will wake up soon, I hope."[51]

Written Friday afternoon, Lena's letter was newsy following a wistful opening: "I'd give anything to know how you are and what you are doing. Of course, I am hoping for the best." She reported having just baked 250 *kichel*, Jewish bow-tie cookies, for a bar mitzvah that weekend and learning from Mrs. Herman about the Malkin House, a pension in Tel Aviv on Allenby Avenue where Hadassah might want to stay. She also gave Hadassah an update on her sisters: Naomi had switched programs (from design to chemistry), Selma was loving Barnard, and Judith had just furnished her new apartment. Lena concluded her letter to Hadassah reminding her, "Accomplish what you set out for + what we are hoping for."[52]

Just before the Sabbath began, Mordecai used fatherly humor to express his confidence in Hadassah and their plan:

> We all keep on thinking about you. It was a wonderful thing that we hit upon the plan of your going to Palestine just in time when you could have such excellent company. We are all waiting to hear the first news from you informing us that you and not the sea had a swell time. It's just like me to come out with a foolish pun, but it will make you realize how good I feel and how happy we are that you are having this glorious opportunity to broaden out in mind and spirit (and a little bit in body too—say about 7½ lbs.).[53]

In a follow-up letter written a few days later, Lena reiterated the family's satisfaction in Hadassah's decision to travel to Palestine. She was particularly pleased that Hadassah was not tempted by a position that Benjamin Greenberg, the Department of Education's district superintendent, had been able to secure for her to be an examiner on literacy tests in Bensonhurst, Brooklyn, near Coney Island, an hour and a half away from the Kaplans.[54] "We don't even know," Lena explained, "whether it was a full paying or half paying [position] + we don't care. We are very, very happy with what you decided and only *hope* that you will make the best of the time you spend in Palestine to gain in knowledge and understanding. Learn to think for yourself. Get new ideas and ideals and broaden out mentally and," she reiterated her husband's message, "even a few pounds physically."[55]

When Hadassah and Reba relatively quickly constituted a foursome with two young, non-Jewish men—William Van Knox and Alvan Henry, known as "Read"—they presumably pursued "new ideas and ideals" in ways other than Lena and Mordecai had envisioned. The young women might have first encountered their male counterparts on deck, but the geography of the dining room cemented their relationships. Hadassah and Reba did not fit at the same table with the Dushkins, Schoolmans, and Jacobses. Instead, they sat nearby with the chief engineer and a couple, heading to Palma, Spain, where the husband was going to work for General Motors. Hadassah was not terribly impressed by the pair, labeling them "rather sane (or maybe same)." In contrast, the young women were drawn to Knox, a handsome young architect who was traveling to Beirut under the auspices of Yale University and the French Academy to build in the desert near Mesopotamia.[56] Knox introduced them to Read, who was traveling to Alexandria with his parents, American-born Robert Henry, known as "Pat," and Elaine. Pat had received his bachelor of arts and law degree from the University of Chicago, traveled to Oxford on a Rhodes Scholarship and then studied in Heidelberg, Germany, and Grenoble, France. He served in World War I as a captain and major before teaching law at several state universities. Following a lecturing stint at All Soul's College at Oxford University from 1920 to 1924, President Calvin Coolidge nominated and King Foud I appointed Henry to become the third American to serve on the Mixed Court. The Mixed Court, which represented fifteen countries, including Egypt, in commercial, admiralty, and real estate disputes, consisted of forty-four international judges.[57] The Henrys were traveling on the *Exochorda* en route to their estate in Alexandria. They brought their son Read with them. He had been living independently for several years while studying in London, at the University of Illinois, and at Yale, where he had befriended Knox. Read planned to live with his parents for the year before returning to Yale. Hadassah noted in her journal (as opposed to her letters home) that Read's girlfriend, Jean Halliday, had committed suicide just before his trip.[58]

Despite such a recent loss, Read developed a crush on Hadassah. From Hadassah's letters, it appears that Reba and Van were dating. The foursome traveled, had drinks before and after dinner together, and regularly held midnight teas. Some others moved in and out of their orbit. Sis Callner and the Haddad sisters, Emireh and Corrine, stayed up all night with them to see the Rock of Gibraltar, which Hadassah described as "looking just like the one in El Greco's paintings" (she gave credit to Hunter College's art history program for helping her to make that connection). Early that morning, the group raided the kitchen to find freshly baked breakfast rolls and coffee.[59]

Although not part of their assemblage in any formal sense, Hugh Parker, a Scottish, forty- to forty-five-year-old father of two who was traveling solo to Alexandria, intermittently spent time with them as well. In Hadassah's letters home, she described the interest he paid to her as "paternal" and suggested that it applied to both Reba and herself.[60] Six days into her trip, Hadassah wrote her family that "Mr. Parker" was "our Encyclopedia—our amuser—+ our "waker upper": "(I overslept once—until 12:00—+ since his room is opposite ours + he offered to knock on the door, I accepted graciously)."[61]

Parker might have penned the following undated and unsigned poem:

> From New York City came a maid,
> So blythe and bright was she,
> 'Twas on the deck one starry night
> I met her first at sea
>
> "Where are you bound, my lonely maid?"
> In mine I took her hand,
> "I journey far kind sir," she said,
> "Unto the promised land,"
>
> "In company with a maiden fair,
> Who has the name of Reba,
> I doubt not you'll mistake her for
> Another queen of Sheba."
>
> "We hope to stay there but one year
> Together with the Jews.
> Then to New York we will return
> With somewhat altered views."

"Perhaps, of course, we may remain
And even longer tarry,
If fate should guide our footsteps to
the men we wish to marry."

O Hadassah! O Hadassah!
You may change your mind,
So like your many sisters—
They are not hard to find."⁶²

There is little record of what Hadassah's mentors thought of Read or Van, but they were, unsurprisingly, quite wary of Parker. When Hadassah first wrote to her family about him, she narrated a heated exchange between him and her chaperone Jacobs. The conversation began when Parker approached Hadassah and Reba as they were reading aloud the British Mandate on the boat's deck. "I wish," he told them, "I could make you a present of Palestine." "Why?" they asked. Palestine, he replied, was only a financial burden and responsibility for England and did her "absolutely no good." Jacobs then entered the conversation, refuting Parker's arguments about Palestine's cost to Great Britain. "Why," he then asked, "[do] the Jews want Palestine anyway?" According to Hadassah's account, Jacobs answered Parker's question with one of her own: "Do you consider an average Jew a good Britisher [sic]?" Yes, he answered, but he then proceeded to add various qualifications, constituting what we might today call microaggressions, a statement considered subtle discrimination against a marginalized group. Jacobs explained that "it was just that—just the qualifications that caused the Jew to feel more at home in Palestine. Because among other Jews, if he does an ordinary fault, it is considered as such + not exaggerated etc." Parker conceded but then moved on to more overtly antisemitic tropes about Jewish control, echoing the type of stereotypes outlined in Adolf Hitler's *Mein Kampf*, which had appeared in an abridged form two years earlier. "The Jews," Parker exclaimed, "overrun the world wherever they are. They always come into power. They control England even now." According to Hadassah, he said this "respectfully" rather than with malice, and she appeared not to have been offended by his proclamation, which she reported in her letter without comment. Presumably Jacobs and the Kaplans did not interpret the non-Jewish, Scottish man's words as lightheartedly as did Hadassah, who continued to engage and regularly consult Parker. When they passed the Rock of Gibraltar, three days later, she wrote home, "My friend Mr. Parker explained all the important things," including the workings of the water supply and the history of a 750-year-old castle.[63]

The following evening, the night before docking in Palma, Spain, the two became even more intimate. In a letter to her family, Hadassah recalled the Captain's Dinner as "New Year's Evish," with "delicious sparkling Burgundy," a "marvelous meal," and "confetti."[64] She reserved more detailed accounts for a diary entry written once she had arrived in Palestine:

> After dinner, Mr. Parker used as an excuse to come to my room—the fact that he wanted benzine for his cigarette lighter. He was very sweet tho—and when he kissed me—I thought it was just the effect of the liquor. We went back to the dining room + Read + I had a dance + then, as far as I can remember (It was so long ago) we went to the bar. After that, Reba and Van, who were quite friendly already, went to the top deck. Mr. Parker and I walked around a bit and then came downstairs. He came to my room to see something—but stayed some time. And the blasé Hadassah was thrilled! I did like him an awful lot. And it was a new experience doing such things with a person 44 years old! He was so perfectly darling about it and spoke so beautifully to me too! No sooner did he leave my room, than Mrs. Dushkin and Schoolman came in "to see how I was." They had looked at me peculiarly when I passed them in the reception room! They were also worried about Reba. But I assured them that she was quite OK![65]

While something sexual clearly occurred between Hadassah and Parker, the exact nature and level of intimacy remain unclear. Their age differential (and Parker's marital status) made their affair unusual, but premarital, episodic dating and sexual experiences (generally short of intercourse) had become common by the 1920s.[66] In a 1924 study of collegiate women in Muncie, Indiana, 92 percent admitted to "petting" (intimate touching) and "spooning" (cuddling front to back).[67] Hadassah's younger sister Selma teased her for the many male friends who continued to phone her in New York and who were upset to learn about her travels. "If they keep phoning much longer," Selma threatened,

"I'm going to say I'm Hadassah—with permission of the copyright owner?"[68] The cultural clash between, on the one hand, Hadassah's mentors and parents and, on the other hand, Hadassah, Reba, and Selma represented an intergenerational shift in attitudes toward what was and was not permissible in premarital relations between the sexes. On the ship, the less guarded younger generation found space to emerge.

Despite Hadassah's seeming self-confidence, notes in her diaries suggest some level of ambivalence about her behavior. Her concern was not about passing, modifying her mannerism and façade to fit into her surroundings and appear to be non-Jewish. Given her destination, her companions, and her mentors, there could be no question about her identity. Instead, what was at stake was her willingness to flirt, date, and engage physically in relationships across religious and other lines, including age, nationality, and even marriage. Even so, Hadassah was considerably more guarded with her contemporary Read than with Parker. Two days after her encounter with the latter, she recorded a terse entry in her diary indicating a conversation between Read and herself. "Stood on bridge," she wrote, "and told Read how I felt concerning Jew-Gentile situation. It was a very good catharsis."[69] Although she does not spell out the exact nature of her stance, given her family's dedication to sustaining Judaism, it can be assumed that she warned Read that their religious differences would limit the seriousness of their relationship. Even if Hadassah was candid with Read, she knew that she was pushing beyond socially permissible behavior in her relationship with Parker.

Hadassah spent Rosh Hashanah touring what she described as the "terribly crowded" streets in Marseille with Read, Van, and Reba. She described the city vividly in a letter home:

> One house is right on top of the other. The streets are about 2 ft. wide and in very many places there are no sidewalks. In the town proper you see thousands of stores—signs—street vendors, etc. There are people sitting in the middle of the street next to baby carriages manicuring their nails & selling fruit, children's dresses, books, etc. There are quite a few moving picture places. And of course, on every block there are at least fifteen cafes—where you sit outside, watch the passers by and drink. There are all sorts of people and officers. Colored Morocco [sic] officers, short fat ones with moustaches and berets. As for the streets! Would you believe

that New Yorkers could be afraid to cross the street. Well—there the cars run fast and furious and toot their horns all over the place. After they've warned you—their duty has been performed + it is your look-out whether you desire to be killed or not.[70]

While Hadassah noted the multicultural nature of the French port city, she does not appear to have attempted to encounter the Jewish community of Marseille, which dates back at least to the sixth century. For example, she did not try to locate the Grand Synagogue in the sixth arrondissement, with its elegant stained-glass windows and Romanesque arches, where presumably services were being held to mark the Jewish New Year. Marseille was one of the largest Jewish communities in South France. By some estimates, in 1933, as many as twenty-five thousand Jews, mostly the working-class descendants of Mediterranean and Sephardic Jews, lived there. They would be joined, in the 1940s, by Jewish refugees and together face discriminatory laws that labeled, segregated, and incarcerated them. In two roundups in 1942 and 1943, French police officers and Nazis gathered thousands of Jews in the small street in front of the Grand Synagogue and deported them to death camps.[71]

Oblivious to what was to come and focused on her personal adventures, Hadassah returned to the ship just "2 minutes before it sailed." She had another drink with the chief engineer—she had also met him in Marseille at a jazz club for drinks and dancing. Then, she spent some time with Reba on the deck before receiving a cable from her family wishing her in transliterated Hebrew a happy New Year and kisses from all of them ("Shana Tova Uneshikot. Mikulanu"). Hadassah herself had sent a similar cable the day before, wishing them a happy New Year and sending them love also in a transliterated Hebrew ("Shana Tova Lekuchem, Beahava, Hadassah"). Nevertheless, Hadassah described their message as starting her "off on a fainting spell" such as she had not had "in centuries": "I went down to the cabin and later Read, Van, and Reba came to see how I was. Read was darling and cheered me up remarkably. It was just what I needed to feel that somebody cared the least bit!"[72]

Whether her fainting spell indicated dehydration or a growing sense of guilt, Hadassah expressed increased concern about spending time alone with Parker. When the *Exochorda* docked in Naples a few days later, Reba and Van planned to take a boat to Capri along with Read and his parents, who wanted to show him where they had spent their honeymoon. Parker invited Hadassah several times to tour Naples, but she was uneasy. In her diary, she wrote, "I didn't know what to do." Presumably, she wanted neither to be a third wheel with Reba and Van nor to travel alone with Parker. There is little indication that her chaperones were closely following her whereabouts. "Luckily, Reba wasn't ready on time and we missed the boat to Capri."[73] Parker—the only one in the group who spoke Italian—then took the three of them to see some of the major local tourist sites, including the volcanic crater Solfatara, the Flavian Amphitheater, the Royal Palace of Naples, the opera house, and a thirteenth-century castle.[74] Hadassah sent home an extensive travelogue and photographs of her journey.

Like Parker, Read also paid special attention to Hadassah, with the journey permitting space where the two could circumvent the eyes of parents and chaperones. Hadassah noted in her diary that Read brought her a "lovely corral necklace" after a day in Capri with his parents. A few nights later, the penultimate evening before both Read and Parker would permanently disembark in Alexandria, Hadassah and Read stayed up to see the sunrise. Hadassah described them in her diary as having alternated between their cabins and walking around the deck, finally retiring to Hadassah's room at 5:15 a.m., when they "found that Van had left + Reba was asleep." Hadassah recorded that she and Read "slept straight through until lunch" without noting who slept where.[75]

The following evening, Parker and Read's last one on the ship, Hadassah recalled in her diary that Parker "acted just like a kid." "He," she explained, "wanted an opportunity to say goodbye to me. I finally went to his cabin for a tin of Luckies + he was very grateful. He's a darling, I have to write him."[76] It is unclear what happened in their room that evening, if Hadassah actually did write to him, or if he replied. In her diary, Hadassah mentioned that she, Reba, and Van returned to Parker's room later that evening to look at his photographs. According to Hadassah's diary, Read could not join them because he was apparently writing letters at the bar to try to avoid seeing the daughter of a Dutch judge, a setup presumably arranged by his parents.

When the *Exochorda* docked for three days in Alexandria, Hadassah and Reba toured the city and traveled to Cairo unaccompanied by their formal chaperones. Instead, Parker, who also spoke Arabic, showed Hadassah, Reba, Van, and Read Montazar's Palace and then helped the young women to purchase train tickets for $4.10 for the 350-mile journey to Cairo. They traveled with Van, Jack Simon—a Jewish Palestinian whom Hadassah and Reba had not spoken to on the *Exochorda* but who would become a close friend over the course of the year—and a few other shipmates.[77] Only in Hadassah's diary did she reflect despondently on her departure from Parker. He had offered to meet them in a day or two when they returned to Alexandria if Read could not, but Hadassah "was quite sure he wouldn't have to" and that they would "never see him again." "No sooner did we get into our compartment (in the train to Cairo)," she recalled, "then I began to feel very sad about leaving Mr. Parker + actually sniffled. Of course I'll 'think of him kindly!'"[78] Hadassah was right. Other than regards from Parker, which Read sent in a letter to Hadassah, she appears not to have seen or heard from him again.[79]

Hadassah's arrival in Alexandria reveals her discomfort with Arabs and Arabic in a way that differed from her attitudes toward the other people she had thus far encountered on her journey. When previously landing in Spain, France, and Italy, she had commented positively or humorously on the languages and people she confronted. In Marseille, she loved hearing French songs (even more than a Russian orchestra that played jazz) and "had so much fun" speaking French and serving as the group's interpreter.[80] In Naples, she joked about not being able to ask for salt for her potato chips and, instead, being served granulated sugar.[81] In Alexandria, in contrast, her confrontations with Arabs and Arabic were more discomfiting. "It certainly was a shock," she wrote in her diary, "to get off the boat and hear only Arabic spoken. Besides, all these men looked so fierce that we were petrified."[82] Hadassah was relieved to be able to fill her train car to Cairo with fellow travelers from the *Exochorda*. "We were very happy," she wrote home, "that we didn't have to double up in that compartment with any Arabs."[83]

Although travel allowed Hadassah and her peers to interact with people from different backgrounds, she clearly understood certain barriers as unassailable. As the comparative literature professor Mary Louise Pratt explains, travel creates "contact zones" or social spaces where cultures and individuals, typically within asymmetrical relationships, meet and clash.[84] Hadassah's attitudes toward Arabs reflected Orientalist ideas based on stereotypical depictions of Middle Easterners that helped to legitimate colonial hierarchies and aggression. Part of Hadassah and her family's thinking about Arabs was shaped by what they had heard about recent violence in Palestine, especially during the summer of 1929.

Hadassah's attitudes toward Arabs were further shaped by her mother's anxieties. Lena repeatedly warned Hadassah to take special care around Arabs. "Please darling," her mother warned, "don't ever go out alone or even with Reba and Sylva (when she comes) among Arabs. Don't laugh at this when you read it. I am very serious about it."[85] Lena's biased racial assumptions were highly problematic but common among white women at the time. Indeed, similar ideas helped wrongly to convict nine African American teenagers—one as young as fourteen—of raping two white women, one of whom recanted her accusation, in the contemporaneous Scottsboro Trials. Mordecai would protest the violation of justice in that case, connecting it with European injustices such as the forced dissolution of the Austrian Parliament and the institution of authoritarian rule by the Italian fascist Benito Mussolini's mentee, the Christian Social chancellor Engelbert Dollfuss. Watching a dramatization of the Scottsboro case, "They Shall Not Die," led Mordecai to question his faith in humanity and God. He assured his diary that if he could leave the rabbinate for "some kind of fighting organization that would hold out the least promise of destroying the present crime infested social order," he would "regain . . . faith in life."[86] What Hadassah or Lena thought about the Scottsboro trials remains unknown. Hadassah, however, appears to have maintained racial divisions even as she crossed other boundaries. In contrast, her younger sister Selma would more easily cross racial lines. When she sailed to London that May, she met the boat's musician, thirty-four-year-old Duke Ellington. They remained friends throughout his life.

In Cairo, Hadassah, Reba, Van, and a few other friends from the ship followed a largely prescribed colonial tourist route. They might have taken one of the popular preorganized tours. Thomas Cook & Son's, for example, encouraged visitors to experience Egypt as a picturesque exhibit displaying ancient ruins as opposed to a modern land with contemporary people.[87] Instead, Hadassah, traveling with her peer group, was both startled by the "thousands of Arabian beggars" and surprised by Cairo's modernity, although she expressed no connections between the two.[88] She, Reba, and Van visited King Tutankhamun's collection at the Museum of Egyptian Antiquities and the Zoological Gardens. Most exciting was their donkey ride to see the Great Pyramid and Sphinx of Giza. "Can you picture us getting on donkeys," Hadassah wrote home, "with dresses, silk stockings + high heels? Well we did—+ rode very comfortably."[89] In her diary, Hadassah recalled the young women's discomfort because of their "girdles."[90]

When Hadassah did interact with local Arabs, it was in service encounters in which she assumed the worst of them. Two disputes over payments in Cairo reveal Hadassah appealing to British officials for protection. In the first instance, Hadassah and Reba paid a taxi driver the amount they had been told their trip to the Zoological Gardens should cost, which was less than a quarter of the amount indicated on the meter. The driver appealed to an official, but the policeman "shoved him aside."[91] The driver then returned to the young women with an interpreter and six other people. "We were sure," Hadassah wrote in her diary, "he [the driver] was going to knife us—but we paid him some more + he went back."[92] According to Hadassah's letter home, the women doubled what they had paid, which was still less than half of what the meter had said. On the way back, she told her family, the women took a streetcar "to avoid the haggling."[93] When Hadassah later saw a dispute between two Arabs, she was highly critical. "Everything was all right," wrote Hadassah, "until one of them started cursing his children (he didn't mind having his mother + father cursed). Anyway they all started yelling + poking each other—but luckily some English officers came over + quieted them." Hadassah appears to have been less interested in how the English officials resolved these conflicts, what happened to the disgruntled Arabs, or how they were compensated than in the British-style restoration of order and her own well-being. Her final comment to her parents illustrated her tendency to generalize about, rather than empathize with and try to understand, Arab circumstances within a colonial structure. "Honestly," she wrote home, "it's remarkable the way those Arabs love to fight. All they ever do is quarrel, yell, + beg. I've never in my life seen people with such temperaments."[94] Hadassah's characterization of Arabs illustrates the type of assumptions that were common within a colonial framework and prevented visitors and colonists from seeing the legitimate grievances experienced by indigenous peoples.

When Hadassah and Reba returned to Alexandria, Read picked them up in his five-year-old car, "the first new Ford in Alexandria," and drove them to his family's place "right off the sea with immense rooms and high ceilings."[95] Read continued to pursue Hadassah, taking her out for "steak and drinks" and giving her an elegant jade necklace.[96] In a letter home, Hadassah emphasized the inexpensive nature of the jewelry, writing that Read bought it after haggling for a "ridiculously low price."[97] In her diary, however, she at least retrospectively eluded to the "elegant green necklace" and Read's lifestyle more generally as excessive, labeling him a "Champagne Charlie," a term referring to a young Frenchman who introduced hard-alcohol-drinking Americans to the refined drink.[98] Once Hadassah arrived in Palestine, Read stayed in touch. Hadassah was surprised that he sent her via Federal Express photographs of their foursome swimming at Cleopatra's Baths with an accompanying letter emphasizing Hadassah's physique.[99] "Make a special note," Read commented, "of the picture of you and me (I already have). The super-Venus like curves and figure are shown off to excellent advantage—very nice."[100]

Perhaps wary of further encouraging him, Hadassah took care to avoid Read's repeated invitation to stay with his family in Alexandria and travel with him to Luxor when she returned to Egypt in December. Although they continued to correspond even after returning to New York—and Read's invitations persisted—Hadassah was more guarded with him than she had been on the ship.[101]

While Hadassah and her peers were on the *Exochorda*, crossing borders where letters could not reach them and evading mentors who were minding their own children, they temporarily escaped both their parents' and their chaperones' close watch to pursue new intimacies. As Hadassah reflected back on her journey after returning to New York, she would remain nostalgic about her encounter with Parker. "I met a very swell person on the boat coming over," she wrote her older sister, Judith. "He had the grandest sense of humor of anyone I've ever met—of course he was a Gentile + married—+ I'll never see him again—but I enjoyed his company a lot on the boat."[102] Controlled transgressive behavior limited to a three-week journey allowed women like Hadassah to explore relationships they would not, under other circumstances, have tried.

Figure 3.3. Hadassah Kaplan and Alvan "Read" Henry at Cleopatra's Bath, Alexandria, Egypt, October 9, 1932. (Personal collection)

While traveling, venturesome, young Jewish women might challenge expectations about with whom they might become intimate. The constrained time and space of the ship permitted experimentation while largely preserving reputations and colonial hierarchies.

4

Getting Settled

The *Exochorda* sailed into Jaffa at 5:00 a.m. on October 9, 1932. Since only a handful of Jews worked at the port, Arab Palestinian fisherman would have rowed the visitors to shore. The port city, one of the oldest in the world, which had long served as the main passageway for Palestine's imports and exports, had grown during the British Mandate into the largest and most prosperous Arab city in Palestine, with a vibrant economic and cultural center.[1] In Arabic, it was known as *umm al-gharib* (mother of the stranger) because of the range of people intermingling on its streets, and *'arus al-bahr* (bride of the sea) for its beauty.[2] Before the founding of Tel Aviv in 1909, Jaffa stood as the center of both Jewish and Arab nationalism, the latter indicated through its third name: *'arus falastin* (bride of Palestine). But by the 1930s, the size of its port, combined with overcrowding and deteriorating conditions, left it struggling to export the citrus fruit grown in the region. Heavy cargo, such as iron and coal, was redirected to Haifa. A year after Hadassah's arrival, Haifa would open a deep-water harbor that would become the country's leading port.[3]

Jostling on the shore to meet the *Exochorda* were Hadassah and Reba's camp friends: the Canadian Miriam Kronick, who was known among friends by just her last name, her mother (Mrs. Kronick), and Helen Schwartz. We do not know what Hadassah and her peers thought of the port. Did they register the city's coffeehouses, theaters, and cinemas?[4] Perhaps they arrived on a market day, when the smells of animal carcasses, rotting fish, and overripe vegetables would have overpowered the more distant fragrance of orange groves.[5] Or maybe they were so focused on catching up with one another that they did not fully register their surroundings until arriving in the neighboring Jewish city of Tel Aviv.

Tel Aviv, which literally means "the ancient mound of spring," a Hebrew translation of the Austro-Hungarian writer and activist Theodor

Herzl's novel title *Alteneuland*, "Old-New Land," duly impressed Hadassah and her peers. The Jewish city adjacent to Jaffa initially began as a self-governing, modern, Western, Hebrew-speaking garden suburb and later became a resort destination—a "Palestinian Atlantic City."[6] Hadassah reported having been "very pleasantly surprised" to find Tel Aviv so clean and light, "having been told by some prejudiced Englishmen that" it was "much worse" than Cairo, a comment that again reinforced colonial assumptions.[7] Presumably the New Yorkers were more struck by Tel Aviv's architecture than its dirt, noise, and disease. Hadassah probably tuned out the city's soundscape of radio, cacophony of languages, stray dogs, cats, and rats "the size of cats" to encounter a city in transition.[8] In the 1930s, Tel Aviv combined Eclecticism—a European "fashioning of 'the Orient'"—including architecture in an array of colors with turrets, arches, and silver-painted domes—with the International style built by immigrants aspiring to re-create European cosmopolitanism and vibrancy in the Middle East through modern, minimalist, white, and angular buildings crafted in the Bauhaus style. The urban center sought to differentiate itself both from Jewish ghettos in Europe and from Arab cities, like Jaffa. By the 1930s, with its waves of immigrants, booming construction, and a growing retail, trade, and creative sector, Tel Aviv had replaced Jaffa as the economic, cultural, and demographic center of the Yishuv, the Jewish population in Palestine.[9]

Forty percent of Jewish migrants to Palestine during the 1920s and 1930s settled in Tel Aviv, but Hadassah was not among them.[10] While Tel Aviv's size nearly quadrupled in the 1930s, from 45,000 to 165,000, Hadassah moved to the other predominantly Jewish city in Palestine: Jerusalem.[11] Arriving the day before one of the holiest times in the Jewish calendar, Yom Kippur, or the Jewish Day of Atonement, might have shaped Hadassah's route. But beyond the calendar, Hadassah was markedly more drawn to Palestine's biblical origins, Holy Land tourism, and archeology than to the more modern Tel Aviv. In this way, Hadassah's itinerary reflected the tendencies of American Jews more broadly, many of whom were pulled to cities, especially to Jerusalem. According to the 1931 Census of Palestine, most American Jews (851) settled in Jerusalem compared to in Tel Aviv (702) and in Haifa (94).[12]

Hadassah, Reba, Van, and Sis joined the New York contingent in Jerusalem when they took a two-dollar taxi to Goldsmit House, a pension at the intersection of King George and Bezalel Streets. Goldsmit's was conveniently located across the street from where Jack Simon lived. Jack was a Palestinian Jew from a Sephardic family who worked as a United Press correspondent. The young women had befriended him at the end of their journey on the *Exochorda*.

The view en route to Jerusalem, the olive trees, and the "first class roads" all inspired Hadassah. She did not, however, comment on the traffic and the range of traditional and modern vehicles sharing the road, with cars jostling for space alongside horses, buggies, camels, and bicycles, and the inevitable stench of horse droppings, gasoline, and exhaust fumes.[13] Instead, Hadassah, who loved driving, relished the taxi driver giving her a turn at the wheel until they arrived at "hair-pin bends in the mountains."[14]

Like many Jewish tourists before her, Hadassah went to the Kotel, the Western Wall, to attend Kol Nidre services, marking the beginning of the Day of Atonement with the chanting of a special legal formula in Aramaic annulling all religious vows (but not professional or personal commitments) made in the previous year. The Kotel is the holiest site in Judaism, where stand the remnants of an ancient wall surrounding the Jewish Second Temple, destroyed by the Romans in Jerusalem's Old City in 70 CE. The Kotel is also the third holiest place in Islam. Al-Haram al-Sharif, as the platform is known in Arabic, contains the Al Aqsa Mosque and the Dome of the Rock, where Muslims believe the Prophet Muhammad ascended to heaven. The British attempted to preserve the status quo maintained by the Ottomans, but the dual history and identity of the site had long fostered disputes over its access and control, conflicts that continue to the present. Three years before Hadassah's arrival, the Western Wall had become the locus for clashes over rising Jewish and Arab nationalism. That October, Jewish demonstrators in Tel Aviv and Jerusalem protested restrictions on their ability to access the thirty-by-five-meter alley in front of the wall and to hold prayer services there. Activists included Revisionist Zionists, a militant group led by Vladimir Jabotinsky that considered clashes between Jewish and Arab nationalism inevitable and sought to expedite the establishment of a Jewish state through British policies conferring state land to Jews.[15] Jewish demonstrations at the Wall—along with ongoing efforts to buy the pavement—exacerbated Arab Palestinian fears of mounting restrictions on their right to pass through the space, as well as broader concerns about territorial rights. Joseph Klausner, a professor of Jewish history and Hebrew literature and an expert in the Second Temple period under whom Hadassah had expressed interest in studying at Hebrew University, led the conflicts in Jerusalem. Klausner, who would later become the great-uncle of the Israeli author Amos Oz, established a Pro–Wailing Wall Committee in 1929 to defend Jewish rights to worship at the Wall. The Grand Mufti of Jerusalem, Haj Amin al-Husseini, published pamphlets insisting that Jews intended not only to retake the Wall but also to rebuild the Jewish temple. Such rumors triggered the burning of prayer books and hand-written prayers that Jews inserted into the cracks in the Wall, in the belief that a divine presence dwelled there that might answer their pleas. The demonstrations, rumors, and book burnings also sparked violence across the country, including massacres in Hebron, Jerusalem, and Safed, killing in roughly equal numbers almost three hundred Jews and Arabs and injuring more than seven hundred people, with Jews—the majority of whom were living in long-standing, non-Zionist, unarmed, religious communities—suffering twice as much of the destruction and as many of the casualties. British armed forces shot most of the Arabs, who were killed while attacking Jewish settlements. Jewish militants also participated in the violence, lynching about twenty Arabs.[16] Visiting Kibbutz Hulda in Central Palestine following the attacks, the Zionist sociologist Arthur Ruppin recalled the damage he witnessed. "On Tuesday," he wrote, "I went from Tel Aviv to visit Huldah, most of which was destroyed and burnt to ashes during the disturbances. Many of the trees have also been burnt. There is nobody there. The place makes a terrible impression."[17]

Despite ongoing violence and political strife, Hadassah hoped to find meaningful Jewish religious life in Jerusalem. She and Sis followed the advice given to them by Goldsmit House residents to go to the Kotel for Kol Nidre services. Although they arrived at the designated time, Hadassah wrote home that "everyone had [already] left" by then.[18] The next day, the young women walked around the city looking for services, following the sound of singing to a Sephardic synagogue, founded by Jews whose ancestors were forced to convert or were exiled from Spain to other places in Europe and the Middle East. Hadassah and Sis found the service "neither particularly inspiring nor interesting," before moving on to an Ashkenazi one, founded by Jews descended from a Jewish diaspora that had migrated from northern Europe to Slavic lands. The two young women, coming from Ashkenazi backgrounds themselves, might have expected to have identified with such a service. Instead, Hadassah noted with disdain the marginalized role women played. According to her, they "just sort of sat and looked." In the Society for the Advancement of Judaism, her father's synagogue, unlike most synagogues at the time, young women could lead and actively participate in ritual life. In contrast, the services Hadassah encountered in Palestine were more typical of Orthodox ones she might have experienced elsewhere, separating women from men literally behind a *mechitza*, a physical barrier, that alternatively put women on a balcony, behind a wall, or in a separate room from the men. Few women attended these services, and when they did, they mostly watched the men rather than engaging in prayer themselves. Hadassah was particularly disappointed by the gender divide in Chasidic services, which she experienced on Simchat Torah, the last of the Jewish High Holidays that marks the end of the annual cycle of Torah reading. "The men," she wrote home, "have a whole room downstairs where they dance around with the Torah + sing beautifully—+ the poor women are stuck up in a tiny alcove where they pile on top of one another in order to be able to see. Honestly—you have no idea how women are treated here. It's pathetic."[19]

More generally, Hadassah was disappointed by the relative absence of religious observance and spirituality, despite both her and her family's high hopes regarding religious life in Palestine and its potential to serve as a spiritual center for diaspora Jewry. "Somehow or other," Hadassah wrote her family following Yom Kippur, "I felt that here in Jerusalem I'd find nobody on the streets [i.e., no one engaged in business and other official activities on the Jewish Sabbath and holidays] and everybody would be praying—instead I found what appeared to be a great lack of religious feeling. Occasionally walking along you'd hear services thru a window—but just as often you'd hear a radio or a victrola [record player]! The only thing there weren't many of was automobiles."[20] Hadassah's disappointment with what she perceived as the shortcomings of religious life and sentiment in Palestine resonated with her peers. The Jewish educator Jessie Sampter, who had studied with Mordecai before settling in Palestine, similarly described Jewish religious observance in

Palestine as unsatisfying. "In Jerusalem," Sampter explained, "one has to choose between anti-religious and fossilized religion." Unwilling to settle with either of those options, Sampter challenged, "But does one have to choose? Is there not a third choice, a new way?" She turned to her friends, including the founder of *Hadassah*, Henrietta Szold, and the Jewish educators Julia and Alexander Dushkin, to forge a more meaningful religious life. They created "gender-inclusive services," meaning ones where women could play an active role liturgically. They also excluded from their rituals what Sampter considered "unappealing theological content, . . . renewing temple sacrifice, for example." Yet, she nevertheless remained underwhelmed by Palestine's spiritual life.[21] Even the Scottish Hugh Parker, Hadassah's paramour on the boat, had criticized religion's commercialization in Palestine. The presence of collection trays in religious institutions particularly offended him. "Anyone who wanted to lose all religion," he insisted, "should go to Jerusalem."[22]

Political tensions exacerbated religious shortcomings. On Yom Kippur afternoon, when Hadassah returned to a packed plaza in front of the Kotel, she witnessed hostilities undergirding Jewish-Arab relations. A year earlier, an international commission in the aftermath of the 1929 disturbances led the British to enact a law aiming to maintain order by banning political speeches and demonstrations at the Wall, as well as boisterous religious ceremonies for both Jews (blowing the shofar, or rams horn) and Arabs (the *zikr* ceremony, including singing and drumming). Earlier prohibitions from the Ottoman regime prevented the bringing of "appurtenances" to the wall, including Torah scrolls on ordinary weekdays, benches for the old and infirm, and screens to separate men and women, like the ones troubling Hadassah. Without a commission or a judicial system adjudicating rights at religious sites, British officials intervened regularly, interrupting religious ceremonies to try to maintain what they considered the status quo.[23] Hadassah watched British authorities stop a Jew from marking the end of the fast day by blowing his shofar, which she described as a crime punishable by three to eight months in prison.[24] "We noticed," Hadassah wrote home, "an Arab at the wall [Kotel] on the other side. He was calling the Arabs to prayer. Just then it came time for the Shofar. But it seems that for political reasons we are not allowed to blow it. Because the Arabs won't have us do anything that wasn't done before the destruction of the Temple."[25]

Here, Hadassah misapplied the international commission's prohibition to Arab Palestinians. "Anyway," she continued, "as he [a Jew] started to blow it [the shofar]—men shouted *Lo* ["no" in Hebrew] to him. He was forced to stop + the British Officers who were protecting there as well as at intervals in the approach to the wall, came over + stopped him + pacified everybody. I'm telling you we might have had a riot there + then."[26] But none ensued. Instead, Hadassah witnessed ongoing negotiations over religious observance in shared sacred spaces and concerning what role British authorities would play in peacekeeping.

Beyond exploring Jerusalem's religious and political terrain, Hadassah spent time with her friends, including Reba, Sis, Jack, Van, and a few other Americans who floated in and out of their orbit. Often they visited in tea shops, such as the Vienna Café, exchanging written notes and spoken comments in Hebrew.[27] Hadassah reported that the Grand Café was best for dancing, with its "excellent orchestra," dance floor, and garden.[28] The recently opened King David Hotel, with its own orchestra and chauffeur service, also held balls and other dances.[29] Hadassah wrote her family that parties in Palestine were similar to those in New York, with regard to dances and songs, except, she said, "that we tried to speak only Hebrew + we sang some Hebrew songs."[30]

With knowledge of the land as a central tenet of Jewish nationalism, Hadassah and her friends toured the country, traveling to Bethlehem and the Dead Sea frequently in Jack's car, with or without him. On the weekends, they traveled to Tel Aviv by bus, which the American journalist Nellie Straus-Mochenson described as a "ramshackle affair," involving long waits, pushing, sweating, and irregular departures depending on when they filled as well as when drivers put down their reading to return to the road.[31] The crew found more reliable lifts from Jack or his South African friend Harry Joffe, a nephew of another former Camp Modinite: Zelda Shapiro. Harry had lived in Palestine with his family for four years, was—according to Hadassah—fluent in Hebrew, and, as she would later learn, was also a member of the Haganah, a Zionist military organization constituted to combat revolts by Arab Palestinians.[32]

One of the biggest enticements of Tel Aviv was its Jewishness. Despite its unattractive exterior, the city was intensely alive with Jewish activity, including public events and celebrations from Sabbath to holidays.[33] When Hadassah and Reba went to Tel Aviv, they would often participate in such celebrations. The crew, who stayed with various camp friends, usually the Shapiros or the Kronicks, often went to Pension Muskowitz after a shofar announced the arrival of the Jewish Sabbath. There they spent time with Bertha Singer Schoolman and Esther Lamport, whose younger daughter, Felicia, had become a bat mitzvah in 1928 at the SAJ in a joint ceremony with Hadassah's youngest sister, Selma.[34] On Friday nights, they celebrated Oneg Shabbat, or the joy of Sabbath, with wine, cookies, dancing, and singing—in Hebrew and Yiddish. They also gathered to mark missed events in New York, such as the elaborate wedding, which Mordecai officiated at the Jewish Centre, between Esther's cousin Sylvia Lamport and the Zionist lawyer and Jewish community leader Ezra Shapiro.[35]

Sometimes when in Tel Aviv, the group watched tennis matches or visited Harry's family home in an orange grove in Rehovot, on the coastal plain, south of Tel Aviv. Despite the ideological Zionist emphasis on, and significant funding of, agricultural collective settlements on nationally owned land, by the mid-1930s, the largely privatized citrus industry accounted for the vast majority of Jewish agricultural output (75 percent), was the leading export industry, particularly of oranges (85 percent), and incorporated the country's most significant economic activity, including 60 percent of customs revenue.[36] Citrus growing also turned an arena in which both Jewish and Arabic Palestinians growers had previously thrived into a mostly Zionist endeavor. Jews purchased growing numbers of orange orchards from Arab landowners, seeing their cultivation both as marketable and as a means to develop a new type of Jew tied to physical work of the land rather than cerebral or purely monetary pursuits.[37] Hadassah recounted the attractiveness of the place to her family: "Rows and rows of orange trees [were] planted in this beautifully red soil against a background of hills + a setting sun. . . . It was like the movies—Not what I ever imagined would be in Palestine."[38] Indeed, the group also actually went to movie theaters, where they saw international films accompanied by subtitles in multiple languages, including Hebrew and English.

Despite Hadassah's frequent weekend forays to Tel Aviv, she preferred Jerusalem. She told her father that he would not recognize the city he had visited seven years earlier, since the streets that were only alleys had subsequently become "quite large and important."[39] In contrast, she described Tel Aviv as "very crowded" and "ghetto like," with some "*very* ugly" houses.[40] Contemporaries agreed with her assessment. The Hungarian-born journalist and novelist Arthur Koestler, who lived in Tel Aviv during the 1930s, explained that the city had "a main street named after Dr. Herzl with two rows of exquisitely ugly houses, each of which gave the impression of an orphanage or police barracks. There was also a multitude of dingy shops, most of which sold lemonade, buttons and flypaper."[41] Although Tel Aviv's infrastructure was less developed than Jerusalem's, Hadassah reported that Tel Aviv's social life was markedly more intense, with packed dance floors and streets.[42] "It's very modern—as you might expect—a city built up over night with no traditions in back of it. It has lots of shops, places to eat etc.—+ is much more free + gay than Jerusalem—but in an emptier way."[43] Tel Aviv was also significantly more homogeneously Jewish than Jerusalem was. An openly Jewish culture developed in its public spaces, including public celebrations of the Sabbath and Jewish holidays. Hadassah had an easier time finding people willing to speak Hebrew in Tel Aviv than in Jerusalem, although it too was a multilingual city.[44] Nevertheless, Hadassah preferred Jerusalem. She planned to begin studying at Hebrew University when the Jewish High Holidays concluded and the semester began.

Mordecai was delighted by his daughter's correspondence. Just before Sukkot, a weeklong harvest festival named after the booths or huts in which Jews are supposed to live and eat, Hadassah sent her father a sprig of leaves with a note: "Use the myrtle in the Lulav [a cluster of four different species of plants shaken in all directions on the holiday] and then press it for me."[45] "You are as good as gold," Mordecai exclaimed. "Your cables and your detailed letters compensated in part for the long time we had to wait before we heard from you. Would you believe that when I got through the 26th page of your letter I was hungry for more? You can't write enough as far as I am concerned. Keep that in mind when writing to us. . . . Believe me, the joy which your cable on Kol Nidre night gave me exceeds the joy from the success of the [Kol Nidre fund-raising] appeal."[46] Mordecai had succeeded in raising $8,000—$1,000 of which would go to the Teachers' Institute—as a result of his plea on the holiest night of the Jewish year. Such a campaign, however, did not give him as much pleasure as his daughter's letters. Still, he asked Hadassah when he could begin to write to her in Hebrew.[47]

Lena, however, was more critical of her daughter. Hadassah's chaperones sent the Kaplans a cable shortly after arriving in Palestine expressing their concerns about her behavior on the ship. Lena's early correspondence to her daughter is rife with anxiety, including racial stereotyping. "Didn't you take a chance," Lena wrote her daughter, "getting into that Spaniard's boat. Supposing he kidnapped you, then what? Anyway be careful with the *Arabs* + even with the [Jewish] Palestinians— Don't be kidnapped. We can't ransom you—+ we have no money for trousseaus—that's a form of kidnapping too."[48] "I would like to ask you," Lena warned in a follow-up letter, "to be careful with whom you go out and where and when. . . . Didn't any of the other folks go to Cairo? You don't even mention them."[49] After three weeks of not hearing from Hadassah, Lena berated her daughter: "I hope I don't have to write any don'ts to you. Now you know what I am worried about. First and foremost your health. Be careful about the food you eat and the water you drink and *Don't drink too much wines* [sic]. It is not good for you. Be careful with whom you go out and where you go—Beware of the Arabs. Never go near their homes unescorted especially at night."[50] "Darling," Lena wrote after finally receiving a letter from Hadassah two days later, "just the things you wrote about in your letter make me worry. I mean going places with people whom you don't know so well. After all how do you know where they are going to take you. Please give me no cause for worry. That doesn't mean you should do things and not write about them. I know I can trust you and that you won't do that." She also reminded Hadassah to cleave to her mentors: "We can't imagine why you never mention any of the women folks that you left with. Didn't Julia [Dushkin] go to Cairo as she had intended?"[51] A few days later, Lena continued,

> I am not so much worried but annoyed at your mode of life since you left home. When you were here you said that you were fed up with night clubs and dancing etc. etc. and here you are whether at Marseilles, Alexandria, Cairo or Jerusalem you are doing the same thing all over again. Really dearie I thought you ran away from that. Do be a sensible girl and settle down and see the land of Israel, get all the spirit and education you can. You will have plenty of night clubs and dances when you get back home. Don't be the social butterfly. Try to be a little of a Halutzoth

[pioneer]. I wouldn't want you to be that altogether either. But combine everything if possible.[52]

Great-Aunt Sophie and Grandma Anna prodded Hadassah to communicate more frequently and directly with them. "I am so overwhelmed with joy about your arrival at your destination," Mordecai's older sister, Sophie, explained passive aggressively, "that I am pardoning your negligence in not writing to me at all, while you wrote to your grandma."[53] Anna used incentives that are particularly poignant to me—Hadassah's granddaughter and mother of her great-granddaughters—to try to persuade her to write. "I would ask you," her grandmother pleaded, writing mostly in English with a smattering of Hebrew, "to fulfill the *mitzvah* [written in Hebrew and meaning "commandment"] of making your grandma [as] happy as possible by keeping me up with a letter as often as you can and perhaps more as you can, and I am sure that in years when God will bless you to be a happy grandma you will have a great deal of *nachas* [joy, also written in Hebrew] from your great grandchildren."[54]

The anthropologist Riv-Ellen Prell has written about the predominance of conflict in representations of overbearing immigrant mothers and their independence-seeking, American-born daughters.[55] Hadassah's intergenerational correspondence suggests that clashes over different conceptions of womanhood reflected not only mythic desires and longings but also those expressed by actual women. Indeed, some modern women saw Zionism as a move away from the traditional world of their mothers. As one pioneer in the 1920s explained to her mother, "I am leaving you not as a heroine who seeks salvation for her nation and land, I wish to save myself, mother. And your existence has directed me to this path. When I behold your everyday life—the cycle of petty worries and continuous anger coupled with lack of joy and happiness—a dark cloud looms over my heart. . . . Reflecting and pondering the idea that this destiny awaits me, I shuddered; my hair stood on end."[56] Certainly, Hadassah would never have written such a thing to her mother, yet some part of her was probably drawn to a different future than Lena's. Hadassah's mother, through her admonitions, sought to use her social capital to ensure her daughter's advancement. In contrast, spending time in Palestine among women who had begun to conceive of themselves as Hebrews as opposed to Jews gave Hadassah the space to rethink her own ideas about who she might become. Surrounded by rhetoric describing not only new Jewish men but also their counterpart—Hebrew women—created opportunities to imagine how she might wish to enact her own identity as a modern, American Jewish woman.

As Hadassah balanced between following her family's dictates and finding her own way, she responded to her elders' pleas and demands rather than dismissing them. In letters that took between ten days and three weeks to travel across the ocean, Hadassah assured her mother that she was "well taken care of all the time."[57] She insisted that she "had the approval of the Dushkins and Schoolmans" for her outings off the ship, noting that her chaperones did not disembark in Cairo and could not do much because they had responsibilities to their own children. Nevertheless, Hadassah insisted that they had chaperones: a Mrs. Barnett, who accompanied and stayed in the hotel in Cairo with Reba and Hadassah along with her own daughters. The Barnetts, Hadassah explained to her mother, were related to New York Jews whom the Kaplans knew: Sarah and Edward Epstein, a Hadassahnik and clothing wholesaler whom Mordecai and Lena had initially planned to have escort Hadassah to Palestine but who, instead, met her there a month later.[58] Finally, Hadassah maintained that she regularly consulted with her mentors, mentioning specific teas and other social gatherings in Jerusalem with Julia Dushkin, Rose Gell Jacobs, and Anna Sherman Grossman, as well as meetings in Tel Aviv with the only one of her chaperones to spend the year there: Bertha Singer Schoolman.[59]

Indeed, Hadassah did see her mentors regularly, particularly those living in Jerusalem. Julia Dushkin and Rose Jacobs probably remained in Jerusalem to be close to *Hadassah* headquarters and Henrietta Szold. Both Jacobs and Libbie Suchoff Berkson, the third Camp Modin matriarch, lived in Talpiot, a garden suburb of Jerusalem. After running the camp's girls' side, "Aunt Libbie" was operating Al Kos Te, a teahouse on Ben Yehuda Street, while her husband, Isaac, directed the Jewish school system in Palestine.[60] When the Epsteins—the Kaplans' friends and Hadassah's chaperone in Cairo—sailed for Palestine later that October, they also settled in Goldsmit House, where Hadassah and her friends first went in Jerusalem. The Palestinian-born Anna Grossman Sherman had also lived there with her relatively new husband, the dentist Earl, and their infant daughter. Anna Sherman had grown up in

New York, where her Zionist family had moved because of her father's poor health. There she had studied under Mordecai at Teachers' Institute, taught Hebrew at the Jewish Theological Seminary for more than a decade, and, before spending a few years in Palestine, served as a personal Hebrew tutor to the Jewish philanthropist Frieda Schiff Warburg, wife of the German American banker Felix Warburg. After having three children in Palestine, Sherman, like her father, would eventually return to New York for health reasons.[61] But she was in Palestine the year that Hadassah was there. And Hadassah regularly sought guidance from her as well as from the broader cohort of at least temporarily Jerusalem-based women.

One of the issues Hadassah solicited advice on was where she should live. She and Reba realized shortly after arriving at Goldsmit's that they did not want to stay there. By many counts, the pension was ideal for Jewish travelers. It had excellent kosher food, was immaculately clean, and boasted a warm environment. Mr. Goldsmit, a Dutchman, was known for his unfailing interest in his guests, and Mrs. Goldsmit, a sabra (Palestinian-born Jew), had a reputation for mothering her lodgers, including hosting them for the holidays. Nevertheless, Hadassah and Reba were disappointed to find little spoken Hebrew at the guesthouse.[62] Goldsmit's borders were more diasporic than Palestinian. When Hadassah and Reba arrived, the residents included an American man and three women: one from France, one German, and the third an English missionary. "None of them are particularly interesting," Hadassah wrote her parents in explaining her move, "+ we don't have the Hebrew speaking that we expected."[63] Lena was concerned about where and with whom Hadassah would live. "Please darling," she wrote, "don't be stingy. See that you stay with nice people + clean people (physically and morally)."[64] Hadassah, particularly because of her parents' worries, consulted with her mentors before moving. She asked Mrs. Grossman if she could stay with her, but with a new baby and a small flat, the family did not have space. Still, Mrs. Grossman discouraged her from subletting her friend Jack's house when he was away.[65] Her mentor might have been concerned about the associated questions of propriety or about the twenty-six-year-old Jack himself. Even Hadassah's camp friend Sylva described him in her memoir as "one of Jerusalem's more colourful characters, albeit something of a scoundrel."[66]

After consulting Mrs. Grossman, Hadassah approached other advisers about renting alternative rooms.[67] She considered staying with a colleague of her father's, the linguist David Yellin, who founded and directed the Hebrew Teachers' Seminary in Jerusalem that trained educators to teach in Hebrew. Instead, Reba wound up boarding with him. Before their trip, Hadassah and Reba had decided not to room together, so they would not be tempted to speak English.[68] Hadassah, with her former roommate settled at Yellin's, also thought about going to Tel Aviv or renting space in someone's house, but she was reluctant to furnish a room.[69]

Julia Dushkin and Bertha Singer Schoolman wrote the Kaplans advising that Hadassah switch to a different pension, which suggests that although Hadassah consulted with her mentors, she did not necessarily follow their advice.[70] Instead, in early November, the night of a dance at the King David Hotel and the day before leaving on a weeklong trip to Petra, Hadassah checked out of Goldsmit's and convinced her South African friend Harry Joffe to haul her luggage from the pension to their mutual friend Jack's place. Harry did it, even though he was already wearing a tuxedo for the dance. Hadassah planned to store her belongings at Jack's while he was traveling to Beirut. She assumed she would figure out her longer-term housing when she returned from Petra.[71]

The day of the dance, Hadassah slept until noon. She planned to rest in the car during her trip to Petra the next day, so she had no qualms about pulling an all-nighter. After the dance, she, Reba, and Harry stayed up listening to records, eating, dancing tangoes and Viennese waltzes, and even horseback riding at 5:00 a.m.[72] When she returned from Petra, Hadassah eventually rented a "neat room with a private entrance" in a doctor's "newly built modern house." There, for $24.50 a month, she joined the family for delicious and well-balanced meals "with vegetables." Apparently, however, the stove did not work in the flat, so that when they tried to boil water for coffee, it never got "more than cool."[73]

Once Hadassah's housing was settled and the High Holidays had concluded, she began thinking more seriously about studying and traveling. By the end of October, she was taking Hebrew lessons six days a week and enrolled in Bible courses at the American School of Oriental Research (ASOR), a Jerusalem-based research institute, which, beginning in 1900, led archeological excavations. Hadassah struggled to find a class at her Hebrew level. Hebrew University's classes were too advanced; ASOR's were too basic. Hadassah and Reba enrolled together in a class with the school's director, Nelson Glueck, an American reform rabbi with an appointment at Hebrew University College who was also a scholar, excavator, and surveyor. During the golden age of archeology, following World War I, a biblical approach to the field predominated, with an emphasis on close textual analysis as a vehicle for documenting Israelite-Jewish origins and peoplehood more generally in the Levant.[74] This interdisciplinary approach to biblical studies, which Glueck pursued, fit well with Mordecai's notion of Judaism as an evolving civilization and promoted a historical—in addition to theological—connection between Jews and Palestine. Today's archeologists, in contrast, have developed more academic methods that illustrate the ways that diverse people coexisted in the ancient world. Hadassah recalled that she and Reba prepared three chapters in the second book of Isaiah "more thoroughly" than they had "ever done anything." But, as she describes it, such intensive preparations were excessive. After arriving in Glueck's class, she remembered, "Lo and behold . . . all he did was have us translate!"[75]

Hadassah's investment in biblical archeology moved beyond the classroom to the field. In early November, she joined a weeklong trip to Petra, which she described fairly tritely as "a rose-red city half as old as Time."[76] The interdisciplinary cohort of almost entirely Hebrew University professors included several characters. Hadassah recalled that every time Friedrich Simon Bodenheimer, the German-born entomologist and Hebrew University professor of zoology, "saw a bug or a fly[,] his car had to stop for him to go and catch it. And if perchance," she continued, "the car had to stop because of a puncture, while we sat cursing, he would go wandering around, nonchalantly searching for bugs." In addition to the naturalist, there was also a geologist, a paleontologist, a medical doctor, a Turkish guide, and some support staff. At least two of the doctors knew Hadassah's father. As one of three young people on the trip, Hadassah volunteered as treasurer; Dan Ben Dor made the fires and handled all logistics (he also ran alongside the car in the desert for some exercise).[77] The third young person on the trip was David Magnes, who helped more generally.

David's parents, Judah Leon and Beatrice Lowenstein Magnes, were on Hadassah's contact list. Indeed, just as she corresponded with her

Figure 4.1. Hadassah Kaplan on an expedition to Petra, Jordan. Hadassah is smiling in the center of the photograph (in the second row to the bottom, four people in from the right). She wears a white long-sleeve top and a black head covering. October or November 1932. (Personal collection)

parents about her trip to Petra, Lena wrote to Hadassah asking if she had yet met the Magneses. "If you care to," Lena continued, "you can call them up and introduce yourself to Mrs. Magnes and say that you would like to meet her."[78] Beatrice Lowenstein Magnes, a New York–born German Jew, had been part of the original *Hadassah* Study Circle with Henrietta Szold and was also a sister-in-law of the prominent lawyer and New York Jewish leader Louis Marshall.[79] Her husband, Judah Leon Magnes, was a San Francisco–born Reform rabbi with a PhD in philosophy from the University of Heidelberg who served both as a pulpit rabbi and also as a Jewish communal leader, founding the Kehillah (Jewish Community) of New York. Mordecai had worked closely with Magnes to improve New York's Jewish education through the creation of the Board of Jewish Education, run by the pioneering educator Samson Benderly. In 1922, after the Kehillah's demise, the Magneses moved to Palestine, where Judah founded and became president of Hebrew University. Through first Hebrew University and later Ihud (Unity), an association for Jewish-Arab cooperation and reconciliation, he promoted the formation of a binational state, in which both Jews and Arabs would live equally. A number of self-identified Zionist intellectuals, including the Austrian philosopher Martin Buber, the German historian Gershom Scholem, and the sociologist Arthur Ruppin, would be drawn to Magnes's approach.[80]

To Lena's chagrin, however, Hadassah found the Magneses' eldest son annoying. In her letter home, she referred to David, who rode in the same car as she did and showered her with chivalrous attention, as "the biggest dope" she had "ever come across."[81] She appreciated his bringing her a so-called Arabian headdress (*keffiyeh* and *agal*) to minimize the sun and sand in her hair and eyes but nevertheless found him overbearing. "He insisted," she explained in a letter home, "on taking care of me. Do this or do that—+ be careful you'll catch cold—And he wouldn't let me do a thing for myself. And you know independent me!—How I love that sort of person!"[82] David would continue to pursue her after the trip. He invited her to an antitubercular fund-raiser dance at the King David Hotel, which was part of a wider effort to survey and control the communicable infection in Palestine. Hadassah, however, was keeping her distance. "I'm not going with him," she wrote home, "even if I don't get another invitation."[83] Hadassah's strong reaction to David's unwanted chivalry resonates with the cultural critic Jennifer Bernhardt Steadman's description of traveling women claiming their agency in opposition to male efforts to control their movement and independence.[84]

Unsurprisingly, Lena was not pleased with her daughter. "How," she wrote Hadassah, "could you turn D.M. down. Don't you think it would be nice to go with him once and thru him meet some very fine people. After all his father is a big shot in Palestine. I imagine they mingle with very fine people and you would get an opportunity to meet them thru him. But of course," Lena attempted to soften her tone with two more sentences she does not appear entirely to have meant, "you know best. You can see for yourself."[85] A month later, Lena again inquired about the "Magnes affair."[86] Roughly two weeks later, Lena still could not let go of her daughter's missed opportunity to connect with the Magneses. In speculating as to what had gone wrong, Lena accusingly wrote, "Is it because you were so rude to David that they have no use for you?"[87]

Franklin Delano Roosevelt had been elected president less than a week after Hadassah returned from Petra. She corresponded with her suitors in the US about the election. Ralph Lieberman, whose marriage proposal Hadassah had declined the previous January, wrote as if she lacked basic civic knowledge. In a parenthetical aside, he identified President Herbert Hoover as "the president of our country just now."[88] Another beau, Sydney Lichtman, bent the other way: "You missed an opportunity of defeating Hoover. I really think," he continued, "you could defeat any man."[89] The day before the election, Lena wondered if it would change the "economic condition of the public."[90] Although Hadassah wrote home that she was not sure whom her parents supported, she congratulated them on FDR's election with a "mazel tov!" Echoing her mother's concern over the election's consequences, she wrote, "I wonder whether it will make very much difference."[91]

Doubts about the future of the US were countered by optimism at least about Palestine's economic prospects. "We hear," Lena wrote, "that there is no depression in Palestine. That prosperity reigns there and that all are happy. How do you find it."[92] In actuality, depression had hit Palestine in 1925 with the devaluation of Polish currency. Hadassah had peers who were struggling to find work, not to mention having encountered Palestinians Jews and Arabs who did not have the luxury of ongoing support from family. She might also have heard about Jewish workers struggling to compete against Arab Palestinians, who tended both to be more skilled and to accept lower wages.[93] Despite such information, Hadassah's account reinforced Lena's mythic image of the place.[94] "You know," the daughter explained,

> here things are so comfortable—you never hear a word about depression. There are just one or two beggars on the streets; there is no unemployment; and people don't vie with each other in procuring luxuries and the like. We dress comfortably—and you don't see a soul flashing clothes, jewelry or anything. It's really grand. And everybody is happy. There are loads of people employed in building. Really—I wish you could see how they do it. A lot of men sit on the ground and chop the bricks. . . . So—people go about their work—6 days a week—+ don't groan about depression. (I know the Hebrew for "depression" only from a newspaper article about N.Y.).[95]

Hadassah's impression of Palestine's prosperity was confirmed by other contemporaries. The Polish writer and visitor to Palestine Ksawery

Pruszynski similarly commented on the shortage of labor, especially in the building industry, its budget surplus, and its capital investment.[96] According to the Jewish Agency's 1931 annual report, unemployment in Palestinian cities was less than 1 percent, a figure that overestimated the employment of Arab Palestinians.[97]

Regardless of the country's financial standing, Lena continued to be apprehensive about her daughter's behavior. Was Hadassah seeing the "right" Israel? Was she connecting with desirable people? Lena urged her daughter to visit "the Colonies," meaning the Jewish agricultural settlements in Palestine, and to "see what ... Hadassah is doing."[98] Beyond the Magneses, Lena wanted to know if her daughter had contacted other female Zionist leaders in Palestine, whom she named as a reminder to her daughter. She specifically mentioned Henrietta Szold, her *Hadassah* colleague Lotta Levinsohn, Jessie Sampter, and another friend and colleague of the Kaplans, Lillian Ruth Bentwich Friedlander, who moved to Palestine with her children and extended family following the 1920 murder of her husband, Israel, a professor of biblical literature at JTS, while he was on a relief mission to Ukraine sponsored by the Jewish Joint Distribution Committee.[99] "All these people," Lena insisted, "can show you Palestine + the Palestine that you ought to see."[100] Lena expected full reports from her daughter about her various encounters. "When you answer this question [about whom you have met]," she continued, "make believe it is an examination paper and see how many of these questions you can answer."[101] Lena urged her daughter to keep tabs in her diary of her meetings and use that as a guide to write letters documenting "in detail what transpired." The mother then promised to keep her daughter's letters as a memoir.[102] Hadassah's diaries detailing names and locations in tiny writing indicate that Hadassah obliged.

Nevertheless, Lena continued to worry: Was Hadassah working on her Hebrew every day? "Once a week isn't enough," the mother wrote.

> Frankly, learning Hebrew isn't enough. . . . I should like you to get into a different circle of people if possible from the circle that goes to cafes and dances all the time. . . . Why in the world did you cut yourself off from the people with whom you left N.Y. Not once did you mention any one of them. What happened to them + to you. I am sure Mrs. Jacobs could have introduced you to some very nice people if you gave her a chance.

+ what about Aunt Julia, she knows so many people. Who is this fellow Jack + where did you meet him + what is he doing. Does he pay for all the places he takes you to? . . . Don't misunderstand me. I don't expect you to work all day long. But what I do want is that you get the thrill of Palestine outside of the cafes and dance halls. . . . See for yourself that what you have been reading in the Bible and most likely thought never existed is actually there and you are there to see it. That too should be a thrill for you. The very fact that you are in Palestine and can see all these things for yourself.[103]

Again, Hadassah assiduously responded to her mother's criticism. She promised her family that she was being "*very* careful" with regard to her health. "The people I go with—[I] haven't met anyone yet that everybody doesn't know." Also, "I write every little detail [to you] so that there is absolutely nothing to fear there. I see Julia and Mrs. Jacobs practically every day + Sis who is older than we—almost 29 years old—so that I am well advised."[104]

Hadassah carefully described to her family her extensive travels through Palestine to see and experience biblical sites. With Sis, Sylva, Kronick, and Kronick's mother, Hadassah visited what was an important trade route in ancient Palestine, Shechem; a well the biblical Jacob purchased in Jenin; and the childhood home of Jesus in Nazareth.[105] The group also toured northern kibbutzim and agricultural settlements, including Ganiger and Afula. Most of the one hundred thousand Jews in rural areas of Palestine lived on private property, such as the orange grove her friend Harry Joffe's family owned. Beginning in the early twentieth century, these were called *moshavot*, translated as "colonies" or family-based settlements.[106] Alternatively, agricultural communities were called *kvutzot*, literally meaning "communal groups," and *kibbutzim*, or "collectives," a term introduced in the early 1920s, connoting a larger settlement and including industry as well as agriculture.[107] By the time Hadassah went to see these collectives, with their fusion of socialism and Zionism, they had come to play an outsized role in Zionist thinking. Such communities had come to represent important new ideas about how working-class Jews might transform themselves by working shared land. Hadassah recalled in her diary not having spent enough time on *kvutzot* "to form any conception" of them beyond commenting that those they visited "seemed to be very messy places."[108] Her friends Kronick and Sylva, who had already lived in such settings, convinced Hadassah to wait until after the rainy season. Then she might arrange a longer visit and see other settlements, such as Kibbutz Ein Harod and Kibbutz Megiddo in the Jezreel Valley. Instead, Hadassah traveled to Tiberias and Mt. Herman, saw the hydroelectric power station built by Pincus Rutenberg Water Works, the Galilee—the lowest freshwater lake on Earth—and the northern town Metulah. In Haifa, she visited the Technical School for Chemistry and Physics, where the children of her parents' friends—Carmel (daughter of Lillian and Israel Friedlander) and Joshua (son of Rose and Edward Jacobs)—respectively taught and studied.

The first time Lena expressed genuine enthusiasm regarding Hadassah's behavior was at the end of November in response to her letter from almost a month earlier describing her studies, plans to travel to Petra, and promise that she had sent separately a letter to her father written in Hebrew. Even before receiving that note, Lena told Hadassah that her father was "thrilled." "I only hope," she continued, showing the persistence of her ambivalence, "you are really making as much progress as your note shows." She then went on to ask for the details about her university courses and to express hope that Hadassah was "getting something out of the lectures."[109] By Lena's next letter, she had shifted from some level of ongoing doubt to jealousy. "We are all," she promised, "quite thrilled with your adventure. Shall I tell you a secret. We are all green with envy. But thank God that one belonging to us is really seeing and doing what you describe so well."[110] Selma confirmed to Hadassah their parents' delight. "Mamma and Papa were thrilled by your last letter," she wrote. Echoing her mother's envy, she explained, "Everybody is jealous of you."[111] Mordecai too wrote of Lena's pleasure in Hadassah's letters. "Your mother knows them almost by heart," he explained, "since she reads them out loud multiple times to all your uncles and aunts." No one else can read them, since, he added, "your handwriting is so minuscule and twisted that only an expert like your mother can decipher it."[112]

Even as Hadassah traveled, she continued to work on her Hebrew. She assured her family that "everyone," including the Jacobses, Epsteins, and Dushkins, was struggling to learn the language. Foreigners tended to speak in French or German.[113] Even native-born Jewish Palestinians tended not to speak Hebrew. Contemporaneous studies indicated that urban middle-class female immigrants often spoke particularly poor Hebrew.[114] Hadassah's experiences confirmed such findings. "Would you believe," Hadassah attested, "that I have to keep asking the Palestinians to talk Hebrew?"[115] In addition to private tutoring, Hadassah teamed up with "a group of about 5 girls or women ... to meet for an hour about 4 times a week with a Hebrew teacher just for the sake of versing and carrying on discussions in Hebrew."[116] Hadassah so liked the Hebrew tutor, Mr. Livny, that she decided to drop out of her class at Hebrew University and just have private lessons with him. "You see," she explained, "the University isn't giving me much—after all what do I know about Hebrew literature in 1600—And I can't learn much from his lectures." Since her Bible teacher, Mr. Katznelson, would not let her speak, she decided to cut back on those lessons too. She switched from six sessions a week with Mr. Katznelson to four Hebrew classes a week with Mr. Livny.[117]

Although Hadassah enjoyed the work, Jerusalem was cold, and it was challenging to study at home—especially without a stove.[118] She considered moving to a kibbutz, but her friends and mentors warned that it was difficult to learn Hebrew there. "As a matter of fact," Hadassah wrote her parents, "you don't ever learn such good Hebrew there. First of all—they talk a lot of Yiddish—and the Hebrew that they do talk pertains mainly to the soil!"[119] She also spoke with Lillian Friedlander about moving to Haifa, where she might live with a family, continue private lessons, and attend school.[120] But instead she remained in Jerusalem, where she sought out friends who were willing to speak and write in Hebrew. She practiced the language while taking long walks and motorcycle rides with mostly young men, including the lexicographer Eliezer Ben-Yehuda's son.[121] She read Hebrew newspapers and, at one point, reported back to her family that from her reading, she was learning "all about Hitler; Lloyd George's proposal to alleviate unemployment, Roosevelt's + Hoover's messages regarding their attitude toward the Balfour declaration; and a fairly complete explanation of the dropping of the £."[122]

For additional Hebrew immersion, Hadassah also attended movies, lectures, and plays. "Let me tell you," she wrote her family, "I grasp every opportunity to listen to Hebrew."[123] "You have no idea," she went on, "what good practice the movies are for Hebrew—I always read the Hebrew captions—+ I learned 3 new words Sat. night."[124] By December, she had developed a rhythm, waking up early (a new experience for the proverbial—and lifelong—late riser), meeting with her tutor at 8:30 a.m., reading poetry as well as novels, practicing her violin, and seeing plays in Hebrew, such as *Rasputin*, about the Siberian peasant who became a spiritual adviser to the tsar. Hadassah had also begun to do some editorial work for Gershon Agronsky, who that month published the first issue of the English-language *Palestine* (later *Jerusalem*) *Post*.[125] With her peers and mentors, she visited some *Hadassah*-sponsored sites, including an agricultural school, playgrounds, and *Hadassah* headquarters. "Mrs. Schoolman," Hadassah wrote home, "incidentally told me to write you that she's been hearing 'lovely things about me.' Doesn't that make you feel good?"[126]

As part of her reading, Hadassah devoured the first volume of what would become a fictional trilogy by the German Jewish novelist Lion Feuchtwanger about the first-century Jewish historian and military leader Flavius Josephus. Josephus defected to the Romans, opposed Jewish rebellion, and urged the Jewish defenders of Jerusalem to surrender to the Roman siege in 70 CE. Rather than emphasizing Josephus as a traitor, Feuchtwanger argued that Josephus rejected both Roman and Jewish particularism and, instead, aspired to become a cosmopolitan citizen of the world.[127] Whether Hadassah considered Josephus a hero or a conspirator, we do not know. She did not explicitly discuss the novel or relate it to the nationalist struggles and efforts at coexistence she witnessed in Palestine. Nevertheless, she called the novel "*grand*."[128] Hadassah's fascination with a Jew who chose Hellenistic assimilation and acceptance of a subaltern position within colonial rule rather than struggling for national self-determination is noteworthy given the combination of her father's work to help American Jews reconcile religious and civic identities as well as Hadassah's own presence in Palestine.

Even as Hadassah studied, read, and worked on her Hebrew, she worried that she would not live up to her parents' hopes. She confessed that she did not speak Hebrew with "anyone except [her] teacher—except on rare occasions (almost once a day)."[129] She also feared "wasting time," as she wrote home, "without accomplishing what I set out for—+ most of all what you [Lena] + papa expect. I know you expect me to be a different person when I come home—Perhaps I am changing, but I am so materialistic I'd like to *see* it immediately. I'll die if you're disappointed when I return. So *please* don't expect too much—remember there wasn't much to begin with!"[130]

Hadassah was nervous too about her written Hebrew. She drafted her first Hebrew letters in her diary and appears to have reviewed them with her tutor or perhaps to have edited them herself before revising and rewriting them on stationery to mail. "I haven't been *writing* any Hebrew," she confessed in an English note dated December 1, 1932, which she sent home alongside her first Hebrew letter. "As a first attempt I hope it's appreciated."[131]

The tone of Hadassah's Hebrew letters is somewhat different from that of her English ones. They are also addressed only to her father. Hadassah's English letters, in contrast, were intended for the family, usually referring to them as "dears" or "darlings." In her first Hebrew letter home, Hadassah described a play she had recently watched in Hebrew as well as the speeches and discussion that followed the performance. She reported on the plot of the play, performed by Habima, literally meaning "stage" and referring to a Hebrew theater company originally founded in Russian Poland in 1912. The play, called *Amcha*, meaning "the folk" or "common person," was a Hebrew translation of a Sholem Aleichem story initially written in Yiddish, "Dos Groyse Gevins," or "The Big Prize." In it, a girl's father wins the lottery, moves to a big house, and forbids his daughter from marrying her love: Motel the apprentice. The father later learns that he never actually won the lottery and lifts the prohibition. The daughter is relieved of her misery, and she and the apprentice live happily ever after.[132] After the show, Hadassah, who did not have a ticket for a reception following the play, nevertheless followed the Jewish journalist Nahum Sokolow to the Vienna Café, where he delivered a speech that Hadassah reported verbatim to her father. "The language [Hebrew]," Sokolow insisted,

> is the most important thing for Jewish national life, and it can create a new world for us. Even if there are people here who do not speak or understand the language, he said, there is hope that they will learn. What is most important is that we be exemplary—that we desire to learn. And things like this play—*Amcha*—which is so realistic and entertaining in

such a vital way, can engender such a desire in people who do not understand everything. It's true, [he said,] this is a translation, but it is still beautiful. It is very difficult to translate without doing away with the spirit of the original, but we still also need real Hebrew literature.

According to Hadassah, Sokolow went on to explain the origin of the play's Hebrew title, *Amcha*, to thank Habima for the work it was doing, and to hope that its plays and organization might function like the Comédie-Française, teaching the Hebrew language and Jewish culture to those who are interested, just as France's national theater educates its public in French. Through her reporting, Hadassah was both informing her father about the types of speeches and events happening in Palestine and also enabling him to participate in the renewal of Hebrew language, culture, learning, and a broader sense of Jewish peoplehood. "Before that [speech]," Hadassah wrote her father in Hebrew, "I never thought you'd be able to be happy here—because life is not as it could be in a place of such surroundings—but I was actually extremely sad that you were not here yesterday evening."[133]

Even more than reports of Hadassah's travels and lessons, the Hebrew letters Hadassah sent home "thrilled" her parents "beyond words." Lena wrote,

> Your Hebrew letter gave us more joy than you can imagine and Papa was thrilled beyond words—He said that it has meant everything in the world to him to have you be able to write such a letter. He said that had you taken six lessons a week for a whole year here in N.Y. you couldn't do that. So there—you see that we are not disappointed but satisfied + happy that you are where you are. . . . So please darling don't for a minute feel that we are going to be disappointed. You have already changed in every way.[134]

"I will tell you, my dear Hadassah," her great-aunt Sophie wrote her in Hebrew, "if you yourself stood on the side and watched carefully your parents' faces as they were reading your letters, if you had seen . . . the joy of their expressions, and especially on your father's face as he was reading your letters written in our holy tongue, then surely you would have uttered from the bottom of your heart, 'this work is rewarded.'"[135] Sophie presumably also took particular pride in her niece's Hebrew. As the only girl to attend a local heder (school) in Vilna, she had learned the language well enough to read to a blind Hebraicist and was probably her younger brother Mordecai's first Hebrew teacher.[136]

By the end of the year, Hadassah was largely settled in Palestine. Stylistically, she had figured out how to navigate between the simplistic appearance preferred by pioneers in the Yishuv and the Western fashion to which she was accustomed. In contrast to her peers' efforts to ape Hollywood-style glamour on the Upper West Side, Hadassah found Jewish Palestinians actively rejecting such fashion for high-quality, inexpensive plain shirts (often white button-down), sweaters, and dark-blue or khaki shorts, pants, and A-line skirts. The simple dress suited the climate and hard labor. It was affordable and embodied the so-called New Jew, who, in contrast to diasporic ones, was healthy, suntanned, hardworking, and practical.[137]

Hadassah was not prepared to go that far. She resisted trading in her silk stockings for nylons and continued to wear head coverings and flowery and fitted dresses. She asked her mother to replace those she had worn through and reminded her that her younger sister Selma's narrow frame was close enough to her own that she could try outfits on for her. Hadassah did, however, put away her jewelry and lipstick, except for in preparation for the occasional formal dance. She also replaced her heels with significantly more comfortable flat, elk-skin saddle shoes that were still more fashionable than the plain brown ones typically worn by Jewish pioneers.[138]

Beyond Hadassah's acquiring conviction in her more casual appearance, she was gaining confidence in her written and spoken Hebrew. She increasingly knew that she could successfully serve as a scout for her father and could also use her time productively in ways that would contribute to a renewal of the Hebrew language and cultural development. Hadassah had not found traditional synagogue life meaningful, nor had she become a Junior Hadassahnik. But she had found genuine friends and mentors. She also was learning and participating in Hebrew and cultural experiences that she found meaningful.

That year, Christmas fell during Hanukkah, or the festival of lights. Initially Hadassah wanted to persuade "the boys"—presumably her male friends from Tel Aviv: Harry Joffe, Sam Shapiro, and Ben Adelman—to drive to Bethlehem for Christmas Eve services. "I don't know tho," she wrote home, "whether they'll be very keen about such a long drive."[139] Instead, she stayed in Tel Aviv for the weekend. At a Hanukkah party, where the "decorations were much more suitable for Christmas Eve," she and her friends joined in a "grand Horah," a traditional Jewish circle dance.[140] Hadassah spent that evening at Mrs. Kronick's, lunched the next day with the Epsteins, and then witnessed a Hanukkah parade of five thousand children that turned an ancient tradition and holiday into a modern collective cultural experience. The contemporary celebration emphasized the political reestablishment of a Jewish homeland more than the recovery of the temple and reinstatement of religious freedom through divine intervention.[141] The connection with a struggle for national sovereignty made Hanukkah one of the Yishuv's most important holidays, celebrated more widely than holidays that traditional Jews consider more significant, such as Yom Kippur (the Day of Atonement) and Rosh Hashanah (the Jewish New Year).[142] "The streets [in Tel Aviv] were mobbed," Hadassah recalled. "Everybody under the sun was there. On the roof of the synagogue was an electric Menorah which was lighted—Sokolow spoke.[143] We couldn't hear tho since we were 2 blocks away. Sky rockets were started—+ then the parade—It was already dark—all the children had either Chanukah candles or torches + paraded thru the streets singing. I'm telling you—the tears just came to my eyes. We stood there thoroughly interested for 2½ hours!"[144]

Finally, Hadassah was participating in the types of public demonstrations, holidays, and performances that Lena had hoped she would and contributing to Palestine's cultural development. Furthermore, the Kaplans were relieved to find Judith, Hadassah's older sister, appearing to be financially secure, married, and working hard as a music teacher in a field she enjoyed and one that promoted Jewish cultural growth. With their older two daughters somewhat settled, Lena turned her attention to her youngest girls. She wrote Hadassah that she feared that Selma was too social, while Naomi never went out. Lena's recounting of Selma's activities was particularly comical. "This afternoon," she wrote,

> Selma is to [go to] a ball game with Sydney F. [Friedberg]. Tonight she is going out with George R. and Sat night with Sydney F. again. This time she asked him to take her to one of the girls' parties. She didn't want to ask a boy from school because she knew they would all be there + she

wanted them to see that she goes out with other boys. Last night she went out with Richard + a whole gang. Can you imagine how I feel and how *she* feels. I don't know what to do. I am going cuckoo—Don't allude to this in any of your letters and don't let Reba see this letter.[145]

Beyond not wanting Selma or Reba to know about Lena's concerns regarding her youngest daughter's active social life, Lena seemed to believe that her correspondence lacked the type of depth that would make it historically significant. "Destroy my letters," she went on to admonish Hadassah, "after you are thru reading them because they really are not worth accumulating."[146] Luckily Hadassah preserved them and, with them, a window into early twentieth-century relationships between Jewish mothers and daughters, with all their written and unwritten expectations, assumptions, and longings.

5

Finding Her Way

The day after Christmas, Hadassah and her camp friends, Reba Isaacson and Helen Schwartz, paid ten and one-quarter pounds and ten dollars for a visa for an eight-day trip to Cairo and Luxor organized by the Young Women's Hebrew Association (YWHA). They rode two third-class trains and a ferry across the Suez, supplying their own cushions to soften the wooden seats that "became hard after a while." They "read, schmoozed, and sang" throughout their travels.[1] Although we do not know what books they brought, one might imagine at least one of them tucking into their bag a 1929 copy of Baedeker's 495-page-long, barely portable, English-language guidebook of Egypt, which would be the last one Baedeker would publish. If so, by traveling with a group, they would have already violated the guidebook's advice "to avoid as far as possible coming into contact with the large parties organized by the tourist agents, . . . [to evade] circumstances . . . in which he [a generic tourist] is pushed to the wall, without any redress."[2] Or perhaps they were less interested in practical advice, having already committed themselves to the YWHA's tour, so instead carried in hand a work they hoped would capture the spirit of where they were going, such as the recently released Modern Library edition of the *Arabian Nights* (1932), an inexpensive reprinting that publishers marketed to Americans. Such young women would not have been alone if they had expected to glimpse on their travels scenes reminiscent of the exotic adventures of characters, such as Aladdin, Ali Baba, Sinbad the Sailor, and Shahrazad, who used stories to avoid being killed by her husband, the king, who had killed all of his previous wives after their first night of marriage.[3]

More than fictional characters accompanied Hadassah, Reba, and Helen to Egypt. Indeed, this was the destination of choice for a group of older American Jews traveling that winter. Rose Gell Jacobs and Esther "Sis" Callner had arrived in Egypt a week or two earlier, as had the non-Zionist philanthropists and Society for the Advancement of Judaism members Frieda Schiff and Felix Warburg. The Warburgs traveled with their niece Gisela, who hailed from Hamburg and was the same age as Hadassah and her Camp Modin crew. According to Hadassah, Gisela was engaged to an Ochs of the *New York Times*–owning family, but they appear not to have married. Instead, Gisela would work in Berlin for Youth Aliya, which responded to rising Nazi power in Germany by transferring children to Palestine and other countries. In 1939, Gisela herself emigrated to the US as a refugee. Four years later, she would marry Charles Wyzanski, a chief judge of the federal district court in Boston, and she would go on to chair UNICEF's Boston-area fund-raiser for a quarter of a century.[4]

This cohort—the Warburgs, Jacobs, Sis, Reba, Helen, and Hadassah— were not drawn to Egypt to experience the modernization, anti-British-and-imperial sentiment, and rising Egyptian nationalism of the nation-state, which a decade earlier had achieved nominal independence from Great Britain even as it remained subject to its control. We do not hear about them attending Egyptian theater, cabaret, street performances, or séances, where, without knowing Arabic, they might have misunderstood story lines but might nevertheless have absorbed aspects of contemporary Egyptian culture, including a search for identity, feminism, and reform.[5] Instead, the travelers bypassed the present for Egypt's ancient pharaonic past. They were particularly attracted to Luxor, especially the Karnak Temple, whose axis aligned with the sunrise on the winter solstice, and the Valley of the Tombs of the Kings, where, a decade earlier, excavations had begun on the tomb of the Egyptian pharaoh Tutankhamun.[6] Like many Western travelers, this cohort was searching as much for the biblical roots of an imagined Western civilization as to find exotic qualities they believed modern society had lost. They were markedly more drawn to Egyptology than to Islamic antiquities. Thus, while they would see the pharaohs' tombs and the Egyptian Museum, they did not explore the Museum of Arab Art or the Comité, which housed monuments of Islamic and Coptic Christianity.[7]

With grand hotels, clean water, efficient transportation, and package tours, Egypt, and particularly Luxor and Cairo, had become the most popular non-Western tourist stop for people traveling from Europe and the United States.[8] As Read Henry explained when he tried to convince Hadassah to meet him in Luxor, "You'll *have* to see *that* before you go back to America as it is the most fascinating place in Egypt."[9] Of course, Hadassah and Reba had already visited parts of the archeological site with the architect W. Knox Van and the developer Hugh Parker when they traveled to Alexandria off the *Exochorda*. But they too, nevertheless, joined the journey.

Read had hoped that Hadassah would visit him in Alexandria first and then tour Luxor with his friend Clell McLelland and Read's seventeen-year-old brother—an English prep-school student whom he had not seen in two and a half years. Hadassah, however, wanted to remain with her friends from Palestine. She might have purposely circumvented Read to avoid misleading him about her intentions. Although the exact details are difficult to determine, his ongoing interest in her and her persistent ambivalence about their relationship are clear. When he came down with the flu and his brother injured his knee, the young men delayed their travels and missed Hadassah altogether. One might imagine that Hadassah was not entirely unhappy about the ensuing misalignment of their schedules.

Sis met their train when it pulled into the station at 10:30 p.m., ready to take them to the inexpensive Central Hotel, where the Y's travel group was staying. Also standing on the platform, in a tuxedo, was a family friend who had other plans for Hadassah. It is unclear how Joseph Levy knew about Hadassah's travels. The multilingual, Jewish, *New York Times* foreign correspondent to Jerusalem, who was born and educated in Palestine but a US citizen because of his father, insisted that Hadassah stay with his family. His wife, Esther Levy, had grown up in New York, where she had attended the SAJ and befriended the Kaplans.[10] Before Mordecai heard that they had connected, he had asked Lena to remind Hadassah to be in touch. Joseph shared Mordecai's assessment that Palestine should serve as a Jewish spiritual and cultural center. He also rejected political Zionism, instead promoting Judah Magnes's vision of Palestine as a democratic, international Holy Land for Jews, Christians, and Arabs.[11]

Joseph and his family immediately adopted Hadassah. She stayed in their home along with another American girl around her age, whom they called "the kid." At the same time, Sis initially lodged at the "very swanky" Grand Continental Hotel, "where the finer people go." She would later move to a houseboat on Gezira Island, located on the Nile.

Figure 5.1. Hadassah Kaplan and Esther "Sis" Callner outside Sis's houseboat, Gezira Island, Egypt, December, 1932. (Personal collection)

Reba and Helen would remain with the Y trip's contingent at Central Hotel, which Hadassah described as a "dump."[12]

At the Levys' house, Hadassah experienced new levels of luxury and privilege. When she left her slightly dusty shoes sitting out, she returned home to find them shined. The Levy family provided the two young women living with them with their own Chrysler. The car, presumably with a driver, took the young women to archeological sites, bazaars, the zoo, public gardens, lunches, tea, movies, and other social affairs. Joseph

Figure 5.2. Hadassah Kaplan, Frieda Schiff Warburg, and her niece Gisela riding camels, December 1932. (Personal collection)

even vaccinated Hadassah against smallpox, along with the rest of his household. The Levys invited the young women to "terribly swanky" parties and cabarets filled with "everybody of any importance," including "very dignified" German, French, and English officers. At such gatherings, Hadassah met the US ambassador and consul to Egypt, a member of the English Parliament, and the twice-divorced Cornelius "Corny" Vanderbilt, who was the great-great-grandchild of the first Gilded Age shipping and railroad magnate and philanthropist of the same name. "Honestly," Hadassah wrote home, "it seemed so funny for me to be on the scene with these Englishmen with monocles whom I usually look at in the movies + snicker at."[13] Lena reminded Hadassah that much of the special attention she received was "due to Papa." "There is something to you too," she continued, "but if you weren't Dr. Kaplans daughter you wouldn't be so popular would you?"[14] Hadassah was, indeed, cognizant of the entrée provided her by her father. "Isn't it funny," she wrote home, "how all these important people pay attention to you over here. If I met them in NY I'm sure they wouldn't look at me. I suppose they feel akin to Americans or something—Besides, papa dear—it's quite all right to have you as a father! I don't mind it much!"[15]

Initially, Lena was intrigued by her daughter entering this paparazzied world. "How about an Englishman or an ambassador," she wrote Hadassah. "Can't you land one?"—or at least become a private secretary to one of them.[16] Even if Hadassah neither married nor found a job with the people she met through the Levys, Lena hoped that the experience would mature her and develop her social skills and knowledge base. "There surely," she wrote, "will be much more to you when you get home than when you left. We see an improvement in you in every letter. You surely will have enough to talk about when you get back. You will have enough material for conversation for months and months to come."[17]

Hadassah, however, expressed skepticism and disdain toward the lifestyle and ways of the people she met. "Thursday night," she wrote, "I got a peep into the character and interests of the wealthy. Cornelius Vanderbilt Jr. is quite dull and I'm sure he'd be nothing if not for his father." Hadassah described him as unintellectual, having neither attended college nor been much of a reader. Instead, she reported that he wrote for the *Saturday Evening Post* and other papers, based on his "observations." While traveling, he met a nineteen-year-old "heiress of a Texas oil man." "Because of her (or the $1500 *weekly* allowance [she commanded])," Hadassah wrote home, "he changed his [travel] plans + is omitting Jerusalem, going to Istanbul instead." Hadassah also conveyed in her letters the casual racism and Orientalism of Vanderbilt's wealthy travel companion, Mr. Brodex. "He believes," Hadassah wrote, "that the best thing to get out of travel is material for entertainment at parties." According to Hadassah's account of the conversation, Mr. Brodex used a racial slur against people of color when describing himself collecting as party favors "golli golli tricks," the costume, songs, and performances of Middle Easterners. "Golli" was the term used to describe a racially stereotyped Black minstrel rag doll. Although Hadassah was unimpressed by Vanderbilt and his friend, she repeated his insulting language in her letter rather than countering or commenting on the hierarchies shaping the privileged world she was witnessing.[18] Still, as it turned out, Vanderbilt was less vacuous than Hadassah suspected. In 1935, he would publish a memoir that exposed Herbert Hoover's Treasury secretary, Andrew Mellon, and his then assistant, Ogden Mills, for heightening the panic—and the ensuing Great Depression—by encouraging Wall Street magnates to move their assets abroad before the US went off the gold standard.[19] Despite the company he kept, Vanderbilt's writing suggested a willingness to document and expose class privilege, if not other forms of hierarchy.

Although Hadassah criticized the Levys' world, she was in no hurry to leave its creature comforts or to return to her cold flat in Jerusalem without central heating. Eventually, however, she planned to go back to Jerusalem on New Year's Day, but she overslept and had to take an overnight train from Luxor, where she was visiting. "When I arrived" in Cairo, she wrote, "I was so dead + so filthy I dreaded the train ride back to Jerusalem that same night." Instead of returning with her friends, she waited until a "respectable hour" to call the Levys, who then insisted she stay over the weekend—including her twentieth birthday—and fly to Jerusalem with Joseph Levy the following week. The next week, Levy flew to Gaza without Hadassah. He traveled to Jerusalem, where he picked up her mail, including birthday wishes. Hadassah knew that her parents would want her to return to Jerusalem as soon as possible. She explained to her family that the Levys were "trying to tell" her that she was "not going home next Tuesday either": "But Mama dear—I still remember you saying 'Enough is enough.' Really, I'm tempted to stay here longer— except that I have my room in Jerusalem—+ I might learn a *little* more Hebrew there. But it's so nice to feel at home for a while—+ I certainly do that here."[20] She also appreciated escaping the economic crisis. Even though she had minimized the Depression in her earlier correspondence, as a pseudo child of the Levys, Hadassah fully escaped financial considerations. "That god damn depression!" she wrote. "Honestly—I hate to be selfish—but I certainly am happy I'm in a place where you hear nothing of it. Don't think I'm not economizing for that reason."[21]

Hadassah's sister Selma was sympathetic: "A beautiful house, distinguished people, regal attendance, pyramids, and excavations—and yet," she wrote her big sister, "you've really returned to Palestine! Oh! Yes—it must be hard to leave all that and go back to all your hard work!"[22] But Hadassah was right about her mother, Lena, judging her. Lena was undeniably frustrated with her daughter for remaining in Egypt as long as she did, not having communicated over several weeks, and her apparent lack of focus on what her parents wanted her to do: work on her Hebrew and participate in Jewish cultural and religious experiences. "How is it," Lena passive aggressively asked Hadassah, "that you never mention anything about religion or services. Is there such a thing as a synagogue in Jerusalem where you can enjoy a service? How about Tel Aviv?"[23] When Lena did not hear back from Hadassah for two weeks—and particularly when she learned from Reba's mother, Rebecca Zismor Zuckerman, that her daughter had already returned to Jerusalem—Lena became positively livid. Where was Hadassah, and what she was doing? "I am convinced," she wrote, "that something has happened to you; either an accident or you are sick or something. Everybody tells me not to worry that it is all the mails etc. etc. But I simply can't stop worrying." She then signed her letter, "your anxious mother."[24]

The financial crisis exacerbated Lena's concerns. She wrote Hadassah that she had canceled her and Naomi's twenty-year insurance policies to get them fast cash, although she kept Judith's policy, which promised $2,000 in ten years.[25] "PG [Please God]," Lena wrote Hadassah, "when you will be that old [thirty-eight] you won't need to worry about a thousand dollars. In the meantime, $50 or $150 can come in much handier."[26] In an effort to economize, Lena also did not send Hadassah a birthday present. Her other daughters scolded their mother for that decision. Lena explained that at $1.96, the "one warm dress—a Selma discard—and *stockings*!!!" that Hadassah had requested were too expensive and would have taken too long (eight weeks) to warrant mailing.[27] Instead, Lena planned to send a new dress that she would have Selma try on for size. Two weeks earlier, in mid-December, Lena had sent Hadassah $50. "I know I need not tell you to be careful. But on the other hand don't stint yourself on food. Please eat enough and more than just enough to keep body + soul together. We don't want a skeleton to *come home to us*, but a nice young lady. You see I say come home to us."[28] Lena explained her gifting strategy as follows: "To send you what you need, would be too much + to send you luxuries[,] I can't afford[,] and trinkets you can buy for yourself. So you will have to be satisfied with our good wishes."[29] "Talking of money darling," Lena wrote,

> I dont know what to say to you. I dont want to spoil your fun. You went away with the promise that you could stay until June if you like it there. We never discussed the money problem. . . . Darling if it is going to

involve much money I am afraid you will have to do without it. You will have to be content with all that you have already seen. We dont want you to economize on the Hebrew lessons nor your food, which by the way I am afraid you are doing when you have tea and toast for breakfast and lunch. So the only thing you will have to eliminate a little is travelling.[30]

In addition to asking Hadassah to cconomize on her travel but not her lessons or food, Lena asked her daughter how her friends could afford their travels and what type of work they were doing. She, furthermore, suggested that her daughter find a job—typing, stenography, or teaching English to children for "a little extra money for travelling." Indeed, Lena herself typed the letter in which she suggested that Hadassah acquire some secretarial experience, mentioning that she was practicing "to help Papa." "We can and will and are able," she continued, "to send you enough to live on as you have been doing but I am afraid more than that we cannot do." Lena warned that Hadassah would need to return to New York as inexpensively as possible by the end of the summer.[31]

"At this end of the world," Lena explained, "money is rather scarce and extra money is not at all available. Therefor[e] darling you will have to be content from now on to cut out some of your trips and concentrate on your Hebrew, so that when you get back it will be an asset to you and enable you to get some kind of a teaching posting if you don't get one in the public schools." "You see," she continued, "I am coming down to *tachless* [Yiddish for "purpose" or "practical details"]. I hope you know what that means. Altho it is true that you haven't cost us so much or in fact nothing much, you have used up the little of your own money that you had and now we have to help you out. . . . Therefor[e] darling please be good and make the best of it educationally."[32]

Indeed, Lena feared that Hadassah was not using her time well and was about to start costing the Kaplans money they did not have. At a tea honoring Frieda Schiff Warburg following her return to New York, she had apparently told Lena that Hadassah was "fine + having a good time. But," Lena wrote Hadassah,

> she [Warburg] asked me to forgive her for saying that she thinks that you are not in the right environment. That you should come more in contact

with the real life of Palestine. . . . Papa + I think the same. We both feel that you had no right to waste so much time in Cairo in the first place. Secondly that if you would go to Haifa as Miss. Friedlander advised or work in a kvuzoth [agricultural settlement] you would get that which you set out for. After all you did not go to Palestine for the social life. You had enough of that here. You simply transferred your mode of life from NY to Jerusalem + Cairo.[33]

Beyond Warburg's criticisms of Hadassah, although she did not specify it, Lena might have been concerned about her daughter spending so much time in anti- or non-Zionist circles. While the Levys were family friends from the SAJ and distinguished members of the community, some American Jews viewed Joseph's reporting as overly critical of Palestinian Jews. Similarly, although the Warburgs were strong supporters of the SAJ and other philanthropic causes, they were also non-Zionists. Even as the family supported economic investment in Jewish agricultural colonies, businesses, and philanthropies, the Warburgs opposed political nationalism and viewed a Jewish state as utopian.[34] It is unclear if the politics of those with whom Hadassah was associating in Cairo further aggravated the Kaplans.

By the time Hadassah received her mother's letter, she had finally managed to leave Cairo, taking a train to Kantara, a ferry across the Suez Canal, a train to Lydda, and finally renting a car to drive to Jerusalem. The letters from home she found there illustrated Lena's growing concern not only about her daughter's behavior and their family's financial standing but more generally about the suffering in New York. "I am sending you a clipping from the paper," Lena explained,

> from which you will see what is going on in N.Y. You are very fortunate to be away from this. You are spared seeing all the hardship and misery one sees wherever one turns. All one hears when one goes out is deficit deficit in all organizations and naturally you know the cause of these deficits. The people have no money to contribute and the work must go on and the work does go on and nobody gets paid etc. etc. Conditions here are really indescribable and therefor[e] you ought to thank your lucky star that you are away.[35]

Lena went on to insist that it was time Hadassah stop traveling and find a job, particularly since she had run through her savings (she had only $25 left) and her parents were hard-pressed to send her an allowance.[36] "You see dear," wrote Lena, "you will have to come down to earth soon. You are living in the clouds now and have no cares and worries. You may have some I know. That is you must evidently always be aware of your finances."[37] In this letter, Lena further assured Hadassah that if she got a job, she could—if she wanted—remain in Palestine: "altho we are all lonesome for you. Every once in a while," Lena confessed, "we miss you terribly. I never want to write that but it did come out this time."[38]

Hadassah must have internalized her parents' growing concerns about money, safety, and how she was spending her time. The following week, in a letter unusually addressed just to her mother, Hadassah relayed an anxiety dream in which her parents showed up in Jerusalem and made her go home immediately, without even packing. While weeping, Hadassah repeated, "I said I'd be in Palestine for the nasty rainy season—+ not ever see it when its lovely—after suffering through all that! I guess I like Palestine," she continued to her mother. "What do you think?"[39]

Even as Hadassah negotiated with her parents to remain in Palestine, her younger sister Selma was advocating for an adventure of her own. She wanted to spend the summer of 1933 and the following fall of her sophomore year studying German in Germany or Switzerland. Such travels were unusual for a young Jewish woman at the time, but they were not unprecedented. Even if the Kaplans did not know the family personally, they were probably aware of twenty-year-old Ruth Gruber from Brooklyn, who, the *New York Times* announced just a month before Hadassah departed for Palestine, was the youngest person to earn a doctor of philosophy from the University of Cologne. She wrote a dissertation on Virginia Woolf in a year.[40] Gruber went on to become a journalist, photographer, and humanitarian who is perhaps best known for her documentation in 1947 of the *Exodus*, a refugee-laden ship that returned to Germany after the British refused its entry into Palestine.

Indeed, international student exchange grew rapidly in the early twentieth century. German universities had, since the 1880s, attracted a range of American postgraduate students, among them W. E. B. DuBois, the Black intellectual and founder of the National Association for the Advancement of Colored People. But during the interwar period, the number of American undergraduate students going abroad skyrocketed, with more than two thousand studying in Europe.[41] Pivotal for that influx was the creation, in 1923, of a Junior Year Abroad at the University of Delaware, followed two years later by a program at Smith College. The typical exchange student was a woman from an East Coast college, like Barnard, studying in France.[42] "Pop" Alexander, one of Selma's Barnard professors, encouraged her to study in Germany, promising her a scholarship, including tuition and lodging. Within four years, he furthermore assured her that she would be hired as an assistant German teacher at New College. Mordecai must have been particularly pleased at the idea of his youngest daughter teaching at New College, which, like his Teachers' Institute, was "an experimental teacher-training institution under the auspices of Columbia University's Teachers College."[43] The Kaplans would have also appreciated the timing, since they too hoped to spend the year in Palestine on Mordecai's sabbatical. Selma was certainly thrilled by the prospect of being paid to teach. Alexander offered her a starting salary of $100 a month. "Gee Hadassah," she exclaimed, "can you imagine me being told about a salary—so you wonder that I'm going around half dazed—Oh! There'll be Communism or something dumb like that before then and I'll be sewing or something dumb like that—and Alexander said he won't mind even if I get married—what an optimist!"[44] That January, Selma boarded the Hamburg America Line for a formal dinner "to taste the food and look over the boat."[45] There was a gym, an orchestra, a dance floor, and a stag party with about 150 young men. "What fun it was," Selma wrote her sister.[46]

But Hitler's appointment to chancellor that month ruled out the option of such travel. Ruth Gruber described in her memoir studying the previous academic year at a German university, where she attended Nazi rallies, participated in lectures that turned into shouting matches affirming Nazi ideology, and was acutely aware of growing antisemitism.[47] "We will on no condition," Lena wrote Hadassah in February as they began to discuss her return trip, "allow you to go to Germany."[48] By May, Lena insisted that Hadassah could not travel on a German steamer. Selma's trip to Germany was canceled, and the Kaplans delayed their sabbatical because of financial and family obligations. Nevertheless, they still allowed Selma to go to London with New College—without a scholarship or the promise of a subsequent job since she would not be learning

German there. Mordecai noted in his diary that the prominent lawyer Samuel Untermyer intervened to ensure that Alexander switched transport for Selma and the seven other Jewish girls to a non-German ship. According to Mordecai, Selma's professor "was very much incensed by all these interferences." He yielded to them, however, particularly after Untermyer sent a $1,000 check to cover the cost of changing plans.[49]

Selma and her peers boarded the British Royal Mail Ship *Olympic* on June 2, 1933, her parents' twenty-fifth anniversary.[50] Judith minimized Selma's complaints about not being able to travel to Germany or ride a German ship. "The whole problem of 'touring,'" Judith wrote Hadassah, "seems so desperately irrelevant when we read of the sort of things that are happening in Germany."[51] Judith was presumably referring to the recent German boycott of Jewish businesses, the dismissal of Jews from civil service jobs, and the burning of books written by Jews and others deemed "un-German." Selma, however, was more focused on gratitude toward her parents. "You know," she wrote Hadassah, "things like this [trip] make me realize how wonderful mamma + papa are—not only the idea of offering to send me when they don't plan to go—that itself is enough—but just the idea of wanting me to go—to study in Palestine or Europe—There are so many wealthier people who'd never think of such an idea—who are smug and content—but they're so different— They're [sic] whole philosophy or psychology. When I realize that I see how much we all have to be thankful for—and how damn lucky we are!"[52] Although Selma described her parents as exceptional for allowing her and her sisters to study abroad, the appreciation Selma felt toward them was similar to the sentiment expressed by her peers: other female students traveling abroad at the time. As one student, named Eleanor Daniels, wrote her parents from a ship en route to Europe in 1937, "Thank you, thank you, thank you for letting me come—it's going to be wonderful, I know."[53]

Hadassah focused less on gratitude after returning from Egypt than on her Hebrew reading and lessons. Dialing down her social engagements, she finished Ahad Ha'am's essays, noting in her diary the need for a spiritual renewal through Hebrew culture and calling for "revival of [the] Hebrew spirit thru [the] creation of [a] concrete Jewish Life in Palestine."[54] Hadassah further read a Hebrew translation of *Alice in Wonderland* and studied a series of pamphlets, including ones issued by

Keren Hayesod (United Israel Appeal) and Keren Kayemeth (Jewish National Fund). She read the organization Junior Hadassah's *Primer on Palestine*, the Hebrew Bible (especially Jeremiah), and David Frischman's *The Golem*, the story of a creature magically brought to life to rescue an endangered Jewish community. She also attended lectures, mostly focused on archeology.

Hadassah traveled in a social crowd but purposely tried to focus on her studies. "There I sat with my Bible in hand," she recalled to her family about a Tuesday evening in March, "and courageously refused" to go to a friend's house. But she broke down after three other friends asked her if she was going. At Helen's house, she remembered that they "sang Yemenite, Arabic songs—drank wine, tea + ate cake—Her room you see," she continued, "is all of 2x4 and so we felt cozy, if nothing else sitting on the floor—windowsills, etc."[55]

Despite some interruptions, Hadassah's reading raised her awareness about, among other things, the problems that might emerge from political nationalism. On Hadassah's reading list that March was Judah Magnes's controversial pamphlet "Like All the Nations?," which he published in 1929 but the Jewish Telegraphic Agency printed in Hebrew and English the following January, five months after the extensive violence experienced by both Jews and Arabs.[56] In the piece, which he later developed into a book, Magnes argued that what lay at the heart of Zionism was not a state or a Jewish majority but instead "immigration, settlement of the land, and Hebrew culture." He called for binationalism—neither a Jewish nor an Arabic state but instead a national-international entity where all residents had equal rights. Magnes also insisted on the centrality of a constitution to establish and protect a democratic order along US lines.[57] Palestine, he contended, should not become like most flag-waving nations, oppressing a majority Arab Palestinian population through military might and denying them their political aspirations for national self-determination. He viewed the protection of the rights of Arab Palestinians as a moral imperative that could not wait. "Israel's question," wrote Magnes, "always is, and whether we want it or not, will always be: Are my own hands clean of blood? Not are his hands clean? Have I done him wrong? Not, has he done me wrong?"[58] Magnes could not imagine a world in which Jews became "successful conquerors and colonizers. Neither the hostile world," he continued, "nor their own soul will let them." Instead, he contended that a Jewish homeland should "defend the prophetic tradition," developing an international, interreligious, and interracial Palestine where Jews, Christians, and Muslims might build an ethical-liberal society marked by "human solidarity and understanding." Such a land would guarantee Jewish immigration, settlement of the land, and the development of Hebrew life and culture, while simultaneously drawing on all available weapons—"spiritual, intellectual, social, cultural, financial, economic, [and] medical"; everything but bayonets—to forge a just land fostering religious freedom and equality before the law, including for women. The pacifist concluded his pamphlet by explaining that although conquering the land and maintaining power through the sword might have been appropriate during the time of Joshua, it is "not in accord with the desire of plain Jews or with the long ethical tradition of Judaism that has not ceased developing to this day."[59] In this final statement, Magnes clarified his prophetic vision. He was not looking for Jews to become politically normalized but instead to form "a society committed to actualizing the Jewish principles of justice and morality."[60]

It is difficult to ascertain how much of an impact Magnes's writing and work had on Hadassah. She recorded the title of the work and its author in her diary, but the notes that follow appear to be quotes from elsewhere—perhaps a lecture. In them, Hadassah outlined principles behind B'rith Shalom, a Jewish organization promoting binationalism that Magnes founded. She wrote that Palestine contains many people who claim the land as their "national home" but contended that Jewish workers (Poale Zion) will convince "the Arab peoples, themselves struggling for freedom, liberty, and independence, that we Jews want nothing for ourselves that we are not willing to give to everyone." In this way, she drew connections between Magnes's approach to "radicalism [labor politics] and nationalism."[61] Hadassah also might have juxtaposed her reading of Magnes against a more didactic work, such as Junior Hadassah's recently released *A Primer on Palestine*. The primer, which Hadassah also read that spring, acknowledged the existence of Arab nationalism but downplayed how representative it was and, instead, highlighted specific examples of growing Jewish-Arab cooperation with help from the British government.[62]

Hadassah did not appear to have associated her reading of Magnes with other conversations, such as one with a friend of her mother's whom she described as having had to leave her home in Rehavia, with a "real American kitchen and bathroom," when "the Arabs started getting funny."[63] Her written reflections show how little she knew about the violence in the summer of 1929. "We had no idea," she commented, "of what was happening over here. It was absolutely a Civil War, it seems."[64] In contrast, we know from Mordecai's diaries that he not only was cognizant of the unrest but also attended a protest rally at Madison Square Garden where he was supposed to have spoken.[65] He might not have discussed his reflections and actions with the family, or the family may not have registered them. Interestingly, although one of the thirteen sections in the Junior Hadassah *Primer* addressed "The Arab," there were only two brief mentions of the crisis in Palestine that summer, neither of which contextualized or explained it. Instead, the primer minimized Arab Palestinian discontent, insisting that moderate nationalists had replaced radical ones and emphasizing the presence of sympathetic "Arabs of all classes" who "rescued and cared for" injured Jews during the violence.[66] The optimistic tone in Hadassah's notes, and her conviction that labor Zionists could convince Palestinian Arabs of their good intentions, suggests that she was more persuaded by the Junior Hadassah *Primer* than by Magnes.

Even if Magnes's writing did not transform Hadassah's thinking, she wanted to connect with those people her parents valued. Shortly after reading "Like All the Nations?," Hadassah telephoned Magnes, Hebrew University's then chancellor, and made a 9:30 a.m. appointment to meet him. Hadassah reported home that the two "discussed Palestine vs. America; America's present tsorus [a Yiddish word for troubles] etc." Hadassah told her parents, presumably proudly, that Magnes asked her to be in touch when she returned to Jerusalem, apparently misunderstanding that she was already based there. Beyond discussing politics, Hadassah continued to concentrate on personal logistics. "I *do* wish," she wrote home when conveying the encounter, "he'd invite me to his Seder!"[67] The Magneses did not. Perhaps, as Lena feared, Hadassah's lack of interest in their son David created distance. Nevertheless, Hadassah connected with the Magneses a few more times—visiting Dr. Magnes a month later and also attending Hebrew University's dedication of its outdoor, white-stone theater.

Hadassah also went to events connected with the organization *Hadassah*, including the graduation of nursing students. She visited places where her *Hadassah* mentors worked, such as a playground near Zion Gate in Old City Jerusalem catering primarily to Arab and Yemenite Jewish children.[68] Hadassah noted gendered and religious inequities between the Young Women's Hebrew Association (YWHA), which sponsored the trip she initially took to Cairo, and the recently opened Young Men's Christian Association (YMCA), an elegant neo-Byzantine complex across the street from the also new King David Hotel. "It's really a crime," Hadassah wrote her family, "to see that place [the YWHA]—where a stove is a luxury because they can't afford the oil for it—particularly after visiting the beautiful new building of the YMCA—which has a pool, tennis courts, track field, chapel, in fact everything! Even in Jerusalem the Jews haven't as much as the others. Because after all—the Ys need donations! Oh well—"[69]

Hadassah continued to explore diverse religious sites, visiting the Citadel and Tower of David, Bethlehem, and Hebron. Using her father's index, she cross-referenced the various places she visited with their descriptions in the Bible and also looked them up in the *Handbook of Palestine*, a guidebook published after World War I emphasizing change over time as varied people ruled and inhabited the region.[70] While she sought out historical churches and mosques—returning for a second visit to the Church of Nativity and witnessing the Ceremony of the Fire at the Holy Sepulchre—the sites that most resonated with her came from ancient Jewish biblical sources. In many respects, Hadassah's travels and writing about them exemplified what Magnes described as the potential significance of Holy Land tourism for Jews. "Palestine," he promised, "can help this people to understand itself, to give an account of itself, to an intensification of its culture, a deepening of its philosophy, [and] a renewal of its religion."[71] At a minimum, Hadassah sought to demonstrate to her parents that she was experiencing the Palestine they wanted her to see. Indeed, as she describes it, the combination of her travels and reading did make Jewish history come alive. "Somehow or other," she wrote about visiting the Citadel and Tower of David, "I had the feeling that I'd just bump into Josephus—so easily could I picture him there after having read that book [referring back to Lion Feuchtwanger's biography of the cosmopolitan Jewish historian]!"[72] In Hebron, she tracked down various places mentioned in the Bible, such as David's pool and the Tomb of the Patriarchs, Machpelah. While Hadassah admired the huge slabs of stone in the Tomb, she dismissed as "superstitious" the Jews who stuffed into the holes between them petitions to ancestors. She was also intrigued by the Crusaders' remains: "Seriously tho," she commented, "lots of what the Crusaders built is still left—+ people even lived in some of the holes, that were made then, until very recently!" Unable to find vineyards, she wrote her parents, "It's supposed to be glorious there in the spring. But I can't put everything off until then. I'll just have to take the Bible's word for it—that there are vineyards there!"[73] While Hadassah traveled and studied historically significant sites, she still worried that she was not doing enough. "I wish," she reflected, "I didn't have such a nuisance of a conscience—I always feel that I'm not seeing + accomplishing 1/100 of what I should be!"[74]

Hadassah's sense of personal deficit was magnified by her growing awareness of the economic crisis in the US. Both her mother and her younger sister Naomi wrote about the family's experience of FDR's Bank Holiday. On his second day in office, the president shut down the banks after a month of nervous people withdrawing cash from US banks in so-called bank runs. The Bank Holiday combined with the Emergency Banking Act restored the nation's confidence in the banking system—and encouraged people to return their hoarded cash—by insuring deposits in the reopened banks.[75] But before then, Lena found herself and her family with access to almost no cash. On Friday, March 3, 1933, she spent her last fourteen cents shopping for the Sabbath. When the banks closed that Monday, Lena was relieved to learn that Mordecai had a few dollars stored away. "Luckily," Naomi wrote, "Papa is one of those criminals who hoards his four dollar allowances to buy books, and he hadn't yet bought his last batch—so he's been our bank—+ we got our allowances this week."[76] Lena, who had not imagined how bad the situation would become, was genuinely concerned about Hadassah's access to cash. She had recently sent Hadassah a second $50 check, which Lena worried Hadassah would not be able to cash. Lena asked if Hadassah could go to their friends from the SAJ, either Joseph Levy—the newspaper editor and publisher whom Hadassah had visited in Cairo—or the Epsteins, to borrow money if she needed it.

Hadassah was still sitting on the check wondering if she should cash it for a diminished rate or wait. Either way, the crisis raised existential questions for her about whether she should remain in Palestine or return to New York. "Is it worth," she asked, "coming back + having nothing to do but worry because I won't have enough money to buy clothes? Or shall I look for a job and stay here. It's true the pay can't be so very much—but I don't have to spend it on clothes!" Hadassah worried that she would not be able to secure a teaching job in New York and that she would not have the resources to live in the way a young woman of her background expected to do in New York. She asked her mother to renew her substitute teaching license and one of her sisters to go to the Board of Education to "find out [her] place on the list." She also wrote to the Board of Education herself.[77] Without serious work prospects in New York, Hadassah recommitted herself to improving her Hebrew. Knowing that she would not have to pay for room and board while living on *kvutzot*, agricultural communes, she also made plans to visit them between the Jewish holidays Purim and Passover. Then she intended to learn shorthand so that she could find a job beyond her occasional work at the *Palestine Post*.[78]

In the meantime, Hadassah decided to reaffirm her celebrations of Jewish holidays in ways unique to Palestine. Although she attended synagogue services only about once a month—and more frequently after returning from Cairo—she still had not found meaningful ones in Palestine. What she appears to have valued most was participating in communal and collective celebrations of Shabbat and Jewish holidays, marking them with friends and mentors and joining in public gatherings and parades. On Tu'B'shvat, the New Year of the Trees, she hosted friends, including her mentors the Shermans and Schoolmans and her camp friends Sylva and Kronick, in her "little yard with a few greens shooting up." "I made round brown bread" sandwiches, she wrote home, "with cream cheese and chives, black current Jelly—; + then I had triangular white bread sardines mixed with hard boiled eggs and mayonnaise. Besides that I had little petite fours + a bowls of almonds, raisins, + figs." She proudly reported having kept her entertaining budget for thirty people to $2.11.[79]

Like Hanukkah, Purim—a minor Jewish holiday recounting Esther saving the Jews of Persia from annihilation by overturning a plot by an official named Haman—conformed well to a national narrative of auto-emancipation. Tel Aviv saw a weeklong whirlwind of events run by its municipality with free outdoor happenings, including a costume parade with elaborate floats created by artists celebrating Tel Aviv's abundance (as well as satire) and a three-day-long street carnival with horse races and a three-story public stage, called "Esther's Palace." By the mid-1930s, more than one hundred thousand participants—international visitors, Palestinian Jews and Arabs, the religious and the secular, pickpockets among them—would make a mass pilgrimage to the festivities, watching dances (or dancing themselves), listening to orchestras, witnessing plays, and enjoying themselves. Indoor parties and costume balls required admission fees and attracted smaller crowds but still drew thousands of revelers. According to the cultural historian Hizky Shoham, Tel Aviv's Purim carnivals were the first cultural practice developed in Palestine and then disseminated to the diaspora.[80]

On Saturday, March 11, two days before banks reopened in the US, Hadassah recalled that "the [Tel Aviv] streets were literally more mobbed than 38th St. + Broadway at lunch hour except—that everybody was happy + carefree."[81] Caught up in the carnival nature of the holiday, which encourages topsy-turvy behavior, Hadassah appears to have observed the floats. But she did not register at least one display protesting the oppression of Jews in Germany. On it, a statue of Hitler wore a sign proclaiming, "Death to the Jews," as he and his horse trampled two bleeding Jews. Formal complaints by the German consul in Jerusalem could not stop a more overt protest against antisemitism at the following year's parade, when a float featuring a monster with a swastika on its back was burned in effigy.[82]

That evening, dressed as a "newspaper girl," Hadassah, along with her friends, watched a Purim *shpiel*, or performance, on a large, grandstand stage, which Hadassah described as "pleasantly* grotesque ... (*Is that possible?)," she went on to ask. The group climbed "fences, roves, and what-not—in order to be able to see something." They then went to a series of parties at friends' houses, in restaurants, and on rooftops. "It was like a New Year's Eve week-end," Hadassah reflected, "lasting, in fact more than a week-end!" But she also implied that she was growing tired of the social scene. One night, she skipped the parties to talk with Sis and go out for coffee at 11:00 p.m. "I think I've really grown old here," she wrote home, "because I cannot dance all night as I used to—and I cannot stand noise and lots of people."[83]

Well before Purim, Hadassah began to think about how to mark Passover, a holiday that commemorates the Israelites' escape from Egyptian enslavement and is based more on at-home rituals than public festivities. As early as December, she twice asked her parents if they might come to Palestine, but Mordecai could not begin his sabbatical until the fall. In turn, Lena twice suggested that Hadassah spend the holiday observing the pilgrimage to Mount Gerizim in the West Bank of a small Jewish sect called Samaritans, who descended from Jews not deported during the Assyrian conquest in 722 BCE. The mother of Hadassah's camp friend Kronick invited her for Seder in Jerusalem, presumably at Goldsmit's pension, where Hadassah's other mentors, Sue Rosen and Rose Gell Jacobs, would be.[84] But Hadassah preferred, if possible, to find a more intimate Seder.[85] Lena had written in November of the anticipated arrival of the forty-seven-year-old philanthropist and former *Hadassah* president, the New York–born Irma Lindheim, who was immigrating to Palestine with her children. Lena promised that Lindheim would "be very happy to have [Hadassah] come and live with her for as long as [she] expect[ed] to stay."[86] Given that the widowed mother of five arrived in Palestine only a few days before the holiday, however, it is unsurprising that no invitation materialized. Instead, Hadassah sublet her room in Jerusalem to Sis, stowed most of her clothing at a friend's house, and, after celebrating Purim in Tel Aviv, traveled to her first of several agricultural collective settlements, or kibbutzim.

Hadassah was unsure of how long she would last in a rural communal setting, but, she confided in her diary, "try I must."[87] Her assumption that she needed to attempt this lifestyle might have been influenced by the high rate at which American immigrants to Palestine volunteered in and visited the colonies; two-thirds of them at least tried to do so.[88] Unlike at least some of those volunteers, however, Hadassah did not come out of an obviously Zionist labor youth group, such as Hashomer Hatzair (The Young Guard), which socialized young people collectively to live and work the land together, to subjugate their individuality to the collective, and to migrate to agricultural settlements as a group. They saw working the land as a vehicle for transforming themselves individually and, in turn, Jewish society as a whole.

Lena wrote Hadassah in February assuring that if she wanted to try living on a *kevutzah*, another term for an agricultural collective, "for a short time," she could. "But," she continued, "on no condition should you do it because you think we want you to do so."[89] By the time Hadassah experienced collective living in Palestine, she was more culturally acclimated and confident in her Hebrew than, for example, her friend Sylva had been. When Sylva ran out of funds shortly after arriving in Palestine, she had gone to Givat Brenner, where she recalled all sorts of surprises, including rooming with members of the opposite sex, eating uncut loaves of bread, and learning to manage with little water, outhouses, and belligerent flies. Hadassah, in contrast, neither focused on such discomforts nor experienced the type of isolation and language barriers that Sylva had. Whereas Sylva described herself as descending into a "world of silence," unable to comprehend the Hebrew newspapers, much less her neighbors' interpretations of current events, Hadassah's Hebrew was on solid grounding by then. Eventually, through immersion on kibbutz, Sylva too acquired basic conversational and then reading Hebrew.[90]

Hadassah first visited Ein Harod, a large kibbutz established eleven years earlier with more than 400 people, including 180 children. Members of Ein Harod embraced vociferous debate and viewed themselves as the Yishuv's avant-garde leaders with regard to both defense and the labor movement.[91] Just three years after the settlement's founding, in 1925, the community's accomplishments so impressed Abraham Cahan, the socialist editor of the *Forverts*, a daily Yiddish paper, that he dubbed its participants "saints and pure people."[92] Prior to his visit to Palestine, the editor had eschewed nationalisms incompatible with socialist cosmopolitanism and internationalism, and his paper had fluctuated between indifference and scorn toward Palestine.[93]

Hadassah was a bit less convinced of the kibbutz's character. In her diary, she attested that "there were too many people there to get to know anyone. In fact," she continued, "at times it felt as tho we were all working in a factory—everyone was too tired at night to even talk."[94] Nevertheless, she wrote the family about how much she enjoyed wearing camp clothes and skipping lipstick.[95] The same young woman who sailed across the Atlantic in heels and silk stockings would spend the next month mostly bareheaded, without makeup or pretense, and permanently wearing clothes that resembled not only summer camp but also the austere, simple dress of the Jewish pioneers: dark shorts, a buttoned-down shirt, and a cardigan. This was, in many respects, the height of her embodiment of Palestine's so-called New Jew, as she shed her dresses, stockings, and hats for practical work clothing, hard labor, and a serious tan.[96] On the kibbutz, she most closely adhered to the stereotype of the New Hebrew Woman in early twentieth-century Zionist discourse. Both were physically and emotionally fit and aspired more to equality, political rights, and military activity than to femininity, charm, and charity work.[97]

"It's easy enough," she commented shortly after her arrival at Ein Harod, "to see how one could be won over to this sort of life."[98] In another letter, she implied that she had, indeed, been persuaded to remain. "I'm so enthusiastic," she explained, "I'm liable to stay." She then continued, expressing some hesitation, "I'm just trying to realize tho whether it's that they still treat me a little like a visitor, that they do a few things for me, that makes it nice—+ whether I'd like it if I actually were one of them."[99] Feeling more persuaded of her initial conviction, she wrote to her parents that she woke up "feeling lousy" after having dreams of returning to New York. "I certainly never imagined," she continued, "*I'd feel the way I do about Palestine.*"[100] Clearly, Hadassah enjoyed her newfound freedom to engage in physical labor, eschew feminine dress and proprieties, and participate unequivocally in the land's upbuilding. But it remained to be seen if her feelings and commitment to such work and lifestyle were fleeting or would endure.

Hadassah described herself to her family as even happier at Geva, a smaller collective than Ein Harod. She appreciated Geva's intimacy and spirit. She also learned about its problems from her guide. An American boy named Eddie told her about "the Arab situation in these parts," which Hadassah did not detail further in her diary. Eddie also outlined "the social condition in the Krutzot." Among other problems, he mentioned the suicides of an older man, a teenage girl, and a "jealous" wife.[101]

Despite such concerns, Hadassah loved the fieldwork at Geva. Women in the collectives, who were generally outnumbered by men, were often assigned to domestic tasks, such as laundry, kitchen, or child care. Some fought gender-based stereotypes to be able to work the land as their male peers did and to participate in the collective's governance. Many of them believed that their manual labor would yield both personal and national liberation, contributing to the construction of a new Jewish woman alongside her male counterpart.[102]

Modern women, like Hadassah, sought ways to contribute to the upbuilding of the nation through motherhood, field work, political rights, and military activity.[103] In 1914, for example, Rivkah Danit, a female laborer, wrote about her struggles to participate in manual—nondomestic—work, building a road in the lower Galilee:

> It was with the utmost difficulty that I, a woman, could persuade [the Histadrut, or General Organization of Workers] to take me along. There were all sorts of objections. The work was too much for a girl. It wasn't nice for a Jewish girl to be working on the open road. There was even one *haver* [friend] who believed that it would be a national crime! But another girl and I stuck it out for the first week and, in spite of renewed objections, stayed on. At the end of the first month, there was a whole group of women at work on the road.[104]

From a brief visit in 1925, the New York–born Jewish philanthropist and educator Irma Lindheim had a more idealistic impression of gender and the service ethic on collective settlements. "For women," she explained to her family, "there is a new freedom in the life of the *Kvutza*. Their tasks are hard but they are defined, and because of their definition the status of women is placed on the same level as that of men. In the division of work the women's equality is undisputed, as it is also when the fruits of her labor are ready to be plucked."[105] By the 1920s, new services including child care, food preparation, and laundry collectivized what had previously been private or familial responsibilities. Lindheim was so impressed by what she observed that, in 1933, she joined Mishmar HaEmek, as a forty-seven-year-old widow. At Geva that same year, Hadassah's experience was closer to Lindheim's vision than to Danit's reality. Whereas Danit struggled to work in the fields, Hadassah primarily labored there. She planted *pardes* (orchards), dug ditches, whitewashed trees, sowed nurseries, tended vineyards, weeded, reduced the number of cornstalks, built cement walls, and patched mattresses. At times, she was the sole woman working among men. The photos of her driving a buggy tractor, hoeing, and mugging with friends indicate how much she enjoyed the experience. Hadassah was particularly satisfied by her work because she understood that the *kvutzot* were understaffed. She, thus, felt as though her labor was even more important.[106]

Despite Hadassah's experiences, gender inequities persisted on kibbutzim, with men responsible for agriculture and women in charge of

Figure 5.3. Hadassah Kaplan on kibbutz, March 1933. (Personal collection)

child care, the emotional labor of mothering, and auxiliary services such as cooking, laundry, and cleaning.[107] Yet such disparities also furthered advocacy for equity. When Hadassah was at Ein Harod—one of the few kibbutzim with roughly equal numbers of men and women—she might have noticed the statue lionizing "The Galilee and Its Women Guards." If she had stayed longer, perhaps she would have become involved in the battle over the role of women in the military and as the kibbutz's guards. Or maybe she would have met and joined Ein Harod's outspoken women, such as the Ukrainian-born Lilia Bassewitz, who drew attention not only to women's rights in the kibbutz but also in the broader labor movement. Bassewitz's writing in Ein Harod's newsletter also addressed the need to value child care and other forms of so-called women's work as well as to elevate the social, intellectual, and emotional lives of all despite the kibbutz's atmosphere of deprivation and frugality.[108] Even if Hadassah did not directly encounter Bassewitz, exposure to feminist ideas and practices on kibbutzim shaped her.

Over the course of a month, Hadassah toured some nine collective settlements, working on three different ones and visiting some six others. When she explored them, she observed shoemakers, laundries, barns, stables, and schools. She particularly noted the presence of leisure

Figure 5.4. Hadassah Kaplan on kibbutz, March 1933. (Personal collection)

spaces. "It's really remarkable," she commented. "No matter what else those kibutzoth [sic] haven't got—they always have a *library, recreation room*, and a beautiful place for the children."[109] From the libraries, Hadassah checked out books occasionally in English but mostly Hebrew translations, including Charles Erskin Scott Wood's 1927 collection of satirical essays originally published in *The Masses, Heavenly Discourses*; Vicki Baum's best-seller *Grand Hotel* (1929); and Pearl S Buck's *The Good Earth* (1931). When she was not working and reading, Hadassah listened to music, sang, and danced with her peers. She was impressed by the way the *kvutzot* governed and discussed work allocations. Hadassah wrote home about how good she felt—sunburnt and well fed—with the "sort of tired stiffness of the *muscles* that one gets after gym or horseback [riding]. I've never," she continued, "felt healthier in my life as you can well imagine—being outdoors *all* day. The food at this kvutzah is really good!"[110] She wanted her family to join her and wrote home that she wished she could "dig up just enough money" for them to go there: "all of you. God—you'd love it!" As if to persuade them further, she sent home clippings from a grapefruit blossom with the "most glorious odor."[111] The family did not take up her offer, but family friends did. Just around Passover, Hadassah hosted her camp friend Kronick's father as well as Irma Lindheim, the wealthy widow whom Hadassah had hoped would invite her for Passover Seder. Lindheim would establish several collective settlements. Hadassah also entertained Helen Levinthal. The daughter of a prominent Conservative rabbi in Brooklyn, Helen would become the first woman to complete all the requirements to become a rabbi at New York's Jewish Institute of Religion (JIR), a seminary training liberal rabbis that the Reform rabbi Stephen Samuel Wise founded in 1922. Lindheim had also enrolled at JIR in its first year of operation, which was also the same year that Judith Kaplan became the first bat mitzvah. The institute had theoretically acceded to Lindheim's request to grant clergy status to trained men and women, but she did not complete the course. When Levinthal became the first qualified person for the position, in 1939, the faculty decided the "time was not ripe," though the Berlin-born Regina Jonas had been ordained the first female rabbi in the Reform Movement in Germany four years earlier (in 1935).[112]

Beyond entertaining guests, Hadassah connected the land she was working with the Bible. She wrote home about seeing Harod's spring, near Ein Harod. In the book of Judges, Gideon tested those men wishing to fight with him against the Midianites, separating those who licked the water from the river from those who first cupped their hands to gather drinking water. God promised Gideon that the latter would be better prepared warriors and told him to send home the other troops.[113]

Hadassah was markedly less aware of the political context of the place than of its biblical connotations. Lindheim, whom Hadassah entertained at Ein Harod, presumably was significantly more mindful of growing tensions. When Lindheim rode horseback through the country in 1925, she commented on how little of the arable land belonged to Jews and argued that the Jewish National Fund (JNF) should buy more land for collective use.[114] Roughly a decade later, the Zionist Organization's land purchasing and development agency would acquire significant land. Between 1936 and 1948, JNF bought six hundred thousand dunams, which is roughly equivalent to six hundred million square meters. Such land created the infrastructure for 130 new agricultural settlements, influencing international decisions regarding Palestine and later Israel's borders.[115] Nevertheless, only a little more than a quarter of all Jewish land at the time was owned nationally; instead, almost three-quarters of it was owned by private entrepreneurs.[116]

Hadassah made few comments about the land's ownership or relations between Jewish and Arab Palestinians. She knew that there was an Arab village near Ein Harod, the first kibbutz where she worked, as well as the first in the Valley of Harod. But she also did not realize that in the 1920s, there had been three Palestinian villages and two hamlets there.[117] Hadassah noted a military demonstration by the British military—with tanks and planes—which she described as a reconnaissance mission in case "God forbid, something happens between the Arabs and the Jews."[118] Might she have used her recent reading of Magnes to interrogate the kibbutz's foundation or its use of power for self-maintenance? At Ein Harod's inception, the JNF purchased the land from the prominent Christian Sarsouk family of Lebanon as part of a wider project to expand Jewish national ownership within the Jezreel Valley for agricultural settlements. Between 1921 and 1923, JNF bought 73,600 dunams, more than tripling national ownership of land (6,352). It removed the area's residents, largely Arab Palestinian tenant farmers who worked the land but had no legal right to it. Later British policies would call for monetary compensation for displaced tenants or, more aggressively, for no land swaps to occur until Arab tenants could be resettled in new areas, but neither approach was sufficiently practiced to make the former residents self-sustaining.[119] Instead, Ein Harod's conflicts with its Palestinian Arab neighbors were ongoing. Battles over the growth of the kibbutz would instigate military engagements, including night raids on Arab Palestinian villages, and their resistance through attacks on kibbutz members and setting fire to their fields. Ein Harod would become training grounds for an Anglo-Jewish commando unit that would raid Arab villages and a sergeants' course that would develop into a center for training Israel's future army, which would play a central role in driving Palestinian Arabs out of the Jezreel Valley in 1948.[120] How would such realities relate to Magnes's vision of an international Holy Land following a prophetic tradition in which Jews proved themselves different from all the nations by building a liberal-ethical society that avoided wronging others regardless of the actions of others?

Rather than registering the tensions and emerging conflicts in the Jezreel Valley in the spring of 1933, Hadassah mostly noted relatively peaceful interactions among Jews, Palestinians, Bedouins, and Brits. For example, she described visiting a Bedouin camp with an American friend who was learning Arabic. She characterized the Bedouins as "very friendly." "We invited ourselves in," she continued, noting the Bedouins' hospitality in serving them coffee and food.[121] Hadassah also wrote about having seen children from an Arabic school visiting a Jewish one and eating oranges together.[122] Such exchanges matched those recorded by her peers. Sylva, for example, conveyed the story frequently retold by members of Kiryat Anavim, where she worked, about how the Mukhtar of Abu Ghosh brought his children to the *kvutzah* in 1929 following the violence that summer "as a gesture of his determination to safeguard ... [its] security."[123]

Perhaps also because of Hadassah's focus on manual labor, she paid markedly less attention to world events than she had previously done during her time abroad. On her first evening in Ein Harod, Hadassah wrote home that she attended a lecture about Hitler and Mussolini, but she admitted that she was "too tired to make it out" after spending a long day planting an orchard (she arrived in the fields at 7:00 a.m.; her peers had been there since 4:00 a.m.).[124] On March 27, when Stephen Wise and the American Jewish Committee organized a protest in Madison Square Garden against Hitler and rising Nazism, echoed by seventy other communities in the US, Hadassah was absorbed in weeding. There is no record of her following contemporaneous protests and efforts by American Jews to boycott German imports or German attempts to boycott Jewish-owned businesses.

Mordecai also did not directly comment on such events. He had not written to his daughter in a month and a half.[125] In his diary during this period, he developed lectures and teaching notes trying to explain the current crisis and offer some solutions. For example, he argued that prophetic Judaism offered a better model than Marxism for how the middle class might awaken from the status quo to use social education and political action to create a more just social order. He was also deeply cognizant of growing antisemitism and the worsening of the economic crisis. "When women of the type of Vivien Bachrach ... and Helen (Gottesman) Borgenicht—women in their late thirties [who were members of the SAJ]—get together, the chief topic of conversation is what they do to prevent their husbands from committing suicide."[126] Presumably, Mordecai was relieved that his daughter was keeping busy and actively engaged in a communal effort. In many ways, she was following the advice she heard from Palestine's Jewish political elite. When she was on kibbutz, she twice listened to Chaim Weizmann lecturing in praise of the labor performed by workers on agricultural settlements.[127] In a speech delivered at Hebrew University that April, Judah Magnes also advised his audience "not to be discouraged because of Germany, etc.—but to spend all our energies here now in order to develop our own cultural life, etc."[128] Hadassah probably appreciated these talks because they reinforced how she had chosen to spend her time.[129]

Even as Hadassah focused on her work, boys continued to pursue her, at times persistently. Before leaving for kibbutz, she went to dances and tea with acquaintances but wrote home, "That's all I see of them—+ that's all I care to see of them. There wasn't one person . . . that I could point to + say—'That looks like the sort of person I want to meet!'"[130] On the kibbutzim, she befriended a few American men, and they regularly spoke Hebrew with one another. But she also continued her relationships with others. Harry from Tel Aviv referred to Hadassah as a "self confessed, dyed in the wool, bred in the bone and empty in the head communist!" and wanted to know, presumably because she was living on a kibbutz, if she was going in for the communal "one for all and all for one, all in one bed idea." He also, more seriously, asked what she thought about the people she was meeting and ideas she was encountering there.[131] Meanwhile, her former New York boyfriend Jack Wilner Sundelson, whose marriage proposal she had rejected a year earlier, mocked her for stopping drinking, while simultaneously warning her not to get "stout with beer." Jack told Hadassah not to worry about lacking a job (since "nobody has one + those that do, don't get paid") and asked if he could meet her in Europe. "Building a few beautiful thoughts about joining you" this summer, he wrote. "It's a matter of guessing," he continued, "as to how good we can be this summer in getting beautiful thoughts translated into action."[132] We do not know if Hadassah wrote back, but she and Jack did not connect in Europe. Another of her New York pursuers, Milton Levine, was more discreet: "You did the right thing in disappearing temporarily from this atmosphere of depression—for jobs are few in New York City—and the city is exactly as you left it. . . . Your home on 1 W. 89th St. still stands as a mute symbol of your majesty every time I drive past it in my Graham [an American automobile]."[133]

Meanwhile, Hadassah's sister Naomi reminded her not to have unreasonable expectations of the people she encountered.

> You always write that the people aren't interesting and exciting. What do you call interesting and exciting? . . . Stop looking for a fairy tale hero. . . . I think you're afraid the people you go with don't come up to the family's standard because you have set up an imaginary unattainable one for yourself. . . . Forget your silly ideas and don't expect to get knocked off your feet by some man who was made for you + for whom you were made—because that's crazy. . . . In the meantime, everybodies [sic] interesting or uninteresting according to the way you look at them.[134]

Naomi equally warned her not to dismiss the women she met and be grateful for Reba and those with whom she had genuinely connected.

Hadassah wrote chastely about the men she encountered in the *kvutzot* in the enduring record. She only infrequently wrote personal reflections in her diary and mostly used the little black books to keep track of dates, people met, and places. But apparently, she wrote in greater detail to her eldest sister, Judith, and her husband, Albert, in letters not preserved. We have only Al's response:

> With reference to the gentleman who tried "to get funny" with you, I daresay you know all about taking care of yourself and I have no doubt that any of us here are much worried on that score. Judy and I agree that if you really have an honest love affair, it would do no harm, proper precautions first having been observed. But we do look with aspersion on simple illicit sex relationships. So just poke them all in the eye until you really feel like giving yourself to a man for more than physical satisfaction. Don't worry about the gossip. . . . Judy and I will defend you well.[135]

Al's advice accorded with the trends that the journalist Ksawery Pruszynski noted regarding "collective love" on kibbutzim at the time. He suggested that monogamous, amorous relationships developed following a "trial period," presumably including sexual experimentation, to determine the compatibility of the partners.[136] Neither Judith nor Hadassah's other sisters appear to have weighed in clearly on the possibility of such premarital activity, but it seems reasonable to assume that

Judith agreed with her husband's acceptance of such relations, as long as they represented a "love affair" as opposed to simply a physical attraction and if "proper precautions" were observed. Although not spelled out by Al, such safeguards at the time probably would have included condoms and douches.[137]

We do not know why Hadassah left Kvutzah Hatzafon, a settlement established by members of the Socialist Zionist youth group Hashomer Hatzair from Detroit two years before Hadassah's arrival.[138] Presumably it had little to do with the man who tried to "get funny" with her, since she remained on kibbutz several weeks after that incident. It is more likely that it was because she had stayed long enough to develop her own assessment of the project, which she called a "wonderful experiment" and quite satisfying for "the older generation" but not the right place for her for the long term. "I know very well," she wrote, "that I'd never be content there for the rest of my life."[139] The day before Passover, she sent a transliterated cable home with traditional wishes for a "Happy Passover and next year in Jerusalem!" from Kvutzah Hatzafon. Hadassah enjoyed a "very pleasant" but "not Seder-like" Passover, including meat and potatoes, soup with "hard knedlach [matzah balls], wine and cakes," followed by singing and circle dances, including the horah and polka, as well as "very funny" skits about people in the settlement. Afterward, she was ready to leave the settlement.[140] Despite missing an entourage of two carloads of Americans driving to the annual feast in Shechem described in the book of Judges, Hadassah would go on to join other celebrations tied to particular geographies and communities. Shortly after arriving in Jerusalem and the day before Orthodox Easter, she connected with thousands of banner-and-painting-toting tourists thronging the ceremony of the Holy Fire, when the Church of the Holy Sepulchre was lit up by torches and candles representing Jesus' resurrection.[141] From there, she celebrated Lag B'Omer, a Jewish celebratory festival held on the thirty-third day of the Omer, breaking up the forty-nine days of semimourning between Passover and Shavuot commemorating suffering under the Romans. Hadassah joined nearly fifteen thousand people on a pilgrimage to Rabbi Shimon ben Yochai's tomb in Meron to see people cutting the hair of three-year-olds and burning it in bonfires. From there, she went to Haifa with her friends and mentors to mark Shavuot, a harvest festival seven weeks after Passover that also commemorates the

Figure 5.5. Shavuot in Haifa, June 1, 1933. (Personal collection)

giving of the Torah. In Haifa, Hadassah listened to speeches, watched the parade, and witnessed Shavuot offerings, which she considered the "most impressive and beautiful celebration" she had seen all year.[142]

Hadassah was eager to maximize her time with friends, watching plays, and listening to concerts and speeches, and she also wanted to figure out how she might return through Europe and extend her time abroad as long as possible. But she and her parents were not exactly on the same page, especially as her family's circumstances changed.

6

Returning Home

When Hadassah left for Palestine, she intended to stay abroad for only a year. As she settled more into Hebrew speaking and life in Palestine, however, she wondered if she should remain, as did many of her mentors and friends. The widowed Irma Lindheim and Lillian Friedlander settled in Palestine, Lindheim on Kibbutz Mishmar HaEmek and Friedlander in her extended family's home in Zichron Ya-akov. The same year that Hadassah spent in Palestine (1933), her chaperones, the Berksons, Schoolmans, and Dushkins, together with other Jewish educator friends, Israel S. and Shirley Chipkin, bought an orchard in Netanya, indicating that they were putting down long-term roots.[1] Some of Hadassah's mentors who returned to the States, like the Hebraist Anna Grossman, did so to settle their affairs before migrating or at least intending to do so. In 1936, the Grossmans would ultimately return to New York to manage Anna's chronic kidney disease.[2] Others went back for long periods but still visited or migrated to Palestine later. Even after Rose Gell Jacobs returned to New York, she traveled to Palestine over the next four years as she served out her term as national president of *Hadassah*. Likewise, although the Dushkins went back to Chicago for a year, the whole family returned to Jerusalem in 1934, at which point Alexander built Hebrew University's John Dewey School of Education. Eventually he would recruit Mordecai to be a visiting professor there from 1937 until 1939. The Dushkins moved to Palestine permanently in 1949.[3]

Among Hadassah's young or single friends, some, like Reba and Helen Schwartz, returned to New York that spring. Helen's mother met her in Palestine, and the two traveled through Europe, with Mrs. Schwartz stopping to visit her mother in Poland. When Reba learned that her great-grandmother had been diagnosed with cancer, she decided to go home. She imagined learning to type, becoming a stenographer over the summer, and then returning to Palestine in the fall, but she did not go back. Other friends of Hadassah's remained in Palestine. The poet Simon

Halkin and his wife, Minnie, had a daughter that September, Hadassah's South African boyfriend Harry Joffe would be badly injured in the 1948 war, and the New Yorker Ted Lurie would remain at the *Palestine Post*, later to become the *Jerusalem Post*'s editor.

Also staying was a contingent of Canadian and American women who worked—often with Henrietta Szold—in child welfare and social work, including former Modinites Zelda Shapiro and Sylva Gelber. After leaving kibbutz, Sylva waitressed at a tearoom run by Libbie Suchoff Berkson, the former head of Camp Modin's girls' side, and volunteered with the *Hadassah* organization as a family caseworker. When Sylva failed to answer her father's repeated requests that she return to Toronto after a year, her mother came to Palestine "not as a tourist to see the sights, but as a mother, charged by her husband to bring his only daughter home." Yet she returned alone after Henrietta Szold persuaded Mrs. Gelber that her daughter was "on the verge of developing a creative career." Shortly thereafter, Szold offered Sylva a scholarship to study full-time at a school of social work. She went on to work for the Jerusalem Yishuv's Welfare Bureau.[4]

Hadassah's ruminations about whether to stay or go reflected those of her parents. Lena, as was her custom, focused on logistics. With Judith, the eldest of her daughters, having married and moved out, and the youngest, Selma, in college and aiming to study abroad, it was possible for the Kaplan couple to consider traveling. Might they go abroad for their twenty-fifth anniversary that June or that fall during Mordecai's sabbatical from the Jewish Theological Society? Lena asked Hadassah to help her figure out how much it would cost for food, water, electricity, taxes, and a small furnished apartment in Tel Aviv as compared to Jerusalem. Alternatively, the Kaplans considered traveling to Geneva, where the League of Nations was headquartered. They believed that it was "the safest country just now + at all times."[5]

Mordecai, however, remained undecided about whether to take a sabbatical and what to do. He believed that the economic crisis had undermined Jewish institutions and causes more profoundly than just prosperity. Mordecai organized a social justice seminar with graduates of JTS to understand current economic problems but felt powerless "to make the least dent in the status quo." "That is why," he wrote Hadassah, "I feel so restless and dissatisfied all the time and am beating about hither and thither in the search for something that would redeem me from the heartbreaking sense of futility and frustration under which I labor."[6] Mordecai was also frustrated with the Society for the Advancement of Judaism, which he had founded and run for twelve years. "By this time," he explained, "all my illusions about it [the synagogue] are gone. I haven't the least idea whether I should break with it or continue to be associated with it. One is as hard as the other." He was particularly concerned about the institution's economic status since the money he was able to raise barely covered the synagogue's mortgage and was not enough to provide for the staff.[7]

Mordecai further questioned his capacity to influence American Jewry and worried about its fate. He had written endless sermons, essays, and articles, but at fifty, he still had not published a book. In 1931, he had submitted to an essay contest an unpublished manuscript, "Judaism as a Civilization." Julius Rosenwald, the president of Sears, Roebuck, and Company, sponsored the $10,000 competition, and Sansom Benderly, one of Mordecai's colleagues and closest friends, accepted sixty-two essays considering how Judaism might best "adjust itself to and influence modern life."[8] The committee disagreed about the merits of Mordecai's writing. After two years, the judges still had not announced a winner. Viewing the contest as a verdict on the viability of his conception of Judaism in US society, Mordecai took this delay personally, confiding to his diary how anxious and tired the waiting made him. The stress made it difficult for him to work, even as he tried to revise two other manuscripts.[9]

While Hadassah wrote home in English every few days, and her mother responded frequently, Mordecai wrote to her infrequently, at most corresponding once a month. Yet he had promptly replied to her first Hebrew letter, sent in December, with one of his own. Mordecai's response—the only letter he appears to have written to her in Hebrew—expressed his loneliness and existential angst. Should he continue his lifetime project of reconstructing American Jewry, or should he, instead, move to Palestine? "All my acquaintances," he wrote in Hebrew,

> are envious of those who moved to Eretz Israel, believing that it is the only country in the world where the cloud of dejection is absent. Is this really true? Pay attention not just to the superficial aspect of life in Eretz

Israel, penetrate into the inner workings of the spirit of daily life. Should a man like me settle in Eretz Israel? I am certain that you are familiar with all my spiritual struggles in this country. Despite the large number of Jews here, I am like a juniper in the desert due to the wide distance between my views and aspirations and the views and aspirations of those with whom I interact at the various institutions at which I invest all my energy.[10]

Hadassah, who wrote several-page-long Hebrew letters once or twice a month specifically to her father, responded in Hebrew to his query in three different letters. First, she offered her own reflections focusing on the importance of her father pursuing his own happiness. She wrote,

> I know that our life philosophies do not agree—because I am certain that all knowledge and work are necessary for someone only in order to make him happy—and what do you think? Does not the best creation arise when one is free of worries? If you try to forget the spiritual state of our people (because certainly a single person or a few people can do nothing to awaken it) and start a different kind of work just for a change—you will surely find a more productive topic to rejuvenate your spirit. And this is more important now than other people's spirit, both for you and for mom and the kids. After all, didn't you work your whole life at the same thing? And didn't you only encounter disappointment and despair? And why should this be?[11]

Hadassah also warned her father of the challenges in Palestine, and the ways that it had changed since he had last been there. She cautioned that Palestine's crisis in the summer of 1929 had altered the overall sentiment in the place. "The emotion and excitement felt before the disturbances," she wrote, "are not visible now."[12] Hadassah furthermore advised that "this is the least religious place in the world," it is difficult to earn a living, and there are few "material comforts."[13] She conveyed relatively little about the water shortages and electricity failures that she regularly experienced that year, but she did describe the difficulties of cooking and staying warm.[14]

Hadassah did not rest after writing her own responses to her father. Instead, she consulted two of her father's friends and colleagues, Henrietta Szold and the Zionist educator Jessie Sampter. Szold feared that Mordecai would find Palestine frustrating. A "man of ideals like [Mordecai]," she explained to Hadassah, "would be disappointed to see the state of affairs over here." In a message from Szold that Hadassah relayed to her father, Szold clarified that "she herself had [not] lost hope in a brighter future, because she knows how much time and patience are necessary for the building of the country—but when she arrived here she was rather surprised."[15] Sampter also expressed some reservations, telling Hadassah that her father already had "an important job abroad." Hadassah, however, countered that she thought her father might best pursue "personal happiness" in a house in Rehovot with a vegetable or flower patch. Sampter then encouraged Mordecai to consider working either with Hebrew University or the pioneers on the types of agricultural settlements where Hadassah had recently visited. "Don't you think," Hadassah wrote her father in Hebrew, "[that] you've already given enough to the Jews, and you need to start living for yourself a bit now?" Mordecai was slow to respond to his daughter's third letter on the matter. "My dear father," she ended one of her letters, "Why aren't you writing to me? I specifically wrote to you in Hebrew to make you happy—and you haven't answered." She signed the letter, "Impatiently, Hadassah."[16]

Like Mordecai, Hadassah was also questioning whether she should remain in Palestine and—if she returned—when she should do so, with whom, where she should go, and what she would do in New York. Her sisters and her brother-in-law wanted her to travel home through Europe and to see as much as she could.[17] Judith warned that there was little good in planning for what she would do back home, since "this year has been one of constant surprises."[18] She and her husband, Al, also agreed that "it would be unwise to travel alone, for many reasons, none of which have anything to do with morals."[19] Presumably, they referred to her safety both as a young woman and also as a Jew, given rising antisemitism.

Hadassah began to think more seriously about staying in Palestine, where she might work and not have to worry about spending as much money to keep up appearances as she would in New York. Her letters, however, illustrated her ambivalence. On the one hand, she loved the "freedom—the feeling that you're in a new country and seeing it being built—and trying to help it grow."[20] She was sure that if she returned to the United States, she would be "dying to come back."²¹ "Must I come home?" she asked her parents at her most self-assured. "I think I'm going to look for a job here. Haifa is grand—I'm really serious! What do you say?"²² But then, two weeks later, Hadassah wrote that she wanted to teach in New York in September and then return to Palestine in February, a calendar that matched her sister Naomi's plans—she was set to graduate from college then—but otherwise was not conducive to an academic school year.²³ At the same time, she worried about leaving her friends and family in the United States. "I often have the feeling," she reflected, "that were I to stay here I'd probably be very happy now—but grow lonely later on."²⁴

Lena fluctuated in her advice to her daughter. Initially, she counseled Hadassah to return home as quickly and inexpensively as possible. "Really darling," she wrote on March 20,

> I am in a quandary. Conditions are very bad [here]. Money is very scarce. You will need so much when you get back. All the rags that you took with you will be good for the garbage pail most likely. I will have to get you everything new from head to foot. That will require lots of money. Therefor[e] don't blame me for wanting you to cut out Europe and come home the quickest and cheapest way. . . . I don't want you to feel that we dished you out of anything. Yet I can't help telling you that it will be a little hard on us financially. I am sure that the children would like to kill me for saying this. They are so anxious for you to see Europe.²⁵

Two weeks later, as Lena mapped out Mordecai's anticipated sabbatical in Palestine, she reconsidered her advice. If Lena and Mordecai were abroad, Hadassah would need to live either with Naomi in a dorm room or with Judith and Al. Instead, Lena recommended that Hadassah find a job and stay in Palestine through the summer until they arrived.²⁶

Meanwhile, Hadassah heard little from her father for four months. "There still rings in my ear," he confessed when he finally wrote to her in English,

> what you said to me on board the boat: Remember, Papa, you must write oftener than you did to me when I was at camp. That was a well-coined

rebuke for past neglect as well as an admonition to do better in the future. I took both to heart and was determined to write to you at least once a month. But somehow I let weeks slip by without carrying out my resolution. It seems that the certainty that mamma keeps you informed of all that I am doing gives me the illusion that I myself am writing to you. But I know this is only an illusion. From now on I shall try to make up for lost time and write to you quite often.[27]

The remainder of his letter explained his concerns about the fate of American Jewry and why that made him unsure about going abroad during his sabbatical.

Hadassah, in contrast, had become fully acclimated to life in Palestine. Her Hebrew was sufficiently strong that she did not feel compelled to resume her language lessons. She also did not return to Jerusalem. Instead, she spent most of her time in Tel Aviv. "In spite of the fact," she explained to her family, "that Jerusalem is supposed to be the center of culture + has a different type of person from Tel Aviv, more goes on here than there."[28] Still, Hadassah felt ambivalent about the city, which she described as "awful" for its materialism and religious dearth. "All you do," she explained, "is walk on the beach on Yom Tov—+ it's more crowded than Coney Island."[29] "I am almost certain," she wrote her father in Hebrew, "that Tel Aviv . . . will soon be like West End Avenue." She blamed such materialism on the city's women and their desire to "keep up with the Joneses." Beyond reinforcing the negative stereotype of women's consumption patterns, Hadassah also worried that acquisitiveness would harm the agricultural collectives and especially the children raised on them.[30]

Mordecai wrote Hadassah only two more letters, both in English. This might have reflected his own insecurity about Hebrew. According to his biographer Mel Scult, Mordecai was at ease writing and reading in classical and modern Hebrew but struggled to speak and did not deliver a commencement address at Teachers' Institute in Hebrew until after his first visit to Palestine in 1925.[31] Whether his language choice reflected self-consciousness or a recognition of the additional effort needed to write in Hebrew, his reticence, coupled with Hadassah's growing Hebrew fluency, further reinforced the value of the language skills she was acquiring in Palestine.

That May, Mordecai finally responded directly to the case Hadassah made for moving to Palestine. Whereas Hadassah highlighted what she thought would make her parents happy, her father concentrated on the bottom line: "What could I live on if I were to make Palestine my permanent home?" Unlike what he encouraged Hadassah to do, he was reluctant to visit or even go to Palestine on a sabbatical if settling there would not be a viable option. "To exercise any influence on the life there," he continued, "one must make Palestine his home. Visiting the land or even staying there for a few months would only be a distraction," presumably from his focus on American Jewry. "I would only become disheartened," he concluded, "by some of the mistakes which you speak of in your last letter, by the westernization of the social life, by the irrational sprawling of Tel Aviv etc. I must therefore make up my mind to do the best I can to help our Jewish life in America, and believe me that's some job."[32]

As Mordecai shored up his stance, the Kaplans hoped Hadassah would too. By April 20, Lena was ready for Hadassah to return to New York. "Here it is in a nutshell," Lena wrote. "We think you ought to come home and not make Palestine your home without us unless there is a reason. If there is no reason to keep you there other than the love of the country + you are prepared to stay there indefinitely without us + can support yourself there, you can do as you please."[33] Two weeks later, Lena was more insistent that Hadassah return straightaway. In a telegram Lena sent on May 5, she advised Hadassah to travel home with Reba and the Schoolmans in four days' time.[34] When Hadassah missed that deadline, Lena urged her daughter to come home the following month for the Kaplans' twenty-fifth anniversary—another due date Hadassah would miss.[35]

While the Kaplans pressured Hadassah to return quickly, they also recognized her agency. "Listen darling," Lena wrote Hadassah a day after her telegram, "it is absolutely up to you. If you want to stay indefinitely go ahead + do so. I am sure you can get some kind of a job to get enough to maintain yourself. But the thing is for how long would you like that. The question is would you like to settle there permanently. If not I think it is best for you to come home. But again I repeat come home only if you want to. Don't do it because we want you to."[36] Two weeks later, her father confirmed that the decision was hers. "Let me speak to you as a father to his child." Mordecai went on to suggest that if Hadassah married and stayed in Palestine, he and Lena would probably eventually join her. Hadassah, however, needed to decide for herself about marriage and migration. "You are the one," he explained, "to decide your future. In deciding, the chief consideration—outside of the personality of the man you would care for—is: which country holds out to you greater possibility of personal development and self-realization, Palestine or America?"[37]

The Kaplans' message to Hadassah, that she pursue her own path, differentiated them from many of their peers. The cultural critic Warren Susman has described the 1930s as a period of social accommodation, participation, and conformity when many Americans looked to adapt themselves to patterns of culture—beliefs, values, and lifestyles—and when the notion of an American dream emerged. In contrast, the Kaplans wanted their daughter to be able to choose where she settled, including if she preferred to adapt herself to predominant modes of thinking, feeling, and action in Palestine or the US.[38]

That spring, Hadassah socialized with a more mature group in Tel Aviv than she had interacted with in Jerusalem. She befriended Minnie Malkin, who was born in the Bronx only five years before Hadassah. The two enjoyed swimming and spending time on the beach, which had become a hallmark for creating a new Jew characteristic of a Jewish homeland. This character was to be "healthy, muscular, [and] tanned, ... the direct opposite of the archetypical sickly, skinny, and pale Jew of the exile."[39] Hadassah, with her capacity to tan and athleticism, easily embodied the female version of this prototype. Yet the social group she joined was decidedly more intellectual. It included two Russian-born men who were roughly a decade older than she was: Simon Halkin and Sam Dinin. On occasion, Shaul Tchernichovsky, another older, Russian-born poet and physician, also joined them. In addition to being married to Minnie, Simon was the brother of Hadassah's former Hebrew teacher, Abe. At the time, the Hebrew poet and educator worked as an English teacher in Tel Aviv. He would become a Hebrew literature professor at the Jewish Institute of Religion in New York, founded by the Reform rabbi Stephen Samuel Wise to train liberal rabbis. Eventually, he would succeed Joseph Klausner at Hebrew University.[40]

Hadassah and her family had known Sam Dinin from New York, although her sisters were not huge fans. "Honestly," Hadassah assured them, "you have no idea how Dinin has changed. He isn't half bad."[41]

Hadassah would not have needed to convince her father of that. Mordecai, along with Benderly, had trained Dinin. He had also followed a similar academic path to Mordecai, earning a bachelor of arts degree from City College. The spring before going to Palestine, Dinin further secured a PhD from Columbia with a dissertation called "Judaism in a Changing Civilization," which resonated with Mordecai's own work. Out of deference, Hadassah generally referred to him in her letters home as "Mr. Dinin" rather than use his first name. It is perhaps unsurprising that in Hadassah's new circle, she spent considerably more time attending concerts, the symphony, Habima performances, Bialik playlets, and exhibits. She also continued to travel, spending time in Haifa, visiting additional collective settlements, and reboarding the *Exochorda*, this time without Reba, to see Beirut and Tripoli.

Part of the Kaplans' concern regarding Hadassah's return was financial. They were worried about how to allocate limited resources, given that they also wanted their other daughters to be able to travel. When the scholarship that Selma anticipated to study abroad fell through, the Kaplans scrambled to provide travel, tuition, board, and lodging, which came to $900 in total plus a weekly allowance of $3. In worrying about how to afford such expenses, Lena wrote Hadassah, "We will have to stint on ourselves from now on unless something comes in unexpectedly."[42] She found herself sending checks (two $100 ones) to Hadassah on the basis of anticipated income from two weddings rather than money already earned.[43] To economize further, the Kaplans postponed Mordecai's sabbatical, and Lena began to do all of Mordecai's typing. "People must think," she explained, "we struck a gold mine somewhere. Everyone is complaining + crying depression and here we are. First one daughter goes to Palestine + now another daughter goes to England. They question, where does all the money come from? I too want to know. But we are very optimistic. We believe that God will provide."[44] "We must hope + pray," she continued, "that all of us + all our near + dear stay well + that God should help the people of the whole world with a little more peace of mind + prosperity."[45]

Lena's faith in the family's financial fortune paid off. On June 1, the evening of Shavuot, the harvest festival celebrating the receiving of the Torah and the night before Selma went to London, sixty people, including family, friends, and almost the entire JTS faculty, gathered at the

Kaplans' house to celebrate their twenty-fifth anniversary. In addition to singing a song that Judith composed, "I Love to Lean on Lena," the group showered the family with gifts, including $174 from friends, $225 from the family, and $550 from the women of the SAJ.[46] That Saturday evening, the day after the Kaplans sent off Selma as well as their actual anniversary, they were surprised by a second party thrown by the SAJ. They had thought it was a going-away party for the junior rabbi, Ira Eisenstein, who was heading to Palestine. Instead, they were surprised by an anniversary party for them including three hundred guests, a wedding march, a wedding cake, and a medley of songs rehearsed for two weeks by Judith and Naomi.[47] Two weeks later, Lena sent $100 to Hadassah in Palestine and $200 to her in Paris (she also told her to dispose of the earlier $100 checks). Their finances were further bolstered that July when Mordecai won first place in the Rosenwald competition, receiving a $3,500 award for his "Judaism as a Civilization" manuscript (the foundation split the prize three ways).[48] "Now," wrote Lena, "we need not worry as to where the money for publishing his books will come from."[49] Mordecai immediately gave the money to Macmillan and Company to pay publication expenses and buy copies, but such funds also allowed the Kaplans to subsidize their daughters' travels.[50]

Hadassah, missing her family, heeding her parents' advice, and not feeling tied to Palestine because of an intimate relationship or meaningful work, decided that it was time to go home. By mid-June, she had paid a travel agent $131; bought a train ticket from Venice to Paris; arranged to travel with her camp friend Helen Schwartz, her mother, and Sam Dinin; and promised her friends that she would "be back very soon."[51] A photograph captures her June 16 departure: following an afternoon of dancing and drinking, Hadassah's thirteen friends who boarded SS *Helovan* with her climbed into a rowboat to head back to Jaffa before the ship set sail. Hadassah must have leaned over the side of the ship to capture the moment. Her friends diagonally move through the frame of the image as men row them back to shore. Sylva sits in the middle, enthusiastically waving good-bye to Hadassah and the SS *Helovan*, the ship that would transport her.

After landing in Tripoli on the second day of the journey, Hadassah drove to Beirut with Zadoc Chelouche, a handsome, wealthy man, fourteen years her senior, from a distinguished Sephardi family. Zadoc was

Figure 6.1. Sylva Gelber and friends on a boat disembarking from the SS *Helovan*, Jaffa, Palestine, June 16, 1933. (Personal collection)

also a friend of her parents' friend Joseph Levy and a married father of two. Without visas, Mrs. Schwartz and Helen remained on the boat, leaving Hadassah and Zadoc unchaperoned. The photographs, particularly the small ones that appear only to have been printed on a contact sheet, imply a level of familiarity that furthers the idea that voyages were liminal spaces where passengers pushed boundaries of social acceptability.

While traveling, Hadassah read about the murder of Chaim Victor Arlosoroff. Just a month earlier, the German-born labor leader and Jewish Agency political director had visited Germany to encourage Jews—particularly parents seeking safety, education, and vocational training for their children—to send their children to agricultural settlements, schools, and youth villages in Palestine. Arlosoroff's support for the organized transfer and wide-scale immigration of German youth, combined with his premature death, helped to spark the organizational framework for what would become known as Youth Aliya.[52] The term *aliya* literally means "ascent" and has been used to describe both immigration to Palestine (and later Israel) and also the blessing before reading from the Torah.

On the starless night of June 16, when Arlosoroff was murdered, the recently returned thirty-four-year-old labor Zionist leader had been strolling with his wife, Sima, on the same beach in Tel Aviv that Hadassah

Figure 6.2. Hadassah Kaplan with Zadoc Chelouche on a day trip off the SS *Helovan*, Lebanon, June 17, 1933. (Personal collection)

had regularly frequented. Two days later, while Hadassah was in Beirut with Zadoc, more than thirty thousand people attended Arlosoroff's funeral. The turnout that day illustrated the short-term political truce in the immediate aftermath of his murder between the left-wing labor Zionists and the right-wing Revisionists, also known as Betar, the Hebrew acronym for the Joseph Trumpeldor Alliance, named after one of the men who died defending Tel Hai in the Galilee in 1920 against Arab Palestinian attacks. The Revisionists, a self-defense youth movement led by Vladimir Jabotinsky, sought to revive World War I–style Jewish Legions, volunteer troops that fought in World War I with the British against the Turkish occupation. The Revisionists blamed Arab Palestinians for the attack on Arlosoroff. In contrast, labor leaders, including David Ben Gurion and the Hebrew poet Hayim Nahmun Bialik, who represented the majority at the World Zionist Congress of 1933, faulted the irresponsible militancy of the Revisionists for the murder. They sought to create a Jewish socialist society in contrast to Jabotinsky's Jewish state on both sides of the Jordan. Members of the Revisionist Betar group were arrested for the crime, including Avraham Stavsky and Zvi Rosenblatt. Blaming Jabotinsky and his youth movement for growing hostilities, left-wing Zionists tried to have the whole movement banned from Jewish life. On the verge of a Jewish civil war, both sides employed lawyers and engaged in extensive examinations, including investigations by the British court, police, and Congress. There were also rumors that Arlosoroff was murdered by a Soviet spy or Nazi agent. Both Rosenblatt and Stavsky were eventually freed (the latter on appeal), and the case remains unresolved.[53] Political friction among Jews, of course, remains a common theme.

For Hadassah and her peers, the assassination was a turning point illustrating the depth of Jewish conflict in Palestine. "I find it astounding," Sylva wrote retrospectively, "that when, as a passionate idealist, I set out on my youthful search for a Jewish Camelot, I was unaware of the political tensions already besetting the Yishuv."[54] Hadassah appears to have shared both her friend Sylva's idealism and her political naivety. She wondered if it had been a Revisionist Zionist or an Arab Palestinian who attacked Arlosoroff. She did not consider the possible involvement of Nazis or Soviets.

Indeed, Hadassah did not dwell on the growing storm in Palestine but instead turned her attention back to sightseeing, as she traveled from Tripoli to Cyprus, Rhodes, Istanbul, and Piraeus. Zadoc regularly joined Hadassah, Helen, and Mrs. Schwartz when they went on sightseeing tours, but he and Hadassah rarely visited on the boat. To Hadassah's chagrin, shortly after the journey began, the ship enforced distinctions between first class, where Zadoc traveled, and other accommodations, where Hadassah and her friends could be found. Unlike on Hadassah's trip to Palestine, there is no indication that a more intimate relationship developed between her and Zadoc—or anyone else.

Mrs. Schwartz remained on the ship to see her mother in Poland. She insisted that her daughter Helen go to western Europe with Hadassah and Sam. We do not know if it was fear of rising antisemitism that led Mrs. Schwartz not to take Helen with her to visit her grandmother or if Mrs. Schwartz merely wanted to be on her own with her mother. Did Mrs. Schwartz have the foresight to arrange for her mother's migration or to convince her to go? Regardless of the purpose behind Mrs. Schwartz's visit, she would not have been the only middle-age American Jew during the interwar period returning to what had previously been their European homeland. Some such travelers sought to visit friends and family, to reconnect with their youth, to recall what they might perceive to be a more authentic Jewish life, and to validate their own migratory choices.[55] Whatever drove Mrs. Schwartz, she proceeded alone, leaving Helen to travel with her friends.

The group of three—Helen, Hadassah, and Sam—disembarked in Brindisi on June 24. From there, they took the train to Naples, Capri, Pompei, Rome, Florence, and Venice, spending a few days sightseeing in each city, including attending synagogue in Florence and visiting the Jewish quarter in Venice.

Figure 6.3. Hadassah Kaplan in St. Mark's Square in Venice, Italy, July 4, 1933. (Personal collection)

One wonders if the friends might have experienced the difference between Italy and Palestine as Henrietta Szold did when she returned from her first trip abroad a little more than two decades earlier. "In Jerusalem," she explained to her sisters, "there was pulsating life, and life coupled with misery, poverty, filth, disease, and there was intellectual life, coupled with idealism, enthusiasm, hope. Here in Italy I have no responsibility, I may enjoy, I need not weigh and criticize and doubt and wonder—or if I do, I wonder only at the rich beauty poured out upon this favored land."[56] Did the threesome enjoy the beauty of Italy unbound by the growing threats of rising fascism and antisemitism, or were their travels weighed down by a different type of responsibility than that Szold articulated?

After roughly two weeks of traveling, on July 8, the group broke up. Helen reunited with her mother in Switzerland. Sam traveled to Vienna. And Hadassah took a sleeper car by herself to Milan, where she joined someone she had met in Naples. Hadassah appreciated her autonomy. "With my map of Milan" and following Baedeker, she explained to her family, "I feel just as at home as anywhere else. As a matter of fact—if I must admit it—it's rather a relief to be alone, and to be able to go wherever I want without having to waste half the day making plans."⁵⁷ Hadassah next went to Switzerland (where her parents had honeymooned twenty-five years earlier) and then took a boat to Geneva. She reconnected with Helen and Sam in Paris a week later, which was the day before Bastille Day, and remained there for almost two weeks, touring, seeing family, and reconnecting with many of her friends and mentors from Palestine, including the Rosens, the family with whom she had lived in Ramat Gan in the spring; the Schwartzes; and at least two young men: Joel Lipsky, the third son of Louis, former president of the Zionist Organization of America who had worked for the newspaper editor Gershon Agronsky, and Al Ginsberg, who had attended the SAJ in New York before becoming a lawyer in St. Paul, Minnesota.

Unsurprisingly, Hadassah's travels heightened Lena's nervousness. Lena warned her daughter not to "spend too much time in Europe" on her way home "with people who do not speak the Hebrew language. You know," she cautioned, "you can unlearn a language much quicker than you can learn one."⁵⁸ More significantly, however, she feared for Hadassah's safety, particularly when she traveled alone. Lena urged her, "be very careful with whom and where you go." "It has become an obsession with me lately," Lena wrote. "I just can't sleep nights worry about both of you [Hadassah and Selma] so you see that is why I say the sooner you get home the better."⁵⁹ She admonished her daughter to come home by July 26, if not before.⁶⁰ She reminded her to "be careful." "Don't stay up too late," she warned, "+ see that your door is locked."⁶¹ She signed her letters, "your anxious Mother."

Hadassah responded to her mother's concerns. She could not return earlier because she only received the last $100 check that Lena sent to pay for her trip home on July 18. She also wanted to see Selma. Hadassah assured her mother that she was well chaperoned: "All the Mrs. are here + not another soul do I go with."⁶²

While antisemitism is rarely mentioned in the family's correspondence, it clearly fueled the Kaplans' concerns. Lena was adamant that none of her children should travel in Germany, but it was not until mid-July that Hadassah began to register antisemitism beyond what she read in the news. On Bastille Day, she relayed a conversation to her parents that she described as both "enlightening and interesting" regarding the "German situation." On a boat from Switzerland to Geneva, Hadassah met Professor Carl Conrad Eckhardt, a modern European historian from the Midwest who spent the year at the University of Munich on a Carnegie Institute fellowship with his wife and teenage children. Like many tourists, students, and businessmen, Eckhardt appears to have been charmed by Nazi propaganda, including the comments of German critics, writers, and historians.[63] Eckhardt rejected the idea that student groups in twenty-two Germany cities had burned books just a few months earlier. According to him, the Germans "did not burn manuscripts or books. . . . They," he continued, "wouldn't burn anything of material worth—they can't afford it!" According to Hadassah, he described anti-Jewish activities as "just a gesture," claiming that he would "go into bookshops + ask for Marx's 'Capital' etc. + they'd have it." In a comment that might have come from either Hadassah or Eckhardt regarding interwar Germans, Hadassah wrote, "Things are so topsy turvy + inconsistent that they don't know what they're doing!"[64] Things certainly were "topsy turvy," but the comment vastly underestimated the consequences of inconsistent rules across fifteen states in Germany, carried out by different agencies and levels of government, regarding which books were permitted and which promoted an "un-German spirit." Fearing arrest, readers, writers, publishers, booksellers, libraries, schools, and universities censored themselves.[65]

It is unclear how much Hadassah knew about what was happening in Germany. Clearly, she could not have foreseen that in twelve years, Nazis would destroy an estimated one hundred million books along with six million Jews.[66] While some newspapers reported on the growing violence more candidly, others were significantly more circumspect, toning down not only their content but also its presentation and analysis. Were such events directed or condoned by Nazis or simply the "lark" of students inspired by Nazi rhetoric? Further exacerbating doubt among Americans was a widespread skepticism toward journalism and the tendency of both Nazi and US officials to discount particularly early reports of violence.[67]

Although almost none of the more accessible daily papers in the United States described the book burnings that May, the Associated Press and *Newsweek* printed the news. Indeed, the large urban papers only began to cover the story of what was happening to German Jews that March, as violence intensified. Even so, they wrote more about attacks on communists and socialists than about violence against Jews.[68] Meanwhile, the *Palestine Post*, the daily (except for the Sabbath), Jewish, English newspaper, for which Hadassah briefly worked, regularly announced book talks and reviewed literature—as well as reporting on Nazi arrests, disappearances, torture, and murder. But it was not until June 13, roughly a month after the book burnings began and three days before Hadassah set sail, that the paper published its first account about the incineration of books that spring. On page 6 of an eight-page paper, the *Palestine Post* reprinted a protest letter that Helen Keller had sent to the Associated Press addressed to German students. "You can burn my books," she insisted, "and the books of the best minds in Europe, but the ideas in them have seeped through a million channels and will continue to quicken other minds. . . . Do not imagine your barbarities to the Jews are unknown here. God sleepeth not, and He will visit His judgement upon you."[69]

At a minimum, Eckhardt must have been aware of the torchlight procession and two book burnings that occurred on May 6 in Munich, where he was spending his sabbatical at the university. Members of Hitler Youth torched most of Marx's works. Four days later, a rally of some eight thousand students initiated a second book burning. This time, three thousand participants, accompanied by "marching bands, faculty in robes," student groups in "colored sashes and distinctive caps, uniformed and beflagged Nazi youth," and some seventy thousand onlookers, listened to speeches given by students, municipal officials, and university representatives while incinerating books and journals written by pacifists and Jews.[70] Presumably the same acts that Eckhardt dismissed as a mere "gesture" were the ones that German writers in exile protested as heralding an attack on Jewish intellectualism and so-called un-German individual expression. Book burnings, combined with the subsequent banning of writers from their jobs, looting of apartments, and restrictions on libraries from lending controversial works, recalled a prescient observation by the German writer Heinrich Heine in his nineteenth-century tragedy *Almansor*, that "where one burns books, one will soon burn people."[71]

In Paris, trusted friends told Hadassah more about what was happening in Germany. Hadassah conveyed few of the details in her letters, but still she wrote, "I just woke up from the most miserable dream of

Nazi attacks. I guess," she continued, "it's because Elaine [a friend of hers from New York who was engaged to a Jewish Frenchman] was telling me of someone she met who had suffered." One way Hadassah appears to have managed what she was beginning to learn about growing antisemitism was by focusing on Palestine—as she did when talking until 3:30 a.m. with a journalist friend about England's policies.[72]

On July 26, Hadassah traveled to London, where she reconnected with her mentors and peers from Palestine. She saw the handsome Zadoc Chelouche from the SS *Helovan*; Helen Schwartz and her mother, who had returned from visiting her mother in Poland; Esther Lamport, who was heading back to New York; Al Ginsberg, a young lawyer whom Hadassah knew from the SAJ; and even Chaim Weizmann, the future first president of Israel. Five days later, Hadassah traveled to Stratford upon Avon to see her sister. "REUNION," the daughters cabled home in an unpunctuated message, "WANDERING SISTERS IN SHAKESPEARELAND PROVES FAMILY LOVE STILL EXISTS NEXT TEST HOME SAIL WESTERLAND TWELFTH HADASSAH SELMA."[73] The sisters spent the next two weeks together, with Hadassah joining Selma in her travels to Warwick, Oxford, and Cambridge, where she saw churches and attended lectures, creating outlines and timelines of key works and events in the history of Western art, Oxford, Cambridge, and English history more generally. Selma and Hadassah also experimented with religious passing, performing new identities and hiding their Jewishness. For example, they double-dated British, Christian men without revealing their own religious identity. "Wait till the day," Selma assured Hadassah after she left for New York, "when I tell him [Robin Crossley] I'm Jewish—AND I WILL do that!"[74]

When travel made boundary crossing increasingly viable, passing taught Jewish women like Hadassah and Selma that their identities—their sense of self—could be fluid and performative rather than essential. If they wanted to play a different role, they could, chameleonlike, change their external appearance to become indistinguishable from their peers. We do not know if, like the Jewish immigrant Leah Morton, who married a non-Jew, the glamorous Selma continued to feel immutably Jewish in her inner core even as she mimicked the appearance of someone more affluent and Christian than she was.[75]

Shortly after the sisters reconnected, they received a letter from their older sister, Judith, that revealed another reason why Lena had pressured

Figure 6.4. Hadassah and Selma Kaplan with their friend Robin Crossley in Cambridge, England, August 9, 1933. (Personal collection)

Hadassah to return quickly to New York. Judith told them that after roughly a year, she and Al were divorcing. "It's the culmination of six months of cognition," she explained. "And when you see how utterly unquestioning and sympathetic both mama + papa are, you'll realize that I did right, and that I'll be a much happier and more complete person than I've been for a long time."[76] "Do you see now why," Lena wrote her daughters in London two days after Judith sent her letter to them, "I am so nervous about both of you. Why I don't want you to go out with any of the boys alone. If after a fellow came into our house every day almost for 3 years before Judith was married, and we were so deceived how can we tell what a fellow is if we see him for the first or second time."[77]

Judith had hinted earlier at tensions in the marriage. In October 1932, she had described some of their struggles in a letter to Hadassah:

> Failed to fast for the first time in my life [presumably about Yom Kippur, the Day of Atonement] + suffered bad pangs of conscience—argued every night for a week until 3 o'clock with beloved husband on the whys and wherefores of religious observance + worship—+ barely escaped ignominious divorce—no satisfactory conclusion arrived at—but separation not in the offing—just sort of the first year's adjustment—together with arguing about eating broccoli and drinking tomato juice cocktail—As it is said—you can know a man for six centuries—but you never know him until your [sic] married to him. And it's just as well. Keeps you in a "discovering" mood—you know—for you usually discover 10 nice things to every not nice one.

In the same letter, she described herself as having cried her eyes out while watching John Barrymore and Katharine Hepburn in the 1932 film *A Bill of Divorcement*, in which an anticipated divorce based on the husband's insanity (a newly legitimated justification for divorce) stalls when the husband breaks out of where he had been institutionalized.[78]

Even if the Kaplans were sympathetic to the divorce, they attempted to hide it from a broader public. Judith warned her sisters not to tell anyone where she was staying in Reno, Nevada. Judith had gone to the nation's divorce capital because it was the only place where, beginning in 1931, one could obtain residency and a divorce in six weeks. That same year, Nevada passed a Wide-Open Gambling Act to counter the economic crisis by legalizing gambling, lowering the residence requirement, and expanding the conditions for divorce. No-fault divorces remained impermissible in other states until 1969, when Governor Ronald Reagan of California approved the Family Law Act. Generally, those who sought to divorce had to prove extreme cruelty, adultery, disappearance for five years, or insanity (the latter based on medical documentation). Only in Nevada could those who sought quickie divorces establish residency in six weeks and see their separations approved regardless of their circumstances. Thus, Judith joined a different set of wayfarers than her sisters, the so-called divorce tourists.[79]

According to Miriam Eisenstein, Judith's eldest daughter, the nature of the deception that crippled her marriage was monetary: From appearances, Judith and Al were doing well financially. They moved into their own apartment, furnished it, hired a maid, and even contributed $50 to the synagogue in anticipation of Yom Kippur.[80] According to Lena, the couple was "getting along beautifully financially."[81] Judith was teaching, while Al was admitted to the bar, moved into a new office, and anticipated winning $1,000 in a court case. Miriam, however, recalled her mother explaining that Al was not honest. According to Miriam, he had lied about his job and was writing bad checks. As she recalled, her mother decided to divorce Al after someone came to their apartment to complain about a bounced check, which Judith then had to cover.[82]

Judith's changed circumstances had multiple consequences but particularly financial ones for the Kaplans. Lena had been urging frugality on her daughters since learning of their changed conditions. She warned Hadassah not to buy gifts (other than some Yardley powder and soap for Naomi).[83] "I know," Lena cautioned, "that you are spending as little as possible, . . . yet even that is too much."[84] In a follow-up letter penned a week and a half later, after Mordecai had written Hadassah explaining Judith's situation, Lena insisted, "Do you see now why all our money is gone + now we will need so much for moving expenses. Judith's moving + storage and her trip to Reno + her stay there plus my hospital [she does not specify the nature of this visit] took every penny we received as anniversary gifts. All that plus $250 from Teachers College. We will have to be very sparing for a little while and then we hope God will keep us. Things must turn out better for everybody + for us too."[85] Hadassah was able to watch her costs, but Selma was markedly less frugal. She frequently mentioned needing more cash in letters to her sister, asking her to send $50 just two weeks after acknowledging the $50 Hadassah had already given her.[86]

On August 12, Hadassah sailed from Southampton to New York on a cabin boat called the *Westernland*.[87] She forewarned her parents that although she had changed, she was still figuring out what she wanted to do and how best to attain her goals. "Now that I'm coming down to earth," she wrote home, "I want to tell you please not to expect me to come home a different person—as I thought I would before I sailed. I know just what I want to know learn [sic] + how to go about it—and I know what I'm interested in—The only trouble is that it's from the cultural aspect that I'm interested in these things. I haven't formed anything I could do instead of teaching __ I can't elaborate now—But remember—I'd rather you wouldn't expect wonders—I'd be afraid to return if you did."[88] Nine days later, Hadassah arrived in New York's port. Selma remained in England through the fall semester, during her time there enduring hospitalization for appendicitis.

Hadassah found the adjustment to New York emotionally challenging. She wrote her older sister, Judith, "Coming back to NY—which is exactly the same—+ having to go shopping is just about enough to spoil the whole trip—As mama put it in her steamer letter—'I'll have to come down to earth'—+ tho I was expecting it + dreading it the bump was pretty darn hard."[89]

Hadassah helped her mother settle the family into their new apartment on 101st Street and Central Park West. The new flat was larger, accommodating a study for Mordecai as well as room for all four of the Kaplan daughters, including newly divorced Judith. It was also just a little more than half a mile uptown from where Hadassah had grown up, slightly closer to Barnard College, where both Selma and Naomi were studying, and between the SAJ and Mordecai's Teachers' Institute, which in 1929 moved into the new Jewish Theological Seminary's building on 123rd and Broadway.[90]

As Hadassah looked for work, she sent holiday cards and heard from her friends who remained in Palestine. On October 9, 1933, a seventy-three-year-old Henrietta Szold responded to Hadassah's note, commenting, "It vividly [recalled] the kaleidoscopic American-Palestinian life we led last winter. The atmosphere now is wholly German, so is the language, so are all our thoughts. The Hitler-induced immigration is bringing great values into the country, also great problems, which we are ill prepared to solve, especially as our national means are ludicrously small to meet such talks as a medieval persecution executed with all the experiments modern technique infuses. Will you be back in the New Year?"[91] Szold's reply to Hadassah reflected how much had changed in Palestine and the world in just a few months. That year, fifty thousand Jews would leave Germany. A similar number would depart in each of the following two years, and even more wanted to go. When Arlosoroff had visited Germany in May 1933, he had estimated that more than forty thousand Jews had gone to the Palestine Office in Germany to investigate moving there with their families. In the meantime, Germans constituted just over one-fifth of the near quarter of a million migrants landing in Palestine in the fifth wave of European migrants between 1932 and 1939. Despite the British Mandate's policy to reduce migration, it allowed more Germans than other Europeans, although most Jews in that migratory wave were actually eastern European. Still, the relative proportion of Germans in Palestine's Jewish community grew markedly, from less than 2 percent in the early 1930s to 12 percent by the end of the decade. German Jews concentrated in Palestinian cities, especially Haifa, Tel Aviv, and somewhat less so Jerusalem. Within those cities, they further congregated in German Jewish enclaves known as "Yekke" neighborhoods.[92]

Like those of Hadassah's American and Canadian peers who remained in Palestine, German migrants to Palestine in the early 1930s largely chose to move from a highly developed, urban, capitalist country to one with a lower standard of living. The early German Jewish migrants tended to be young professionals who brought with them a substantial portion of their capital as well as their skills, experience, professions, technology, and even, at times, machinery. Both as customers and as consumers, they profoundly reshaped Palestine, bringing with them European commerce, including sausage, chocolates, cheese, furniture, fashion, and coffeehouses. They also transported many physicians (twelve hundred between 1933 and 1939), teachers, and a revolution in culture and art. Despite the positive professional, social, and economic aspects, new German migrants came in such high rates that it was difficult to settle them. Indeed, so many immigrants arrived in the early

1930s that families slept on Tel Aviv's beaches for a lack of housing.[93] Szold's letter was a reminder of how much the Palestine that Hadassah had left behind had changed and would continue to do so.

By the time Hadassah received Szold's letter, she had landed a teaching job at PS 89 on 135th Street and Lenox Avenue after a two-month search. In the same way that Szold described her variegated view of Palestine expanding from American and Jewish Palestinian to include the rapidly expanding population of new German immigrants, Hadassah's conception of Manhattan grew as she either walked or rode one of the many buses up Seventh Avenue and then trekked one block east to Lenox, which was then considered the heart of "Negro Harlem." Along her route to work, she would have encountered soapbox orators and mobile lunch stands. In the 1930s, Lenox Street, which was renamed in 1987 after Malcolm X, was home to the offices of Black lawyers and doctors as well as the community's "leading institutions," including the recently opened Harlem Branch of the Young Men's Christian Association, the New York Public Library (with its Schomburg Collection focused on Black history), the National Association for the Advancement of Colored People, the New York Urban League, and the *Amsterdam News* newspaper.[94]

The records that Hadassah kept after her year in Palestine are sparse, so we do not know how much she engaged in her students' lives and communities beyond, for example, attending Parent Association meetings.[95] Nevertheless, PS 89 was proximate to important religious communities that would have been instructive to the Kaplans about how another group of hyphenated Americans lived. Three blocks away from Hadassah's new school was the Abyssinian Baptist Church, which was then the world's largest Baptist church. At the time, it was jointly led by pastors Adam Clayton Powell Sr. and his son, an emerging civil rights leader who would go on to serve for twelve terms in the House of Representatives. Hadassah's school was also within ten blocks of an enclave of Black Jews, mostly Ethiopians but also converts, at the Commandment Keepers' Congregation. Finally, PS 89 was near a recently opened residential hotel, known as a "heaven," established by the Christian theologian and movement leader Father Divine, who provided members with lavish daily banquets to illustrate God's abundance.[96] Encountering such communities would have shed light on both the worlds of Hadassah's students and also on the parallels and differences between American Jewish and African American experiences.

Because Hadassah kept her personal letters, we know more about her social than her professional life. Men continued to approach her, including ones who had pursued her before she went abroad. She turned down Read Henry's invitation to visit him in New Haven and attend the Army-Yale football game. Hadassah was reluctant to date people who did not interest her and uncertain of how to proceed. "I never liked those Bohemians of Greenwich Village," she wrote Judith, "but right now their sort of life appeals to me so much—oh Hell—I can't write—my thoughts are all mixed up + I don't know what I'm thinking or saying."[97] Her younger sister Selma tried to cheer her up with assurances from London: "I know," she wrote, "that your trip seems like a dream to you now—but you can't live on dreams all the time—and you ought to be able to see twice as much in ordinary things after having seen so many wonderful unusual things."[98]

The apartment of Sidney Musher's parents on Ninety-First Street and Central Park West was just ten blocks south of Hadassah's parents' new place. She recalled thinking of him often when she passed the building. It was not until a year and a few months after Hadassah's homecoming, however, that she finally bumped into him again. In early November 1934, Hadassah was on a date with Ralph Lieberman, the wealthy brother of her good friend Virginia, whose proposal she had declined before going to Palestine. The two had ventured to Tavern on the Green, which Robert Moses had just transformed into a restaurant from a shelter for sheep that had grazed since the 1880s in Central Park's Sheep Meadow.[99] Sidney was also on a date, with a daughter from the Manischewitz family, whose company, best known for selling sweet ritual wine, helped to make kosher food widely available.[100] When Hadassah passed Sidney to get to the dance floor, he reintroduced himself. The two danced a few times. Three weeks and nine dates later, Sidney proposed to her in her family's living room on Thanksgiving Day. Two holiday dinners—one with the Kaplans and the other with the Mushers—followed. They capped off the evening with drinks at Tavern on the Green. He had a daquiri or two; she had a Scotch.[101]

On December 3, the *New York Times* announced their engagement.[102] Hadassah received a slew of congratulatory messages, including from former beaus. Among the notes was a dismissal from PS 89's principal,

J. C. Gluck, who had previously twice reported that her service was "exceptional."[103] "Dear Miss. Kaplan," he penned two days after the *Times*' story, "I have been giving some thought to the situation both here and at 83rd St. [where the New York City Department of Education was located]. I feel that since you certainly will have not much interest in your work, as witness your own statements, it might be just as well to sever your connections with the school as your future husband wants. Not in the future but at present."[104] This correspondence would put an immediate end to Hadassah's position, which, according to her "Substitute Teaching Record," she had held for 221.5 days.[105] Despite the definitive and dismissive tone of Gluck's letter, as well as not knowing what Hadassah's "own statements" were, the accompanying scraps of undated, yet preserved, handwritten notes imply a more intimate relationship between Hadassah and the principal and a more complicated story. When Hadassah asked Gluck to give the bearer of her note a key for her locker after she lost hers, Gluck replied, "Your second installment [i.e., paragraph] shows that you are capable of affection. I certainly hope that some of it is reserved for me."[106] In another message, Gluck proposed renting his apartment to Hadassah's parents, who were interested in downsizing after Judith remarried Ira Eisenstein, her father's disciple and colleague. Gluck also offered to drive her home from work.[107] When Hadassah straightforwardly requested spectacles for a student in another note, Gluck replied solicitously, "You know very well that whatever you want me to do, I'll do."[108] The principal further recorded in another series of folded small pieces of paper that he was looking forward to a meeting with her with "eagerness and anxiety." He mentioned a test he wanted her to take. When she asked casually what he meant by "test," his written response was overly emotional: "That," he retorted, referring to her note, "is the nicest thing you have done. At least you show some feeling, emotion, which were lacking thus far. There was no test," he continued. "I was terribly disappointed and I did not want to show it. Just a foolish pride."[109]

We do not know exactly what transpired between the two or what specifically upset Gluck. Hunter women typically expected to continue teaching after marriage. Judith, Hadassah's sister, had done so following both of her marriages. No actual marriage bar mandated Hadassah's discharge, although a national effort to oust married female teachers was under way. Five years later, in 1939, Mayor Fiorello La Guardia would ban married couples from both being on New York City's payroll. But in 1934, married and even pregnant teachers were technically allowed to continue teaching in New York, which was significantly more liberal than most areas.[110]

Perhaps Sidney—aware of the principal's flirtations with his now fiancée—did not want Hadassah to continue teaching, or maybe Gluck was jealous about the news of her engagement. Sexual harassment was more subtle among white-collar workers than for manual laborers. For example, Anna Novak, a Chicago-based canner, complained about the pressures women experienced at the time to please foremen. "You could get along swell," she recalled, "if you let the boss slap you on the behind and feel you up."[111] Clearly, the dynamic between Hadassah and Gluck was less explicit. Nevertheless, some type of incident and the assumptions of the day—that married women would leave the workforce unless their husbands lost their jobs—appear to have instigated Hadassah's immediate firing one month before she and Sidney married in the Kaplans' home. It was another reminder that in addition to the difficulties young Jewish women faced in obtaining the few available professional positions, sexual harassment was routine, and it was rare for married women successfully to maintain white-collar jobs.[112]

* * *

By the time Hadassah found herself yet again unemployed, her year in Palestine was long past. Nevertheless, the experience—and an ongoing relationship to the place where her parents, sisters, and she would continue to travel and spend time—remained vital for her personal development and self-conception. In recalling why she and Sidney had not connected more seriously when they first dated, Hadassah reflected, "I really think he ditched me because I was a giddy kid." She recalled Sidney complaining that she kept him "up all night." "It was Palestine," she went on to explain, "that matured me."[113] "I changed all of my standards," she attested, "all of my ideas. . . . I met people who had a different set of values, . . . who were so inspired by what was being done."[114] Hadassah remembered her experiences in Palestine, the ideas she encountered and internalized, and the relationships that she built— with mentors, friends, and intimates—as pivotal to her maturation.

Although Hadassah would live another eighty-one years, the informal education she acquired during her year traveling and studying in Palestine as a nineteen-year-old was formative in turning her into the sophisticated American Jewish woman she would become. Retrospectively, Hadassah referred to her year abroad as "the year of [her] life."[115] It was then that she met new people she otherwise might not have encountered. By eluding chaperones and living at a distance from her parents, Hadassah was able to flirt, date, and explore more intimate relationships, particularly with older men. She also gained insight into the lives of a range of single and married women beyond her sisters and mother. For a young woman coming of age, Hadassah's exposure to their lives was a serious education, offering diverse models as to how one might arrange, maintain, and sometimes eschew marriage. She, furthermore, saw models for mothering while still pursuing one's own personal, professional, and intellectual interests. Hadassah's time abroad also increased her global consciousness. Particularly as she traveled home through Europe, Hadassah began to internalize the firsthand experiences of friends with growing European antisemitism and its consequences. While she continued to look to Palestine to remain connected to a vibrant Jewish culture, she did not see it as a panacea or imagine herself or her family moving there. Her time in Palestine exposed her to how communal celebrations of Jewish holidays and collective agricultural settlements might look. But her travels also laid bare the country's shortcomings: the material hardships, the dearth of religious practice, and the growing conflicts among British officers, Palestinian Arabs, and especially between Palestinian Jews separated by national, cultural, and political backgrounds.

The knowledge and skills Hadassah acquired while traveling prepared her to become a Jewish educator or work for a Zionist organization, in addition to her earlier training to teach in a secular school. But several factors discouraged her from full-time professional pursuits: the combination of widespread opposition to married women (and even more so to mothers) working, Hadassah's experience with her former principal's flirtations and her firing, Sidney's work travel and eventual earnings, and her cognizance, based on her sister's recent divorce, of marriage's fragility. Instead, like many women of her generation with the means to do so, Hadassah focused on her family and brought much of what she had learned in Palestine—her Hebrew, travel savviness, and commitment to building a Jewish civilization—to her teaching, volunteer work, and lay leadership.

Conclusion

Israel on My List

In the early twentieth century, Zionism was critical for a cohort of American Jewish women, including Hadassah. Women such as Henrietta Szold, the founder of the organization *Hadassah*, Israeli Prime Minister Golda Meir, the fund-raiser and educator Irma Lindheim, and the writer Marie Syrkin played overt roles in Palestine and later Israel's development. In a world where relatively few professional and paid positions and opportunities for exploration were sanctioned, women became pioneers in a range of settlement communities, from the religious Hashomer Hadati to the secular Habonim. They served as social workers, nurses, and teachers in the Jewish Agency (the international body representing the World Zionist Organization) and as union activists in the Histadrut (the General Federation of Labor organizing workers in Israel). American Jewish women played leadership roles in Na'amat (the Labor Zionist women's organization in the US), the Mizrachi Women's Organization (now Amit, focused on training and supporting religiously observant Jewish girls in Palestine), and *Hadassah* (the largest Jewish women's organization in the world, providing health and medical benefits to women and families in Palestine and later Israel regardless of their religion). Through Zionism, women discovered what the sociologist Shulamit Reinharz and the historian Mark Raider have called an "opportunity to revolutionize their own lives and, in the process, participate fully in the construction of a new Jewish social reality."[1]

American Jewish women like Hadassah found in Palestine and Zionism an educational source and a means for personal development and communal contribution.[2] As Hadassah's parents had hoped, traveling to Palestine provided a relatively safe space for maturation and adventure for their rambunctious daughter. Hadassah and her peers, through their journeys, broadened their awareness of the world. They challenged social, cultural, religious, and sexual norms, while remaining within the confines of social acceptability as "good" mothers, wives, and daughters. For young women, time spent in Palestine created pathways for meaningful work balanced between tradition and innovation.

American Jewish women's interest in Zionism and what became the State of Israel only grew in the aftermath of World War II. Zionist activities and travel became more accessible than they had been during the interwar period for women like Hadassah. American Jewish women increasingly embraced Israeli culture and consumption and enhanced their involvement in Israeli philanthropy, lay leadership, and Jewish politics.[3] The paid and volunteer efforts of a generation of women working in schools, camps, community centers, synagogues, not-for-profit organizations, the arts, and their homes helped to forge connections between what became Israel and American Jews. Like Hadassah, many of those educators spent time in Palestine, where they learned a literal language (Hebrew) as well as symbols, rituals, and culture to make Judaism vibrant. Their time abroad fostered living traditions that were forward, rather than backward, looking and constituted what Mordecai called "contemporary Judaism in action."[4] The formal and informal work of such women—teaching Jewish traditions, language, and history while organizing religious, cultural, and educational events—profoundly influenced Jewish communities. These women shaped institutional priorities, making Israeli arts, language, and culture vital to contemporary understandings of Judaism. In doing so, such women served both as intercultural and intergenerational bridges.

Women, Zionism, and the arts were central to the new form of Judaism that Mordecai conceptualized and imagined his daughters and their friends helping to build. In 1932, when Mordecai wrote about the need to change the traditional status of women, he identified Zionism, adult education, and the organization *Hadassah* as key. He argued that women were not prepared to counter assimilation because they were never given a serious Jewish education beyond what they imbibed from the "general atmosphere." Zionism, he wrote, provided a vehicle for realizing that Jewish life was worthwhile and a "thing of beauty."[5] Other religious and political leaders echoed Mordecai's rhetoric about using Zionism to develop American Judaism, even if they did not specifically focus on its impact on women. "We need *haluzim* [Zionist pioneers]," explained the

Reform rabbi Samuel S. Cohen, "not only to drain the malarial swamps and to fertilize the deserts of Palestine, but also to remove the poisons of indifference, cynicism, and irreligion that are destroying Jewish life in America. . . . Pioneers are needed again to breathe new spirit into the dry bones of the house of Israel, to reawaken our dormant spiritual energies."[6] Zionism, Cohen suggested, might do as much to help American and other diasporic Jews as it did for those who moved to Palestine.

To shape American Jewry, women like Hadassah and her sister Judith created and taught Jewish music, folk dances, games, art, and stories to the next generation.[7] Drawing on song lyrics that Hadassah had copied into her diary as well as ones her older sister gathered on her own visit, Judith composed music and developed five books of Jewish folk songs, beginning in 1937 with *Gateway to Jewish Song*. Such works included transliterated Israeli songs accessible to American Jewish audiences regardless of their ability to read Hebrew. In addition to Judith's teaching, she also created, performed, and published several English cantatas, narrative choral pieces with musical accompaniment, which allowed singing communities collectively to learn about and explore biblical as well as historical Jewish experiences, including the Holocaust.[8]

While Judith taught the music of Jewish pioneers to educators at her father's Teachers' Institute, Mordecai hired another former student of his as a visual arts educator: Temima Nimtzowitz (who would eventually adopt her husband's last name, Gezari). In 1935, Mordecai commissioned the Russian émigré, who had grown up in Brooklyn and recently returned from two years as an artist in residence on a kibbutz in Palestine, to create a mural in the sanctuary of his synagogue, the Society for the Advancement of Judaism.[9] He wanted the work to represent visually Judaism's reconstruction based on voluntarily chosen folkways and spiritual values rather than prescriptive laws. Labor Zionism was at the core of Temima's three-panel mural: *Elements of Palestine, Old and New*. The artist included more than fifty figures of Palestinian Jews, from mostly older Ashkenazi and Sephardi Jews studying ancient texts to young men and women reading and working in industry, science, and agriculture. Temima's mural idealized pioneers building the land and relegated diasporic Jews—like the SAJ's congregants—to spectators, participating only inasmuch as they visited, volunteered, or moved to Palestine. Mordecai's congregation, however, was less offended by their sidelining than by the work's violation of the Second Commandment's prohibition against graven images. By the mid-1950s, without mention in the institution's meeting minutes, the mural had moved to the social hall, where it remains to this day.[10] Palestine and later Israel would remain central to Temima's long career as an artist and arts educator, spanning forty-two years of teaching at Mordecai's Teachers' Institute and almost sixty directing the Board of Jewish Education's Department of Art Education.[11]

The idea that Jewish educators and artists should spend time in Palestine and use the language and culture of the land to inspire their students developed beyond the walls of the SAJ. Other Jewish educators, such as the Hebraist Anna Sherman and the children's author Libbie Braverman, employed their experiences in Palestine to introduce their students and readers to a dynamic Judaism with living customs and traditions integrated into daily life.[12] A 1944 survey on Zionist education of adults in the US, written by Samuel Dinin, Hadassah's companion home from Palestine, fit well with female educators' pedagogy (although no women were on the committee producing the report). Dinin contended that Zionist education should not promote propaganda about Palestine but should, instead, cultivate the arts—music, plays, visual arts, clothing, furniture, and even jewelry—to teach Jews, wherever they live, "to live a life of Jewish self-knowledge, self-respect and self-affirmation, enriching [their] value as a citizen and as a human being."[13] According to the Jewish educator Barry Chazan, teaching about Palestine through the arts, especially folk songs, lore, and dance, facilitated progressive education and experimentation in the classroom and generally made classes more enjoyable.[14] Scholars contend that early twentieth-century educational, liturgical, and publicity materials, as well as children's books, games, records, radio programs, and films, focused on Palestine lionized *halutzim* (Jewish pioneers) in largely nonpolemical ways. Such works emphasized Klal Yisrael, the whole Jewish community, and the importance of the Land of Israel and Zionism for American diasporic Judaism, but they also tended to downplay ideological and partisan divisions around Arab-Jewish conflict, gender roles, Jewish disputes, and British resistance.[15] Such representations might have reflected how their creators experienced the land and its people: what they decided to communicate reproduced what they chose to see.

One way to avoid the type of propaganda that Dinin warned against in representations of Palestine was through ongoing travel and exchange, which the Kaplans and their peers pursued. Mordecai and Lena spent the summer of 1935 in Palestine and then returned from 1937 until 1939. During Mordecai's delayed sabbatical from Teachers' Institute, he taught pedagogy at Hebrew University. Judith and her second husband, Ira Eisenstein, honeymooned in Palestine the summer after Hadassah returned (1934). They would return with their daughters, Miriam and Ann, when Ira took a sabbatical from the SAJ, from 1949 to 1950. Ira considered permanently remaining in Palestine—Judith had more reservations—but since he was unable to find sustainable work, the four returned to New York at the end of the year.[16] Meanwhile, the Dushkins lived in Palestine intermittently, from 1919 to 1922 and 1934 to 1939, and then migrated permanently to what was then Israel in 1949.[17] Mordecai too moved there in 1975, at the age of ninety-four, with his second wife, an artist born in what was then Palestine, Rivka Rever. They returned to New York five years later to be closer to Mordecai's family in his final years.[18]

Unsurprisingly, Mordecai's conception of Palestine and its potential to transform American Jewry shifted over time. In 1936, when he revisited the issue of women's status, which he had written about four years earlier, Mordecai barely considered Zionism as a vehicle for change regarding gender. Instead, he contended that traditional Judaism needed to transform itself to avoid alienating gifted women (like his daughters). It needed to become equitable religiously and legally both in Palestine and in the diaspora. He called for women to emancipate themselves so that they might (to use Marxist language) demand ownership of their own property, control of the product of their labor, and changes to discriminatory Jewish laws, including those surrounding divorce, which required men to grant women a *get* (religious divorce) before they might remarry and have Jewishly legitimate children.[19] Although he does not explicitly write about witnessing the divorce and remarriage of his eldest daughter, Judith, it presumably influenced his thinking on this matter. Perhaps Hadassah's experiences in Palestine and his own also made him less confident that Zionism and Zionist activities would serve as a panacea for Jewish women.

Despite Mordecai's progressive writing about female autonomy and equality, the reality of gender disparities remained even in his congregation. It was not until the 1950s that the SAJ allowed women to participate fully religiously. Mordecai paid tribute to Ira, who had recently returned from a sabbatical with his family in Israel, for convincing the congregation to approve the change.[20] But historians contend that it was the audacity of young women at the SAJ, inspired by the experience of leading services, whether reading megillah or Torah, that led them to demand reform. Teenage girls in the mid-1940s who had become bat mitzvah and led services in Hebrew schools and camps went on to insist that their right of passage should, as for their brothers, mark the beginning of their leadership of Jewish rituals rather than its height. Having developed new skills, they insisted that they too should be able to carry the Torah on holidays, have *aliyot* (blessings said before and after reading Torah), and count in a prayer quorum, minyan.[21] Marking the revised policy, on December 2, 1950, Judith and Lena represented two of the four women called for an *aliya*. When Lena was called to the Torah, it marked the first female adult bat mitzvah. Her husband recalled her anxiety beforehand. "Lena," he wrote, "was in a state of nerves last night for fear that she would forget the benediction or not chant it properly."[22] Five months later, a third generation became bat mitzvah, as Miriam Eisenstein, Judith and Ira's eldest daughter, celebrated her right of passage. Her celebration was especially poignant. She was both the daughter and the granddaughter of the SAJ's rabbis (Mordecai Kaplan and Ira Eisenstein), a recent survivor of polio, which she had contracted the year before while in Palestine, and a masterful reader, who chanted the entire first section of Kedoshim and the haftorah. Mordecai recalled that a "happy spirit . . . pervaded the synagogue": "some of our friends remembering what Miriam had gone through a year ago in Jerusalem—made the occasion a memorable one."[23] Such celebrations ushered in a more general practice of women at the SAJ, regardless of their education, standing on the bimah (the platform where services are led), counting for a religious quorum (minyan), having *aliyot*, holding and chanting the Torah and haftorah, becoming board members, and being elected officers of the board.[24]

The SAJ embraced gender equality in ritual practice well before other denominations did. Nevertheless, the social realities for

Reconstructionist women during the 1950s remained "constrained by postwar domestic ideals," according to Deborah Waxman, a historian, rabbi, and president of Reconstructing Judaism, the movement Ira developed out of Mordecai's ideology. Most women at the SAJ in the postwar period focused on fairly conventional areas such as education, organizing kiddush, and managing other domestic aspects.[25] Mordecai was more successful at theoretically advocating for gender-based equality than putting it into practice. Feminist transformation would—and continues to—require the liberation of Jewish women and their collective struggles to reshape families and institutions, both Jewish and not.[26]

The recently married Hadassah initially focused on her family, given her choices, talents, and circumstances. The newlyweds, like many of their peers, originally moved into the apartment of Hadassah's in-laws. Eventually, they would rent an apartment down the block. Their first son, Jeremy, was born just before their first anniversary, followed three years later by Daniel and, in another four years, by the baby, my father, David. Throughout that time, Sidney traveled regularly for work. First, he made a deal with Quaker Oats. Then, from 1938 to 1939, he traveled to England, France, and Denmark to expand internationally Quaker Oats' market for preservatives in butter, candies, ice cream, and parchment paper. During this period, Sidney was also applying for patents for new techniques in oxidation and rancidity that could be used to preserve fruit and vegetables and make olive oil, oatmeal, and baby formula. He would eventually receive nearly two hundred patents.[27]

Especially as Hadassah's children grew, she combined domesticity with other forms of paid and unpaid labor. She also continued her education. In 1938, just as she was expecting her second son, Daniel, she completed a ten-week Board of Education "course in fundamental economics and social philosophy." Ten years later, when her youngest son was six, she returned to teaching, working as a substitute in public schools through the early 1960s. In 1958, when she was forty-five years old, Hadassah enrolled in a master's program in art history at Hunter College.[28] She would continue taking art and Jewish history classes at Hunter throughout her life.

Although Hadassah never finished the master's, higher education represented a vehicle that her sisters capitalized on to an unusual degree for professional advancement. Indeed, before marrying, each of them earned a graduate degree. Just before Hadassah went to Palestine in 1932, Judith earned a master's from her father's Teachers' Institute and Columbia University's Teachers College two years after having received a bachelor's degree from those institutions. When she was fifty years old, Judith returned to school, this time to Hebrew Union College–Jewish Institute of Religion's School of Sacred Music, were she earned a PhD in musicology.[29] Like Judith, Naomi began a graduate degree shortly after earning a bachelor's. When her parents were on sabbatical in Palestine, she attended the American University of Beirut as a twenty-three-year-old. She went on to graduate from New York University's College of Medicine as a psychiatrist, to marry when she was a thirty-year-old resident at Bellevue, and then to become a psychoanalyst.[30] The youngest Kaplan, Selma, earned a master's degree in education from Teachers College in 1939. She would teach high school English at her private high school alma mater, Fieldston, instructing the poet Laureate Howard Nemerov and his sister, who would become known by her married name as the photographer Diane Arbus. Selma would later produce a TV version of Thornton Wilder's *Our Town* (she married Saul Jaffe, an entertainment lawyer to Frank Sinatra, Grace Kelly, and Doris Day).[31]

Rather than drawing on a graduate degree, Hadassah looked to the informal education she had acquired in Palestine to shape the Jewish world in which she raised her children and, especially, the institution that was most central to her family's and especially her father's Jewish engagement, the SAJ. Hadassah imbued her love of Jewish art, music, dance, and the Hebrew language into the synagogue's Women's Division and the Hebrew school's parent-teacher association, which she led. She organized art auctions, trips, and women's luncheons, including one in 1955 in honor of her father's seventieth birthday, with keynote speaker Eleanor Roosevelt, who had until recently chaired the UN Commission on Human Rights. Hadassah's love of Jewish arts and language helped to influence the SAJ's Women's Division and synagogue, shaping its culture and the nature of the Judaism it embodied. In an interview, Hadassah described herself as "selling Reconstructionism to women."[32] She also recalled decorating the synagogue and selecting fabrics and chandeliers. "I had to do an awful lot," she quipped, "as an unpaid worker."[33]

Mordecai noted his daughter's impact on the synagogue in his diary. Following Purim festivities in 1951, marking the holiday celebrating when Jews avoided destruction decreed by the Persian court official Haman, Mordecai described the six boys and four girls from the Hebrew school who expertly chanted in Hebrew almost the entire story of Esther, the heroine of the tale, in front of a large congregation of parents and children. Although no record was preserved of Hadassah's reflections on the holiday, one can imagine her recalling the carnival and floats she, dressed as a "newspaper girl," had witnessed in Tel Aviv in 1933 and looking to convey that spirit to her children and their peers. The atmosphere at the SAJ, Mordecai attested about the 1951 celebration, was "more genuine ... than any of the previous Megilla nights." Megillah literally means "scroll" and refers to the story of Purim told in the book of Esther. "My Hadassah," Mordecai continued (Esther was originally called Hadassah too), "has no small share in helping Jack [Cohen, who ran the SAJ's Hebrew school] to build up the school spirit through the P.T.A., which she has been heading."[34]

As Hadassah's children grew and her father aged, she shifted her focus from building the SAJ to assisting the philanthropic work of her husband, Sidney. Beginning in the late 1930s, Sidney aligned with the American Economic Committee for Palestine (AECP) to transfer innovations that he and others were developing in the food and pharmaceutical industry to Palestine. For example, he arranged for the then-young filmmaker Stanley Kramer to record long chicken houses in South Jersey to teach Jews in Palestine more efficient techniques for raising poultry, so that they could handle two thousand to twenty-five hundred hens as opposed to the six hundred or fewer that they had been doing. Kramer would later become a liberal movie icon producing and directing films, such as *Inherit the Wind* (1960), *Judgment at Nuremburg* (1961), and *Look Who's Coming to Dinner* (1967). Under Sidney's supervision, for six months in 1948, the AECP shipped guns to Palestine in crates labeled "agricultural machinery."[35]

In 1965, when Sidney turned sixty, he retired from Cooper Laboratories to work full-time as the managing director and chairman of the Palestine Endowment Fund (PEF), a not-for-profit founded in 1922 by prominent American Jews, including the Supreme Court justice Louis Brandeis, the Reform rabbi Stephen Wise, and the child-labor advocate and lawyer Robert Szold. The group channeled funds to scientific, educational, cultural, and religious entities in Palestine, matching philanthropists with specific projects and programs geared to their interests (what today is called "donor-driven philanthropy"). They did not solicit funds, hold fund-raisers, or publicize the organization. They regularly sent those who were generally interested in contributing to Israel to the United Jewish Appeal (UJA), an umbrella organization that pooled resources to support Jews in Israel and abroad. Instead, the PEF team of thirty volunteers and one twenty-hour-a-week secretary worked by word of mouth with those who wished to give funds to specific causes in Israel, investigate various institutions, and channel resources, funds, and knowledge to specific needs.[36] Despite different fund-raising approaches at the UJA and PEF, both participated in a broader post–World War II American Jewish project using state power, in the form of exemptions and deductions, to support foreign Jewish communities especially in Israel.[37]

Sidney's volunteer work in retirement took him into the PEF's one-room office every day for twenty-five years. While the office work was primarily Sidney's domain, Hadassah was intimately involved in his efforts in Israel, where the two traveled once or twice a year beginning in 1969. There they met with officials including Jerusalem's long-term mayor (from 1965 to 1993) Teddy Kollek; Israel's first prime minister, David Ben Gurion; and its sixth one, Menachem Begin, as well as organizations (especially Hebrew and Ben Gurion University) and friends. Hadassah became particularly involved in a number of institutions of higher education and scientific research, such as Ben Gurion University, Hebrew University, and the Weizmann Institute, as well as cultural entities, including Batsheva Dance company, the Israel Sinfonietta, Tel Aviv Museum of Art, and the America Israel Cultural Foundation, which gives scholarships and grants to Israeli artists.[38] But much of the couple's time traveling in Israel brought them to investigate and draw funds toward small and lesser-known organizations. As one journalist wrote in a quotation that focuses on Sidney's work but also alludes to Hadassah's presence, if not her contributions, "Eleven years after retirement, [Sidney] Musher is still coming to Israel several times a year, spending nearly all his time on the road, checking leaky youth club ceilings and trout fisheries and worrying about how to catch drop-outs before they fall. He and his wife rest their heads on hotel pillows, 'but I can't learn in a hotel,' he said."[39]

After Hadassah was widowed and well into her eighties, she continued to travel to Israel each year. She also remained an active Hebrew speaker.

Even when her other faculties diminished, her caretaker Carmen Varner reported that for three weeks near the end of her life, Hadassah entirely switched to speaking Hebrew, seemingly having forgotten her English.

For Hadassah's eightieth birthday, in 1992, one of the two songs that her then seventy-seven-year-old sister Selma wrote for her describes her perpetual vitality as well as the ongoing role that Israel, Israelis, art, and politics played in her life:

> If you're looking for Hadassah and don't want to run around,
> I've got a little list, yes, I've got a little list,
> of locales and institutions where she's likely to be found,
> Spots she really can't resist, that she never could resist.
>
> There's the choir at Hunter College, & the Weizmann Institute
> I've got them on my list, I've got them on my list.
> The Hebrew University and Ben Gurion to boot,
> They're also on my list, they're also on my list.
> The New York Public Library at Forty-Second Street
> Or riding out to Kennedy for guests she has to greet,
> Beer Sheva Chamber Orchestra or openings at the Met,
> The Tel Aviv Museum, and be sure you don't forget
> The Board of P.E.F. and The Reconstructionist,
> She can't possibly resist, so I put them on my list.
>
> You might find her on the dance floor doing fascinating feats,
> I have it on the list, I have it on the list,
> Or besieging Mayor Dinkins about cleaning up the streets
> I've got him on my list, his office on my list.
> Runs a home away from home for Israelis young or old
> And she'll write itineraries that are wondrous to behold,
> In New York or in Jerusalem she'll tell you where to go,
> In galleries or fine boutiques there's nothing she don't know.
> But you'd best do what she tells you, make no effort to resist,
> Or she'll put you on her list, she'll put you on her list.[40]

With an eternal checklist of things to see and do and people to meet, Hadassah remained a bundle of constant activity well into her senior years. Despite her energy, she never became a political leader, a feminist activist, a major Jewish thinker, or even president of a local chapter of the American women's Zionist organization *Hadassah* (although she did volunteer with the organization, local chapters of which both her mother in New York and her mother-in-law in Washington, DC, had helped to found and lead).[41] Instead, the time she spent in Palestine as a young woman cemented her ongoing interest in building bridges between American and Israeli Jews. Through her unpaid work at her father's synagogue (the SAJ) and in collaboration with her husband (PEF), Hadassah connected American Jews and Israelis with a living Jewish culture and institutions dedicated to its promotion.

Hadassah's efforts were inspired by her father's aspirational vision of a Jewish homeland. Rather than shirking away from the term "Zionism," Mordecai embraced it. In a book published shortly before the founding of the State of Israel in 1948, Mordecai explained that Zionism represented much more than political sovereignty. It symbolized a "Reconstruction of the Jewish Way of Life" and "Jewish democracy in action."[42] In the mid- to late 1950s, following the establishment of the state, Mordecai called for a "new" and a "greater" Zionism, by which he meant not expanding geographical territory or responding politically to antisemitism and the refugee crisis but, instead, a concept beyond statehood: the creation of a spiritual movement that might "salvage" the Jewish people and "regenerate" their collective spirit.[43] He contended that Jews were in a unique position to forge an ethical, as opposed to chauvinistic, militaristic, or expansionist, nation. In the aftermath of World War II, they might "demonstrate to a broken and sorrowful world that nations will never live in peace unless they adopt this new conception of nationhood, . . . that a nation must work for the good of its individual members by striving to bring out the best that is in them."[44] By endorsing a heterogeneous and pluralistic society, Zionism might contribute to world civilization.

Despite Mordecai's hope regarding the Jewish community of Israel and its capacity to develop and sustain Judaism, he and Lena were aware of the internal strife and violence in Palestine. More than Hadassah, whose formative year in Palestine was peaceful, her parents' attitudes toward the country were shaped by living there through the Arab Revolt of 1937 through 1939. Despite efforts by the mandatory government to restrict Jewish land purchases and migration to Palestine, the country's Jewish population nearly doubled in the early 1930s as a result of migration from Germany and Poland. Arab Palestinians protested through strikes, boycotts, and violence.[45] Lena worried about both growing antisemitism and Arab nationalism. Her letters to her children described frequent shootings on her street by both Jewish and Arab Palestinians, daily curfews, water shortages, and feelings of loneliness and estrangement. Lena mourned the fate of Jews as Germany's violation of the Munich Agreement forced the Czech Republic to cede the Sudetenland. Despite hardships in Jerusalem, Lena pressured her husband to remain there throughout his sabbatical. She worried that rising antisemitism in the US might result in their needing to stay and wanted him, if necessary, to be able to work at Hebrew University long term. "If conditions are heading the same way as in Germany," she wrote her children, "we may as well all of us come here and if we have to suffer and be killed let us be killed here in what we hold to be our homeland." Lena—who had repeatedly warned Hadassah to watch out for Arabs—was, nevertheless, highly critical of the ongoing violence between Jewish and Arab Palestinians. Although she insisted that her husband try to secure a position in Palestine, she was dismayed to learn that her children—and potentially grandchildren—wanted to spend time there. When Ira earned a sabbatical (this would not actually happen for over another decade), he and Judith wrote the Kaplans that they hoped to spend it in Palestine. "How," Lena retorted, "would you like to live in a country where one has to work 6 days a week about 10 to 12 hours a day for the very munificent salary (teachers' highest) of 60 dollars a month. You must pay for the children's schooling and then they are taught hatred and contempt first for the Arabs and then each sect for the other." Lena further harangued them, asking if they "would be happy to bring up [their] child in such an atmosphere."[46] Mordecai too feared unending violence, expressing concern about its consequences not so much for the individuals attacked as for Zionism as a political project, for both Israel and world Jewry. "Even more specifically and immediately," he wrote in 1955, "Zionism should make it its objective to find a solution for the Arab refugee problem which is at present the greatest threat that hangs over the State of Israel." Keeping the focus on how the struggles of Palestinians affected Jews and Israel rather than their own community, he continued, "As Zionists, we must realize that whatever threatens the State of Israel is a threat to the life of the Jewish People throughout the world."[47]

Mordecai and Lena were not alone in their discomfort with the emerging state. After seven years in Palestine, from 1927 to 1934, Camp Modin founder Libbie Berkson had left Palestine with her husband following a scandal when she refused to fire an Arab Palestinian dishwasher who worked for her teashop on Ben Yehuda Street, Al Kos Te. She rejected as discriminatory pressures to hire only Jews, a political tactic to counter British restrictions on Jewish immigration and deadly violence. Instead, Libbie gravitated to binationalism and eventually returned to the US.

Similarly, Hadassah's friend from camp Sylva Gelber, who trained and worked in Jerusalem as a social worker for fifteen years, left Palestine in 1948 shortly before the founding of the state. In her memoir, *No Balm in Gilead*, named after the prophet Jeremiah's chastisement to his people for their infighting and also adopted by the organization *Hadassah* as its motto, Sylva recounted her concerns regarding heightened violence on both sides. In it, she recalled her "sense of alienation from all the actors in the Palestine drama, the British, the Arabs, the Irgun/Stern" (an extremist, anti-British, terrorist group), and the Haganah, a Zionist military organization originally designed to combat Palestinian Arab revolts against Jewish settlements, which Sylva described as having abandoned its moderate stance of self-defense for using "violence to achieve political ends."[48] Although she did not include it in her memoir, Mordecai recorded what she explained to him in 1951 during a visit to the family in New York. "In 1947," he wrote, "when Haganah joined the Irgun in the campaign of terror against the British and the Arabs she [Sylva] was asked to enter the campaign. She is a person of unusual courage, but she categorically refused to engage in terrorism. She was ready to go onto the ambulance and medical force. But they would not have her on those terms. She had to leave Jerusalem."[49] Mordecai did not clarify Sylva's motivation for departing: Did she leave because of pacifist convictions or a fear of retribution for refusing to join the Jewish rebels? Either way, Sylva returned to Canada, where she become a leading women's rights advocate.

Libbie, Sylva, and the Kaplans feared the ongoing cycles of violence in Palestine, but they did not relinquish the possibility of a utopian vision there. Instead, Sylva and Libbie joined a wide range of women,

CONCLUSION | 195

Hadassah among them, in contributing philanthropically to specific organizations in Israel. Sylva endowed an award for students at Jerusalem's Rubin Academy of Music and Dance.[50] After Libbie retired in 1958, she supported a book drive for Israeli children (the Ben Zvi Book Fund) and also developed Neot Kedumim, a biblical landscape reserve between Jerusalem and Tel Aviv meant to portray biblical and Talmudic life.[51] Even as they criticized Israel, they maintained connections with people and institutions there.

Today, the bond between American Jewish women and Israel has become significantly more tenuous. Hamas's deadly October 7, 2023, attack on Israel, including the killing of over one thousand men, women, and children, the perpetration of sexual violence, and the taking of 250 hostages, reframed solidarity between American Jews and Israel. The atrocities combined with rising antisemitism in the US and abroad brought together a wide array of Jewish groups in support of Israel.[52] Nevertheless, Israel's war in Gaza, the international condemnation of the high Palestinian death toll, and the absence of a clear geopolitical plan for peace have tempered such unity, particularly among young Jews. Many liberal American Jews are especially alienated by the racism articulated by members of Israel's far-right governments and their efforts to undermine political solutions. A nation and ideology that once largely united Jews in Israel and the diaspora now increasingly fragments them.[53]

Just when the forces dividing us—Jew from Palestinian, and American Jew from non-Jew alike—seem strongest, it is worth remembering Mordecai's vision of ethical nationhood and the creative efforts of a generation of women to implement it. Mordecai promoted an ethical nationalism, grounded in democracy, not theocracy. He advocated a separation of church and state, support for minority rights, and religious pluralism, so that Jews could live Jewishly and others might follow their respective dictates. He further believed that such a community could serve as a moral force for world Jewry. Rather than reinforcing Orthodoxy, he hoped to forge a new and creative Judaism based on group consciousness, self-government, and education.[54] According to Mordecai, the establishment of a free, just, and cooperative society would bring salvation "not through the agency of the State, but through the abundance of cultural and spiritual values which it is bound to produce in its day-to-day coping with the realities of life."[55] Thus, he yearned for an aspirational homeland and an ethical nation that could help diasporic Jews to embrace their dual identities, as both Americans and Jews.

Recovering the dreams of an adventurous daughter, an overprotective mother, a visionary father, and a cohort of largely female educators, nurses, artists, and activists helps to illustrate what Palestine and later Israel meant for American Jews in the early to mid-twentieth century. For many, particularly Jewish women, that relationship was built not on military might and territorial expansionism but rather on a search for personal and communal engagement, opportunities to learn, and a chance to participate in significant labor when many other professional channels were closed to them. Their often-idealistic representations of a Jewish homeland inspired younger generations to look toward Zionism for a living Judaism. In minimizing the competing national aspirations of Palestinian Arabs and the conflicts among Jews, however, they oversimplified the difficulties in creating a shared society, particularly one that is both religious and democratic. Despite such shortcomings, the journey of young Jewish women, such as Hadassah, in search of learning, community, and self illustrates the struggle, constrained by one's time and place, to construct a meaningful life.

ACKNOWLEDGMENTS

Many people and institutions have helped to make this project possible and supported me through its research and writing. Their questions, comments, and ongoing interest have been invaluable to me, enriching a process that might otherwise have been isolating.

Nearly a decade ago, when I was just beginning this project, Joseph Benatov, director of the Modern Hebrew Language Program at the University of Pennsylvania, translated the Hebrew material in Hadassah's archive: her letters to her father, Mordecai Kaplan; his letters to her; and some diary entries. Those elegant translations can be seen throughout this book, bringing to life Hadassah's and Mordecai's voices.

This project would not have been possible without time and resources. I am grateful to Stockton University and my colleagues in Historical Studies for providing me with occasional course releases and sabbaticals to allow me to research and write. My research assistant, Alexa Novo, helped enormously with the final stages of this project. I also want to express my gratitude to the Herbert D. Katz Center for Advanced Judaic Studies, which provided me with an intellectual community, absolutely critical access to the University of Pennsylvania's library system, and even a summer office. Special thanks to Steven Weitzman, Natalie Dohrmann, and Anne Albert.

Archivists and librarians have provided me with critical guidance and made available resources to me without which this project would have been challenging. Stockton's archivist Heather Perez helped me to think through access and search issues. At Penn, Arthur Kiron made me aware of the range of works at the Katz Center that would supplement my research, and Bruce Nielsen and Joseph Gulka helped me obtain them despite the COVID-19 pandemic. At Barnard and Columbia, even at the height of the pandemic, archivists and administrators, including Martha Tenney, Jocelyn Wilk, and Marybeth Kemm, checked admission and graduation records for me.

Conversations with colleagues and invitations to speak about my work have also been vital. Thanks to Melissa Klapper for organizing an excellent roundtable discussion on "grandmother history" at the Association for Jewish History and to Natalia Aleksiun for the opportunity to reflect on personal history in her "Family Series" at the Center for Jewish History. Early in my work, Brent Sasley graciously invited me to speak as a Kornbleet Scholar in Fort Worth, Texas. Other mentors who have provided guidance include Linda Kerber, Alice Kessler-Harris, and Paula Eisenstein Baker.

From relatively early on in this process, the enthusiasm and warm support of two senior scholars, both of whom knew Hadassah, were indispensable. Mel Scult, the preeminent biographer of Mordecai Kaplan, generously shared his oral histories, transcribed by Jane Susswein, as well as his insights and suggestions on Mordecai's diaries, Hadassah, writing agents, and publishers. Deborah Dash Moore's close reading and feedback on my introduction and first chapter helped me to rethink my writing voice and to make the text more generally accessible. Her candid guidance in navigating the publishing world was also invaluable. Bonny Fetterman generously helped me reconsider my book pitch.

At New York University Press, Jennifer Hammer has ably guided the publication process. My blind readers provided me with excellent feedback. Their suggestions both strengthened my argument and enhanced the reader's perception of the world I am describing. Any mistakes or oversights remain my own.

Marilyn Price generously digitized and shared videos of her interviews with Hadassah and Selma conducted in 2002. Those oral histories provided not only insight into the lives of the two but also a poignant reminder of their mannerisms and who they were as individuals. Writing this book kept the voices of women I loved in my ears for nearly a decade longer than I expected. I am deeply grateful for their company.

I am thankful also for the support and input of my family and the descendants of those discussed in my book. Cyrille White, the niece of one of Hadassah's chaperones, Rose Gell Jacobs, clarified the experiences of Rose's daughter, Ruth. I am even more appreciative of the discussions and connections that this book encouraged me to have with family members, who have enthusiastically and steadfastly supported this project despite the time it has taken to complete it. Thanks to my siblings and in-laws: Sarah and Matt Brenner, Abe and Dara Musher-Eizenman, Leora Eisenstadt, Mike Uram, and Katie Eisenstadt. I am grateful to my aunt and uncle Karol and Daniel Musher and cousins Miriam and Ann Eisenstein and Adam and Mark Wenner for their observations, recollections, and sharing of sources. My parents, David and especially Ruth Musher, devoted weeks to sorting through and organizing the papers of Hadassah, Sidney, and Lena, making it possible for me to imagine this project and profoundly enabling it. Thank you to my entire family, those named here and not, for sharing your wisdom and knowledge and for your support.

My friends have sustained and distracted me, told me when my title was too long, brainstormed catchier ones, helped me to finish, and reminded me not to be too hard on myself. Special thanks to Leona Goldshaw, Doug Goldstein, David Greenberg, Rebecca Kobrin, David Lerman, Melissa Lerman, Deb Susser-Stein, Ilana Trachtman, Ruth Watson, and Ivy Weingram. Simone Gorko's coaching was indispensable.

No one has facilitated the writing of this book more than my husband, Daniel Eisenstadt. He has understood my need for writing retreats, my challenges in multitasking, and that his handling of family responsibilities was crucial. Thank you for being my sounding board and for making space for me to tell my stories.

Above all, I wrote this book for my daughters: Elena, Ariella, and Rachel. I want them to know where they come from and am eager to see where they will go.

NOTES

INTRODUCTION

1. M. Kaplan to L. Kaplan, April 6, 1925; "Opening of the Hebrew University—The Ceremony," April 1, 1925, in Kaplan, *Communings*, vol. 1, 204. All Kaplan family correspondence from the author's personal collection.
2. Note that Mordecai M. Kaplan's diaries and papers are also now available digitally through the Jewish Theological Seminary, available at https://digitalcollections.jtsa.edu.
3. Markowitz, *My Daughter*, 29, 77, 107.
4. Hadassah Kaplan, diary, October 5, 1932, personal collection.
5. The datebooks that Hadassah used beginning—at least in terms of what she kept—in 1926, when she was thirteen, were published by her father's synagogue, the Society for the Advancement of Judaism. In 1978, she switched to using calendars published by the Jewish Reconstructionist Federation, which was established in 1940 to promote reconstructionist ideas through publishing.
6. On the gendering of archives and history, see Scott, *Feminism and History*; and Smith, *Gender of History*.
7. The one exception to this is where Mordecai's family life and ideas intersected, particularly regarding his eldest daughter, Judith, whom he treated as a disciple. Mordecai's diaries document the intellectual sparring between the two.
8. Judith and Ira Eisenstein interview, cassette 24a, 21:23 (minutes:seconds).
9. Mordecai M. Kaplan, diary, December 15, 1915, Mordecai M. Kaplan Diaries, August 1915 to January 1916.
10. Ulrich, *Midwife's Tale*.
11. Hadassah kept a diary erratically for seven years, beginning when she was nine years old and again when she was nineteen into her early twenties. Unlike her younger sister, Selma, Hadassah did not join her school's newspaper or literary magazine. She does not appear to have sought to write professionally, yet she did imbibe her father's practice of journaling.
12. Imhoff, *Lives of Jessie Sampter*, 14; Shandler and Wenger, "Site of Paradise," 11–12.
13. Shapira, *Israel*, 469; Kaplan, "Truth about Reconstructionism"; Divine, *Exile in the Homeland*, 7–9, 13.
14. Krasner, *Benderly Boys*, 189–190; Ingall, "Three Cheers for Anna!," 14.
15. Kaplan, "Status of the Jewish Woman," 12. The article was reprinted in *The Reconstructionist Papers* (1936) and in Kaplan's *The Future of the American Jew* (1948).

16 Mordecai Kaplan, diary, October 12, 1930, in *Communings*, vol. 1, 427–428; A. Goren, "Celebrating Zion in America," 41.
17 Kaplan, "Truth about Reconstructionism" (quote); Scult, *Judaism Faces the Twentieth Century*, 309–312; Pianko, *Zionism and the Roads Not Taken*, 96, 122, 127. Note that I am purposely using a lower case r when describing Mordecai Kaplan's vision as opposed to the Reconstructionist movement, which I will capitalize. Rather than initiating reconstructionism as a movement, Kaplan sought to establish it as an ideology that would influence and unite Jews across denominations, including those who identified with the Orthodox, Conservative, and Reform movements. Indeed, Reconstructionism only became its own movement in 1968, under the guidance of Ira Eisenstein, Kaplan's protégé and son-in-law (and my great-uncle). The Reconstructionist Rabbinical College opened five years after Kaplan retired from a more-than-fifty-year career as a teacher and administrator within the Jewish Conservative movement's rabbinical school, the Jewish Theological Seminary. See D. Musher, "Reconstructionist Judaism."
18 Scult, *Radical American Judaism*, 101.
19 Ofer Aderet, "Hebrew Language in Israel Was Difficult beyond Words," *Haaretz*, February 20, 2022, www.haaretz.com. Original research in Shavit, "What Did Hebrew Children Speak." Note that the decimation of European Jewry during the Holocaust in the middle of the nineteenth century hastened the decline of Yiddish, but the revival of spoken Hebrew happened well before that time. On language multiplicity in Palestine, see Halperin, *Babel in Zion*, 4–5, 10–12, 17.
20 For a critical evaluation of Ben-Yehuda's contribution to the revival of spoken Hebrew, see Kuzar, *Hebrew and Zionism*, 84–120. For the relationship between Ben-Yehuda and his second wife and her contributions toward Hebrew revival, see Berlovitz, "Hemdah Ben-Yehuda."
21 Pianko, *Zionism and the Roads Not Taken*, 10.
22 For a thoughtful discussion of the challenges young German refugees faced in acclimating to Palestine and learning Hebrew and the efforts made by their hosts to accommodate their needs, see Hacohen, *To Repair a Broken World*, 279, 281–282, 284–285; and Halperin, *Babel in Zion*, 1–4.
23 There were, of course, exceptions within the Orthodox world, especially Rabbi Abraham Isaac Kook and the Mizrachi, religious Zionist, movement founded in 1902. For a more nuanced discussion, see Reinharz, "Conflict between Zionism and Traditionalism."
24 Knee, *Concept of Zionist Dissent*, ix, 229 (quote).
25 N. Cohen, *Year after the Riots*, 22.
26 Gruber, *Ahead of Time*, chap. 14.
27 Relevant literature examining women's contributions to Zionism includes Bernstein, *Pioneers and Homemakers*; Raider and Raider-Roth, *Plough Woman*; Reinharz and Raider, *American Jewish Women*; Kark et al., *Jewish Women in Pre-State Israel*. Recent biographies of female Jewish travelers and women in Palestine/Israel

include Hacohen, *To Repair a Broken World*; Imhoff, *Lives of Jessie Sampter*; Lahav, *Only Woman in the Room*; Kessner, *Marie Syrkin*; and Sinkoff, *From Left to Right*.
28 1931 Census of Palestine, November 18, 1931, accessed at Economic Cooperation Foundation, https://ecf.org.il; K. Stein, *Land Question in Palestine*, 81, 100–101, 115, 118, 142, 146, 216.
29 Marzano, "Visiting British Palestine," 197–199.
30 M. Pratt, *Imperial Eyes*, 5.
31 Mel Scult has written and edited the bulk of the literature about and by Mordecai Kaplan. See, for example, Scult, *Judaism Faces the Twentieth Century*; Scult, *Radical American Judaism*; Kaplan, *Communings*, vol. 1; Kaplan, *Communings*, vol. 2; Kaplan, *Communings*, vol. 3.
32 To find Julia Dushkin's papers at the Archive of the History of the Jewish People, one needs to look under the name of her husband, Alexander. Similarly, the papers of Mathilde Schechter are folded into the Solomon Schechter Family Collection at the Jewish Theological Seminary. As these examples suggest, the papers of wives are often hidden among those of their husbands and require purposeful reclamation. Imhoff, *Lives of Jessie Sampter*, 12.
33 See, for example, definitions of antisemitism by the International Holocaust Remembrance Alliance, the Nexus Document, and the Jerusalem Declaration on Antisemitism. International Holocaust Remembrance Alliance, "Working Definition of Antisemitism"; Israel & Antisemitism, "Nexus Document"; Jerusalem Declaration on Antisemitism, home page.
34 Pianko, *Zionism and the Roads Not Taken*, 3.

CHAPTER 1. CHOOSING TO GO
1 Moore, foreword to Gurock, *Jews in Gotham*, xi, xiv. See also Rischin, *Promised City*.
2 Moore, foreword to Gurock, *Jews in Gotham*, xi, xii.
3 US Holocaust Memorial Museum, "Jewish Population of Europe in 1933."
4 Moore et al., *Jewish New York*, 189.
5 Moore, *Urban Origins of American Judaism*, 101; Moore et al., *Jewish New York*, 77–99, 201.
6 Gurock, *Jews in Gotham*, 30.
7 Scult, *Judaism Faces the Twentieth Century*, 28–29.
8 Lena Rubin, US Federal Census, 1900, accessed November 8, 2022, www.ancestrylibrary.com.
9 Scult, *Judaism Faces the Twentieth Century*, 94–95; David Musher interview.
10 Hadassah K. Musher, obituary, *New York Times*, March 13, 2013, www.legacy.com; Antler, "Zion in Our Hearts," 134; Katsburg-Yungman, *Hadassah*, 1, 18. Here and throughout the book, I have italicized "Hadassah" in reference to the organization to distinguish the woman Hadassah from the organization.
11 Katsburg-Yungman, *Hadassah*, 1.

12 "Historical Note," Teachers Institute/Seminary College of Jewish Studies Record, Jewish Theological Seminary Archive, Special Collections, https://archives.jtsa.edu, citing David Kaufman, "Jewish Education as a Civilization," in *Tradition Renewed: A History of the Jewish Theological Seminary*, ed. Jack Wertheimer (New York: JTS, 1997).
13 Federal Writers' Project, *WPA Guide to New York City*, 275, 284.
14 Federal Writers' Project, 275, 284. In 1930, Teachers' Institute moved into JTS's Unterberg Building in Morning Side Heights, which ensconced Mordecai more firmly in the Upper West Side.
15 Judith tutored with both the Hebrew poet and educator Hillel Bavli and also Max Kadushin, a rabbinical student of Mordecai's who would soon become a rabbi and leading scholar. Scult, *Judaism Faces the Twentieth Century*, 165. Judith and Ira Eisenstein interview, cassette 24a, 6:18.
16 Judith and Ira Eisenstein interview, cassette 24a, 10:15, 13:05.
17 Baker, "Judith Kaplan Eisenstein."
18 It is somewhat surprising to see such an honest expression of uncensored anger, given that Hadassah knew that her father had read her older sister's diary. Indeed, in 1922, the ten-year-old Hadassah responded to her father's request to read Judith's diary, which he had already done, by offering to bring it to him. Judith herself eventually gave the diary to her father, but not before removing the pages where she had written critically about him. Hadassah Kaplan, diary, April 18, 1926 (quote), personal collection. See also Mordecai Kaplan, diary, December 7 and 10, 1922, in *Communings*, vol. 1, 171–172.
19 Mark Wenner interview.
20 Selma Goldman, "We Luv," in *When We Were Very Young . . . and a Little Later, Too*," n.d., personal collection.
21 Mark Wenner interview.
22 Gurock, *Jews in Gotham*, 55.
23 Scult, *Judaism Faces the Twentieth Century*, 189–194, 192 (quote).
24 The Kaplans had actually pulled nine-year-old Judith from the Jewish Center's Hebrew school shortly after enrolling her. The program was insufficiently rigorous for the young scholar. Scult, 353.
25 Hadassah Kaplan Musher interview (Price).
26 Kaplan, "Status of the Jewish Woman," 12. This work was later revised and reprinted in *The Reconstructionist Papers* and in Kaplan's *Future of the American Jew*.
27 Moore, "Judaism as a Gendered Civilization," 172; Waxman, "From the First Bat Mitzvah."
28 Eisenstein, "Judith Kaplan Eisenstein Becomes the First Bat Mitzvah," 30–31.
29 Eisenstein, 32.
30 M. Kaplan, diary, March 28, 1922, in *Communings*, vol. 1, 159. The bat mitzvah occurred on March 18 at 41 West Eighty-Sixth Street.
31 Mordecai Kaplan, quoted in Moore, "Judaism as a Gendered Civilization," 180.

32 Green, *Ready-to-Wear*, 23, 47–48; Selma Goldman interview.
33 Hadassah Kaplan, "Bas Mitzvah Pledge," SAJ, January 5, 1924, personal collection.
34 Waxman, "From the First Bat Mitzvah."
35 H. Kaplan, diary, January 5, 1924.
36 Goldman interview.
37 R. Stein, "Road to Bat Mitzvah in America," 225; Joselit, *Wonders of America*.
38 Judith Kaplan, diary, September 12, 1922, personal collection.
39 J. Kaplan, diary, September 13, 1922.
40 "Biographical/Historical Information," Wadleigh High School Collection.
41 J. Kaplan, diary, September 12, 1922, and October 23, 1922.
42 Judith and Ira Eisenstein interview, 28:53, 23a.
43 Baker, "Judith Kaplan Eisenstein."
44 M. Kaplan, diary, December 15, 1927, in *Communings*, vol. 1, 252.
45 H. K. Musher interview (Price).
46 H. Kaplan, diary, July 5, 1921, personal collection.
47 Wenger, *Uncertain Promise*, 63.
48 Grunfeld, "Hunter College."
49 *The Wistarion* (Hunter College of the City of New York) 29 (1931).
50 Gurock, *Jews in Gotham*, 50.
51 Markowitz, *My Daughter*, 19, 16; Wenger, *Uncertain Promise*, 23.
52 Wouk, *Marjorie Morningstar*; Markowitz, *My Daughter*, 32; Irving Rapper, dir., *Marjorie Morningstar*, film (Beachwold Productions, 1958); Newhouse, "Marjorie Morningstar"; Maxwell Geismar, "The Roots and the Flowering Tree: Mr. Wouk's New Novel Explores the Clash between a Girl's Heritage and Her Dreams," review of *Marjorie Morningstar*, by Herman Wouk, *New York Times*, September 4, 1955, https://timesmachine.nytimes.com.
53 Hadassah Kaplan Musher interview (author).
54 Scult, *Judaism Faces the Twentieth Century*, 352.
55 H. Kaplan, diary, October 5, 1932.
56 Reinharz and Raider, introduction to *"Em Leemahot,"* 216. Hadassah promised her grandmothers that she would not drive faster than thirty miles an hour in the Willy's Knight, an assurance she no doubt recanted. Although no concrete record clarifies either from whom she bought the car or where she kept it, family myth suggests that she purchased it from a boyfriend and kept it in Deal, New Jersey, where her parents rented a summer home. For the manufacturer's suggested retail price of a Willy's Knight in 1929, see www.nadaguides.com.
57 H. K. Musher interview (author).
58 Markowitz, *My Daughter*, 29.
59 H. K. Musher interview (author) (quote).
60 Greenberg and Zenchelsky, "Private Bias and Public Responsibility," 308. For a similar story at the University of Minnesota, see also Prell, "Antisemitism without Quotas," 160.
61 Markowitz, *My Daughter*, 29, 15.

62 Judith taught music at Teachers' Institute, Selma taught literature at Fieldston, and Hadassah substitute taught in public schools.
63 Kobrin, "Teaching Profession in the United States."
64 Weinberg, "Longing to Learn," 110–114.
65 "Only 376 on License Number One List," *New York Sun*, March 12, 1932, personal collection.
66 Markowitz, *My Daughter*, 86, 24.
67 Gurock, *Jews in Gotham*, 31–32.
68 J. Cohen, *Jews, Jobs and Discrimination*, 17–18.
69 J. Cohen, 19 (emphasis in original).
70 Wenger, *Uncertain Promise*, 20, 23–24, 61–62; Gurock, *Jews in Gotham*, 51–2; Fermaglich, "Too Long, Too Foreign," 45.
71 Markowitz, *My Daughter*, 87–88.
72 M. Kaplan, diary, April 20, 1928, in *Communings*, vol. 1, 258.
73 Gurock, *Jews in Gotham*, 50.
74 Mykoff, "Summer Camping in the United States."
75 Wenger, *Uncertain Promise*, 58–59; Currell, *March of Spare Time*, 13.
76 Quoted in J. Cohen, *Jews, Jobs and Discrimination*, 26.
77 Fermaglich, "Too Long, Too Foreign," 34–35, 43.
78 Wenger, *Uncertain Promise*, 23–24; Markowitz, *My Daughter*, 18, 70, 90.
79 Judith Addelston to H. Kaplan, March 20, 1933, 4–5. All Kaplan family correspondence from the author's personal collection.
80 For examples, see L. Kaplan to H. Kaplan, August 14, 1932, and January 5, 1933; Judith Addelston to H. Kaplan, November 22, 1932; John Sundelson to H. Kaplan, December 8, 1932.
81 Miriam Eisenstein interview.
82 Baker, "Judith Kaplan Eisenstein"; Markowitz, *My Daughter*, 132.
83 Markowitz, *My Daughter*, 134, 140; Kessler-Harris, *In Pursuit of Equity*, 56–61.
84 L. Kaplan to H. Kaplan, January 9, 1933, 1; Sundelson, "Budgetary Methods in National and State Governments"; Clark and Sundelson, *Economics of Planning Public Works*; "Janet Racolin to Be a Bride," *New York Times*, February 26, 1939, 44, https://timesmachine.nytimes.com; H. K. Musher interview (author).
85 Ralph Lieberman to H. Kaplan, October 17, 1932; Jack Wilner Sundelson to H. Kaplan, March 20, 1933; H. Kaplan, diary, October 5, 1932.
86 H. Kaplan, SAJ Diary, 1931–1932, September 20, 1932, personal collection.
87 H. Kaplan, diary, October 5, 1932; Selma Kaplan to H. Kaplan, January 22, 1933, 6.
88 H. K. Musher interview (author); Sidney Musher, oral history, 10, 19. Sidney Musher, Milk Substitutes, A23C11/04, patent application, July 28, 1931, US Patent Office, https://patents.google.com.
89 Judith Addelston to H. Kaplan, March 20, 1933, 3–4.
90 Wenger, "Budgets, Boycotts, and Babies," 192.
91 Wenger, *Uncertain Promise*, 60.
92 Weller, "Unattached Woman," 54.

93 Reinharz and Raider, introduction to *"Em Leemahot,"* 216.
94 Moore et al., *Jewish New York*, 198.
95 Wenger, *Uncertain Promise*, 15–17, 47 (quote), 48, 85 (chart), 94; Wenger, "Budgets, Boycotts, and Babies," 185.
96 Wenger, *Uncertain Promise*, 170–171.
97 Scult, *Judaism Faces the Twentieth Century*, 357.
98 L. Kaplan to H. Kaplan, January 17, 1933, 1.
99 Ira Eisenstein, oral history. Eisenstein considered leaving the SAJ many times, but Kaplan threatened to close the institution if he did. Eventually, in 1954, the Eisensteins left for Chicago with their young family.
100 Jonathan [Rubin?] to H. Kaplan, February 22, 1933.
101 Quoted in Scult, *Judaism Faces the Twentieth Century*, 163.
102 Panitz, "Jewish Theological Seminary."
103 Scult, *Judaism Faces the Twentieth Century*, 348; Seymour and Naomi Wenner interview, 1:45.
104 Scult, *Judaism Faces the Twentieth Century*, 348; H. K. Musher, oral history. Note there is a chance that Hadassah was referring to her own mother, Lena, as an occasional accountant rather than her grandmother.
105 L. Kaplan to H. Kaplan, January 1, 1933, 4–5.
106 H. K. Musher interview (author).
107 See, for example, L. Kaplan to H. Kaplan, December 5, 1932, 5, and January 12, 1933, 3.
108 L. Kaplan to H. Kaplan, January 31, 1933, 2.
109 H. K. Musher interview (author). In a letter, Mordecai made a slightly different promise to her than the one she recalled. In that account, he offered her $100 if she put on eight (rather than ten) pounds. Reinforcing the importance of her gaining weight, Mordecai continued by commenting on the occasion of New York police commissioner and politician John Voorhis's one hundredth birthday. "I am sure," Mordecai explained about Voorhis, "he never tried to look thin. He must have eaten good wholesome food and didn't worry about reducing. . . . The bell has rung." Mordecai concluded, "The lecture is over." M. Kaplan to H. Kaplan, July 28, 1929. Advertisements for healthy models at the time suggested that an ideal woman would be about five foot four and weigh roughly 120 pounds. "Too Fat or Too Thin—1933 & 1934," *Witness2Fashion* (blog), May 22, 2016, https://witness2fashion.wordpress.com. Considering contradictory official documents testifying to Hadassah's height, at nineteen, she was probably five foot five. When she was fourteen, she reported to her parents that she was the only one at camp who was determined to be neither over- nor underweight (although she did not include either her weight or the criteria for those categories). H. Kaplan to M. Kaplan and L. Kaplan, July 8, 1926.
110 H. Kaplan to family, January 24, 1933, 1.
111 L. Kaplan to H. Kaplan, February 14, 1933, 1.
112 H. Kaplan diary, n.d.

113 H. Kaplan to family, March 7, 1933; H. K. Musher interview (author).
114 Wenger, *Uncertain Promise*, 10.
115 M. Kaplan, diary, December 11, 1930, in *Communings*, vol. 1, 432.
116 Markowitz, *My Daughter*, 18.
117 Rosenberg, *Changing the Subject*, 4, 140–142, 144.
118 Prell, "Antisemitism without Quotas," 158; McCaughey, *Stand, Columbia*; Oppenheimer, "Columbia and Its Forgotten Jewish Campus."
119 Scult, *Judaism Faces the Twentieth Century*, 53, 79–81.
120 Naomi and Seymour Wenner interview, 3:34; M. Kaplan, diary, January 31, 1925, in *Communings*, vol. 1, 195.
121 Naomi and Seymour Wenner interview.
122 Israel Unterberg to H. Kaplan, September 19, 1932.
123 L. Kaplan to H. Kaplan, February 14, 1933, 1.
124 Glass, *From New Zion to Old Zion*, 23, 327.
125 Feingold, *Time for Searching*, 199.

CHAPTER 2. THE ATTRACTION
1 Mordecai Kaplan, diary, January 9, 1932, in *Communings*, vol. 1, 466–467.
2 M. Kaplan, diary, June 13, 1931, 449.
3 M. Kaplan, diary, June 13, 1931, 449.
4 Rose Jacobs's younger brother also studied at City College New York and participated in the Menorah Society with Albert Schoolman and Alexander Dushkin. Cyrille White (Jacobs's niece) interview.
5 Krasner, *Benderly Boys*, 269, 274–301.
6 Dushkin, *Living Bridges*, 67–68.
7 Quoted in Krasner, *Benderly Boys*, 320. Note that Gribetz was referring to his impression of Zionism at Cejwin in this interview, but inasmuch as he was speaking more generally about the religious and ideological bent of the Schoolmans, the comment is also applicable to Modin.
8 H. Kaplan to L. and M. Kaplan, July 5, 1927 (quote), and July 14, 1926. All Kaplan family correspondence from the author's personal collection.
9 H. Kaplan to family, May 7, 1933, 3.
10 Hadassah Kaplan, diary, August 28, 1923, personal collection.
11 H. Kaplan, diary, n.d. (circa 1926).
12 Sylva Gelber to H. Kaplan, September 12, 1926.
13 H. Kaplan, diary, July 26, 1927; H. Kaplan to L. Kaplan and M. Kaplan, July 27, 1927.
14 M. Kaplan, diary, August 21, 1927, in *Communings*, vol. 1, 250.
15 Deborah Waxman, "Lady Sometimes Blows the Shofar," 87.
16 Gelber, *No Balm in Gilead*, 3.
17 Carr, *Hebrew Orient*, 23, 211–222.
18 Salomea Neumark, "Palestine without Zionism: A Non-political Viewpoint," *Jewish Exponent*, August 15, 1924, 1, ProQuest Historical Newspapers.

19 Berkowitz, *Western Jewry*, 138–139.
20 Krasner, *Benderly Boys*, 319; A. Goren, *Politics and Public Culture*, 168; Berkowitz, *Western Jewry*, 103 (quote).
21 Carr, *Hebrew Orient*, 9–11, 41.
22 Joselit and Mittleman, *Worthy Use of Summer*; Fox, *Jews of Summer*.
23 Ingall, "Three Cheers for Anna!," 149; Scult, *Judaism Faces the Twentieth Century*, 113, 148, 189; Wenger, *Uncertain Promise*, 193, 194.
24 Shandler and Wenger, "Site of Paradise," 11–13.
25 Lord Lionel Walter Rothschild to Arthur James Balfour, November 2, 1917, Balfour Declaration, 1, https://balfourproject.org.
26 Scult, *Judaism Faces the Twentieth Century*, 330 (quote); M. Kaplan, diary, December 29, 1918, in *Communings*, vol. 1, 133.
27 Dushkin, *Living Bridges*, 25.
28 Rennella and Walton, "Planned Serendipity," 372.
29 Klapper, "Great Adventure," 86.
30 Coons and Varias, *Steamship Travel in the Interwar Years*, preface.
31 Soyer, "Revisiting the Old World," 19.
32 Berkowitz, *Western Jewry*, 130 (quote), 134 (quote); Hazbun, "East as an Exhibit"; and Kark, "From Pilgrimage to Budding Tourism."
33 Berkowitz, *Western Jewry*, 129 (quote), 131, 140, 146 (quote).
34 Quoted in Berkowitz, 141–142.
35 Berkowitz, 125, 144 (quote).
36 Klapper, "Great Adventure," 93, 86–87. Young Black women similarly were impacted by international travel. See, for example, Witmire, "Experience 1930s Europe."
37 Schwartz, "Rebecca Aaronson Brickner," 67, 68 (quote).
38 Ingall, introduction to *Women Who Reconstructed American Jewish Education*, 2.
39 Glass, "American Olim," 210.
40 Davidson, *America's Palestine*, 2.
41 Glass, "American Olim," 209, 210.
42 Simmons, "Playgrounds and Penny Lunches," 272–273; Reinharz and Raider, introduction to *American Jewish Women*, xxi.
43 Antler, "Zion in Our Hearts," 140; Reinharz and Raider, introduction to *American Jewish Women*, xxi–xxvi.
44 See, for example, Gal, "Zionist Vision of Henrietta Szold," 30–31, 35–36.
45 L. Kaplan to H. Kaplan, November 21, 1932, 3.
46 Gelber, *No Balm in Gilead*, 5–8.
47 Gelber, 10.
48 Central Conference of American Rabbis, "Declaration of Principles: The Pittsburgh Platform."
49 Sarna, "Converts to Zionism in the American Reform Movement," 189; Central Conference of American Rabbis, "Guiding Principles of Reform Judaism."
50 Berkowitz, *Western Jewry*, 125.

51 Glass, "Settling the Old-New Homeland," 192–193.
52 Glass, *From New Zion to Old Zion*, 19, 21–22, 25; Glass, "Settling the Old-New Homeland," 193.
53 Glass, *From New Zion to Old Zion*, 328; Mickenberg, *American Girls in Red Russia*, 1–6, 19–20.
54 Glass, *From New Zion to Old Zion*, 13.
55 Glass, 29; Glass, "Settling the Old-New Homeland," 193.
56 Glass, *From New Zion to Old Zion*, 309, 325; Glass, "Settling the Old-New Homeland," 194.
57 Krasner, *Benderly Boys*, 84–85. For more on Deborah Kallen, see Schmidt, "Deborah Kallen."
58 Eisen, "Mordecai Kaplan's 'Judaism as a Civilization' at 70," 6.
59 Kaplan, *Judaism as a Civilization*, 439–442.
60 Scult, *Judaism Faces the Twentieth Century*, 151–153; M. Kaplan, diary, January 25, 1914, in *Communings*, vol. 1, 63.
61 For a more detailed discussion of the evolving relationship between peoplehood and nationalism in Mordecai Kaplan's thinking, see Pianko, *Jewish Peoplehood*, 29, 31–34, 39–53.
62 Scult, *Judaism Faces the Twentieth Century*, 169.
63 Halpern, "Americanization of Zionism," 22.
64 Wenger, *Uncertain Promise*, 193.
65 Reinharz and Raider, introduction to *American Jewish Women*, 7; Reinharz and Raider, introduction to "*Em Leemahot*," 216; Berkowitz, *Western Jewry*, 56.
66 Kaplan, *Future of the American Jew*, 361.
67 Scult, *Judaism Faces the Twentieth Century*, 25–26, 308–309; Pianko, *Zionism and the Roads Not Taken*, 10–11, 131–132; M. Kaplan, diary, October 12, 1930, in *Communings*, vol. 1, 428 (quote).
68 Kaplan, *New Zionism*, 26.
69 Scult, *Judaism Faces the Twentieth Century*, 309–312; Krasner, *Benderly Boys*, 77, 78; Mordecai M. Kaplan, diary, October 4, 1914, 94, Mordecai M. Kaplan Diaries, October 1914–January 1915 (quote).
70 M. Kaplan, diary, October 12, 1930, in *Communings*, vol. 1, 427–428; A. Goren, "Celebrating Zion in America," 41.
71 M. Kaplan, diary, November 30, 1926, in *Communings*, vol. 1, 235 (quote).
72 Noam Pianko argues that Mordecai Kaplan was an antistatist and multiculturalist who argued for ethical nationhood grounded in religious traditions and shared values. While I agree with Pianko's understanding of Kaplan's emphasis on cultural Zionism and ambivalence toward nationalism, Pianko does not sufficiently take into consideration Kaplan's and his family's lived experiences, including the years they chose to spend in Palestine and later the State of Israel. See Pianko, *Zionism and the Roads Not Taken*, 96, 122, 127.
73 Gurock and Schacter, *Modern Heretic*, 53–56.
74 Scult, *Judaism Faces the Twentieth Century*, 103–104.

75 See, for example, M. Kaplan, diary, August 14, 1932, in *Communings*, vol. 1, 300.
76 N. Pratt, "Transitions in Judaism," 699.
77 H. Kaplan to family, April 25, 1933.
78 Kaplan, "What the American Jewish Woman Can Do," 139.
79 Kaplan, 140, 142 (quote), 145 (quote).
80 M. Kaplan, sermon at Jewish Center, September 29, 1918, Reconstructionist Rabbinical College Archives, quoted in Scult, *Judaism Faces the Twentieth Century*, 169.
81 Pianko, "Reconstructing Judaism," 49–52.
82 M. Kaplan, diary, December 29, 1918, in *Communings*, vol. 1, 134.
83 M. Kaplan, diary, March 20, 1925, 201.
84 Kaplan, *New Zionism*, 12, 26, 99.
85 M. Kaplan, diary, August 30,1929, in *Communings*, vol. 1, 358.
86 N. Cohen, *Year after the Riots*, 11 (quote).
87 "Pogroms in Palestine."
88 "Revolt of the Oppressed Arab Masses."
89 M. Kaplan, diary, August 30, 1929, in *Communings*, vol. 1, 427.
90 M. Kaplan, diary, November 20, 1929, 377.
91 Hacohen, *To Repair a Broken World*, 116.
92 M. Kaplan, diary, November 26, 1929, in *Communings*, vol. 1, 380–381. His ongoing ambivalence can be seen a few years later, after hearing the historian Hans Kohn discuss Arab nationalism and his objections to Zionism. "I became convinced by his main talk," Kaplan reflected, "that we Jews are in an awful mess with prospects in Palestine no less than with our economic and spiritual prospects throughout the world. . . . The Jews have gotten themselves into such a tangle that by persisting to stand out as a distinct group they are contributing in no small measure to the conclusion that human life is the most senseless and meaningless phase of reality." M. Kaplan, diary, December 21, 1933, *Communings*, vol. 1, 465.
93 Scholars disagree about what to call the events that took place in Palestine in August 1929. Some call them the "Wailing/Western Wall" or "Al-Buraq" riot, but since the violence spread well beyond Jerusalem to Hebron, Safed, Haifa, and Jaffa, that title does not adequately capture the extent of the unrest. The historian Naomi Kaplan's more geographically expansive term, the Palestine "riots" or "crisis" of 1929, is more apt, but the term "riot" emphasizes the lawlessness and disorder of the events rather than the discontents motivating them. Seeking to provide political legitimization for growing Arab nationalism and to draw attention to Arab Palestinian protests against Jewish migration and land acquisition, other scholars consider the events of 1929 a rebellion, revolt, or uprising. Indeed, the scholar Hillel Cohen locates the origins of the Arab-Israeli conflict in the violence of 1929, rather than 1948, Israel's War of Independence, or 1967, the beginning of Israel's occupation of Palestinian lands following the Six-Day War. There is more consensus regarding what to call a second round of violence between Palestinian Jews and Arabs just a few years later: the "Great" or "Arab Revolt of 1936 to 1939."

At that point, Arab violence against Jews in Palestine was coupled with economic activism, including a general strike or boycott of the Jewish market, paralleling the global Jewish anti-Nazi boycott effort, as well as political organizing, such as the Arab Higher Committee's demands to end Jewish immigration and land sales and create a representational government. In contrast, the violence in the summer of 1929 was not accompanied by significant political and economic organizing. In an attempt to acknowledge the national aspirations of Arab Palestinians, while also recognizing the bloodshed that Jews (and Arabs) endured that summer, I refer to the events of the summer of 1929 as a crisis, disturbance, or violence as opposed to a riot or uprising. N. Cohen, *Year after the Riots*, 93; H. Cohen, *Year Zero*, xi, 18; Anderson, "State Formation," 39–41.
94 Dushkin, "Sanity in the Teaching of Palestine," 66.
95 Hadassah Kaplan Musher interview (Price).
96 "Launches New Boat Today," *New York Times*, October 18, 1930, sec. S, 35, https://timesmachine.nytimes.com.

CHAPTER 3. THE JOURNEY
1 Fiell, *1930s Fashion Sourcebook*, 22.
2 Helman, *Coat of Many Colors*, 13, 40.
3 Fiell, *1930s Fashion Sourcebook*, 22.
4 *The Wistarion* (Hunter College of the City of New York) 29 (1931).
5 Rennella and Walton, "Planned Serendipity," 377.
6 Quoted in Rennella and Walton, 369.
7 Rennella and Walton, 377 (quote), 366 (quote), 367 (quote).
8 Short, introduction to "Women Writing Travel," 5; Steadman, *Traveling Economies*, 20.
9 Steadman, *Traveling Economies*, 4–5; Melman, *Women's Orients*, 316; Carr, *Hebrew Orient*, 31 (quote).
10 "Launches New Boat Today," *New York Times*, October 18, 1930, sec. S, 35, https://timesmachine.nytimes.com. To view the interior of *Exochorda*, see Maritime Timetable Images, last modified October 8, 2006.
11 Hadassah Kaplan to family, September 26, 1932, 15. Note that Hadassah dated the letter she wrote to her family while sailing to Palestine only with days of the week. The dates recorded here are added retrospectively. All Kaplan family correspondence from the author's personal collection.
12 American Export Lines, "Mediterranean De Luxe Passenger Service," brochure, April 1932–June 1932, Maritime Timetable Images, last modified June 24, 2019.
13 Hadassah Kaplan, "budget," diary, n.d., personal collection.
14 H. Kaplan to family, December 16, 1932, 2. Hadassah wrote her family about Sylva's trip, but she might have misunderstood. Sylva recalled in her memoir having sailed an Italian liner called the *Vulcania* to Naples and then transferring to a small Lloyd Triestino ship to sail to Palestine. Lena and Judy would have seen her onto the *Vulcania*. Gelber, *No Balm in Gilead*, 10.

15 Naomi Kaplan to H. Kaplan, October 26, 1932, 2.
16 "Ship Fares Reduced to Mediterranean," *New York Times*, December 23, 1930, 43, https://timesmachine.nytimes.com.
17 "Holland America Line Cuts Fares" *New York Times*, January 8, 1930, 55, https://timesmachine.nytimes.com; "Reduces Ocean Rates," *New York Times*, January 10, 1930, 43, https://timesmachine.nytimes.com.
18 "Steamship Agents in Cruise Rate War," *New York Times*, February 3, 1932, 39, https://timesmachine.nytimes.com.
19 "Saturnia to Carry 1,500," *New York Times*, May 28, 1930, 51, https://timesmachine.nytimes.com; "Reports Travel Increase," *New York Times*, March 27, 1953, 43, https://timesmachine.nytimes.com.
20 "Vagabond Mediterranean Cruises," brochure, June 1934–May 1935, Maritime Timetable Images, last updated June 24, 2019.
21 Swiggum and Kohli, "Fleets."
22 "Cruise Bookings Set 5-Year Mark," *New York Times*, February 1, 1935, 43, https://timesmachine.nytimes.com.
23 H. Kaplan to family, September 26, 1932, 16.
24 For more on male homosexuality on cruises, see Baker and Stanley, *Hello Sailor*; Nilsson, "Cruising the Seas."
25 Snider, "Entropy and Exclusivity," 126; Kupferschmidt, "Who Needed Department Stores in Egypt?," 175, 176. The Hannauxs' stores were attacked by arson in 1948 and 1952. Following the Egyptian Revolution (1952), Nasser nationalized them.
26 Karlinsky, *California Dreaming*, 61–62; Tolkowsky, "Jewish Colonisation in Palestine"; Tolkowsky, *Gateway of Palestine*.
27 H. Kaplan to family, September 23, 1932, 4.
28 H. Kaplan to family, September 23, 1932, 4–5.
29 H. Kaplan to family, September 23, 1932, 11.
30 H. Kaplan to family, September 23, 1932, 4.
31 The Francis Newton on the passenger list is spelled with an *i*, whereas the missionary has an *e*. This either is a misspelling or might represent someone else. Marion Rubinstein, "'Mystery Woman' Smokes Pipe and Runs Haifa YWCA," *Appleton (WI) Post-Crescent*, October 17, 1934, 14, ProQuest Historical Newspapers: Wisconsin Collection.
32 "Inquiry Commission to Examine Grand Mufti Monday in Own Home," *Jewish Telegraphic Agency*, December 1, 1929, www.jta.org; Newton, *Fifty Years in Palestine*; Newton, *Palestine*. Newton wrote a pamphlet, *The Truth about the Mufti*, published by the Anglo-Arab Friendship Society in 1946. Newton, *Searchlight on Palestine*.
33 H. Kaplan to family, October 3, 1932.
34 Roberts, "Reba Rottenberg," 152 (quote).
35 Geni, "Fred J. Isaacson."
36 Rose Gell Jacobs's sister was married to Sis's brother.
37 Mordecai Kaplan, diary, March 12, 1925, in *Communings*, vol. 1, 197.

38 Antler, *Journey Home*, 204–214.
39 Note that I use this term to differentiate Palestinian Arabs from Palestinian Jews. At the time, both groups employed the term "Palestinian."
40 According to the minutes of a 1941 *Hadassah* committee meeting, David Ben-Gurion had discouraged the committee from investigating Arab-Jewish relations because of the war and the absence of Palestinian leaders willing to collaborate. According to Jacobs's account, Ben-Gurion did not want to deal with meddling American women, believing that they should, instead, leave this work up to the Jewish Agency. Z. Segev, "From Philanthropy to Shaping a State," 141.
41 Antler, *Journey Home*, 204, 207, 212–214.
42 Cyrille White, conversation with author, June 15, 2020.
43 Livingston Ferrand, quoted in Engst, *Jewish Life at Cornell*, 13–14.
44 Dushkin, *Living Bridges*, 47–57.
45 Rosen, "Bertha Singer Schoolman."
46 H. Kaplan to family, September 23, 1932.
47 H. Kaplan, "budget."
48 H. Kaplan to family, September 23, 1932, 4.
49 H. Kaplan to family, September 26, 1932.
50 Selma Kaplan to H. Kaplan, September 21, 1932.
51 Naomi Kaplan to H. Kaplan, September 21, 1932.
52 L. Kaplan to H. Kaplan, September 23, 1932, 2.
53 M. Kaplan to H. Kaplan, September 23, 1932.
54 Louis S. Posner to M. Kaplan, October 5, 1932.
55 L. Kaplan to H. Kaplan, October 3, 1932, 2–3.
56 H. Kaplan to family, September 23, 1932, 9, 10 (quote).
57 Henry to University of Chicago Alumni, Tulsa, Oklahoma, "Letter Box," 241.
58 H. Kaplan, diary, October 5, 1932. Although Hadassah dated this entry October 5, she probably actually wrote it later that month. Hadassah did not land in Palestine until October 9. Nevertheless, in the beginning of the October 5 entry, she describes herself writing about "more than a month" of her "adventure" in Jack Simon's "big chair" in his apartment in Palestine "(while he's on his way to Amman)." It seems that the diary represents a recap of the previous month's travel including dated subentries beginning on September 9. When available, I have included dated diary entries by those subheadings. Readers should recognize that this diary was written, at least initially, retrospectively. At times, dates are conflated, including descriptions of a few days.
59 H. Kaplan to family, September 28, 1932, 22–23.
60 H. Kaplan to family, September 26, 1932, 12–13.
61 H. Kaplan to family, September 26, 1932, 15.
62 "From New York City Came a Maid," poem, n.d., personal collection. This poem is undated and unsigned, but its placement in the archive suggests that the author penned it near the end of the trip. We do not have any written record from Parker

to compare, but the content and tone of the letter suggest that he wrote it. The handwriting does not match Read's.
63 H. Kaplan to family, September 26, 1933, 12–14, and September 29, 1933, 24.
64 H. Kaplan to family, September 29, 1933, 25.
65 H. Kaplan, diary, September 28, 1932. Hadassah probably wrote this on October 5 or later.
66 Spurlock, *Youth and Sexuality*, 58.
67 Zeitz, *Flapper*, 46.
68 Selma Kaplan to H. Kaplan, October 5, 1932.
69 H. Kaplan diary, September 30, 1932.
70 H. Kaplan to family, n.d. (circa October 1, 1932).
71 Ryann, *Holocaust and the Jews of Marseille*, 10, 220.
72 H. Kaplan, diary, October 1, 1932.
73 H. Kaplan, diary, October 3, 1932.
74 H. Kaplan to family, October 4, 1932, 2.
75 H. Kaplan, diary, October 3, 1932. This is an example of a diary entry that describes more than one day.
76 H. Kaplan, diary, October 3, 1932.
77 H. Kaplan to family, October 12, 1932.
78 H. Kaplan, diary, October 3, 1932.
79 Alvan "Read" Henry to H. Kaplan, October 27, 1932.
80 H. Kaplan to family, n.d. (circa October 1, 1932), 5–6.
81 H. Kaplan to family, October 4, 1932.
82 H. Kaplan, diary, October 6, 1932.
83 H. Kaplan to family, October 12, 1932, 4.
84 M. Pratt, *Imperial Eyes*, 5.
85 L. Kaplan to H. Kaplan, October 17, 1932, 1.
86 M. Kaplan, diary, February 25, 1934, in *Communings*, vol. 1, 515–516.
87 Hazbun, "East as an Exhibit," 18.
88 H. Kaplan to family, October 12, 1932.
89 H. Kaplan to family, October 10, 1932.
90 H. Kaplan, diary, October 6, 1932.
91 H. Kaplan, diary, October 7, 1932.
92 H. Kaplan, diary, October 7, 1932.
93 H. Kaplan to family, October 6, 1932, 5.
94 H. Kaplan to family, October 12, 1932, 4.
95 H. Kaplan to family, October 11, 1932.
96 H. Kaplan, diary, October 7, 1932.
97 H. Kaplan to family, October 10, 1932, 6.
98 H. Kaplan, diary, October 7, 1932.
99 H. Kaplan, diary, October 21, 1932.
100 Alan "Read" Henry to H. Kaplan, October 19, 1932, 1.

101 Alan "Read" Henry to H. Kaplan, October 12, 1933, 3.
102 H. Kaplan to Judith Kaplan, n.d. (circa August 1933), 2.

CHAPTER 4. GETTING SETTLED
1 T. Goren, "Struggle to Save the National Symbol," 864; T. Goren, "Relations between Tel Aviv and Jaffa," 2; LeVine, *Overthrowing Geography*, 2.
2 Monerescu and Hazan, *Twilight Nationalism*, 7.
3 LeVine, *Overthrowing Geography*, 34, 46–47, 89; T. Goren, "Developing Jaffa's Port," 179–181.
4 LeVine, *Overthrowing Geography*, 89.
5 A. Shavit, *My Promised Land*, 10.
6 Shandler and Wenger, "Site of Paradise," 13, 15.
7 H. Kaplan to family, October 10, 1932, 1. All Kaplan family correspondence from the author's personal collection.
8 Helman, *Young Tel Aviv*, 34.
9 Helman, 2–3, 15–16, 42, 105.
10 Shandler and Wenger, "Site of Paradise," 13, 15.
11 T. Segev, *One Palestine, Complete*, 380; Karlinsky, *California Dreaming*, 4.
12 Glass, "Settling the Old-New Homeland," 195; Helman, *Young Tel Aviv*, 160.
13 Helman, *Young Tel Aviv*, 19.
14 H. Kaplan to family, October 10, 1932, 2–3.
15 Shapira, *Israel*, 82.
16 H. Cohen, *Year Zero*, xxi, 26, 29; Mattar, "Al-Haram al-Sharif."
17 Quoted in Hacohen, *To Repair a Broken World*, 245.
18 H. Kaplan to family, October 10, 1932, 1.
19 H. Kaplan to family, October 21, 1932, 3.
20 H. Kaplan to family, October 10, 1932, 4.
21 Quoted in Imhoff, *Lives of Jessie Sampter*, 55–56.
22 H. Kaplan to family, September 23, 1932, 13.
23 Townshend, "Going to the Wall," 30–33.
24 Jewish Telegraphic Agency, "Shofar Sounded at Western Wall as 10,000 Israelis Participate in Closing Yom Kippur Rites," *Daily News Bulletin*, October 16, 1967, www.jta.org.
25 H. Kaplan to family, October 10, 1932, 2.
26 H. Kaplan to family, October 10, 1932, 3.
27 H. Kaplan to family, October 23, 1932.
28 H. Kaplan to family, October 12, 1932, 3.
29 Shandler and Wenger, "Site of Paradise," 15.
30 H. Kaplan to family, November 6, 1932, 1.
31 Quoted in Helman, *Young Tel Aviv*, 21.
32 Hadassah Kaplan Musher interview (author); H. Kaplan to family, November 28, 1932, 3.

33 Helman, *Young Tel Aviv*, 45–46.
34 H. Kaplan to family, November 28, 1932, 6.
35 H. Kaplan to family, November 22, 1932, 7; L. Kaplan to H. Kaplan, November 28, 1932; "Sylvia Lamport Wed to Ezra Z. Shapiro," *New York Times*, November 28, 1932, 12, https://timesmachine.nytimes.com; Case Western Reserve University, "Ezra Zelig Shapiro."
36 Karlinsky, *California Dreaming*, 5, 13.
37 LeVine, *Overthrowing Geography*, 89.
38 H. Kaplan to family, October 22, 1932, 4.
39 H. Kaplan to family, November 6, 1932, 1.
40 H. Kaplan to family, November 28, 1932, 5.
41 Quoted in Dauben, *Abraham Robinson*, 33.
42 H. Kaplan to family, October 22, 1932; H. Kaplan to family, November 28, 1932.
43 H. Kaplan to family, November 28, 1932, 5.
44 Divine, *Exiled in the Homeland*, 194–195, 197–198.
45 H. Kaplan to M. Kaplan, n.d.
46 M. Kaplan to H. Kaplan, October 17, 1932.
47 M. Kaplan to H. Kaplan, October 17, 1932.
48 L. Kaplan to H. Kaplan, October 12, 1932.
49 L. Kaplan to H. Kaplan, October 25, 1932.
50 L. Kaplan to H. Kaplan, November 1, 1932.
51 L. Kaplan to H. Kaplan, November 3, 1932, 1.
52 L. Kaplan to H. Kaplan, November 7, 1932, 3–4.
53 Sophie (Kaplan) Israeli to H. Kaplan, October 20, 1932.
54 Anna (Haya Nehama) Kaplan to H. Kaplan, October 21, 1932.
55 Prell, *Fighting to Become Americans*, 5–9.
56 Stern, "He Walked through the Fields," 164.
57 H. Kaplan to family, November 14, 1932, 3.
58 H. Kaplan to family, November 14, 1932, 3.
59 H. Kaplan to family, November 14, 1932.
60 Krasner, *Benderly Boys*, 87.
61 Ingall, "Three Cheers for Anna!," 143–146.
62 Bar-David, *My Promised Land*, 63.
63 H. Kaplan to family, October 28, 1932, 2.
64 L. Kaplan to H. Kaplan, October 17, 1932.
65 Hadassah Kaplan, diary, October 19, 2022, personal collection.
66 Gelber, *No Balm in Gilead*, 157–158.
67 H. Kaplan, diary, October 20, 2022.
68 H. Kaplan to family, October 15, 1932.
69 H. Kaplan to family, October 23, 1932, 1; H. Kaplan to family, November 5, 1932.
70 L. Kaplan to H. Kaplan, November 21, 1932, 2.
71 H. Kaplan to family, November 6, 1932.

72 H. Kaplan to family, November 6, 1932.
73 H. Kaplan to family, November 14, 1932, 1; H. Kaplan to family, November 25, 1932, 5; H. Kaplan to family, October 28, 1932; H. Kaplan to family, November 22, 1932, 7.
74 Nelson Glueck School of Biblical Archeology, "NGSBA Mission."
75 H. Kaplan to family, October 28, 1932.
76 H. Kaplan to family, November 2, 1932.
77 H. Kaplan to family, November 6, 1932.
78 L. Kaplan to H. Kaplan, November 14, 1932.
79 "Magnes (Beatrice L.) Family Papers and Photographs, 1861–1977," Magnes Collection Database. Beatrice Lowenstein Magnes's memoir is *Episodes*.
80 Kotzin, "Attempt to Americanize the Yishuv"; Barak-Gorodetsky, *Judah Magnes*; Hacohen, *To Repair a Broken World*, 207.
81 H. Kaplan to family, November 6, 1932, 5.
82 H. Kaplan to family, November 6, 1932, 5.
83 H. Kaplan to family, November 22, 1932.
84 Steadman, *Traveling Economies*, 4–5.
85 L. Kaplan to H. Kaplan, December 8, 1932, 1–2.
86 L. Kaplan to H. Kaplan, January 4, 1933, 2.
87 L. Kaplan to H. Kaplan, January 20, 1933, 1.
88 Ralph Lieberman to H. Kaplan, October 17, 1932.
89 Sydney Lichtman to H. Kaplan, November 12, 1932.
90 L. Kaplan to H. Kaplan, November 10, 1932.
91 H. Kaplan to family, November 14, 1932, 4.
92 L. Kaplan to H. Kaplan, November 10, 1932.
93 Divine, *Exiled in the Homeland*, 12, 136–137.
94 H. Kaplan to family, November 8, 1932.
95 H. Kaplan to family, November 28, 1932, 1–2.
96 Pruszynski, *Palestine for the Third Time*, 11–13.
97 Cited in Junior Hadassah, *Primer on Palestine*, 96.
98 L. Kaplan to H. Kaplan, November 21, 1932, 3 (author's emphasis).
99 For more on Friedlander, see Bentwich, *Lillian Ruth Friedlander*.
100 L. Kaplan to H. Kaplan, November 14, 1932, 1.
101 L. Kaplan to H. Kaplan, December 5, 1932, 1–2.
102 L. Kaplan to H. Kaplan, November 21, 1932, 2.
103 L. Kaplan to H. Kaplan, November 10, 1932, 1–4.
104 H. Kaplan to family, November 22, 1932, 7.
105 H. Kaplan to family, November 20, 1932.
106 Halperin, *Oldest Guard*, 14.
107 Near, *Kibbutz Movement*, 31; Imhoff, *Lives of Jessie Sampter*, 17.
108 H. Kaplan, diary, "Krutzoth" (colonies), n.d.
109 L. Kaplan to H. Kaplan, November 21, 1932, 1.
110 L. Kaplan to H. Kaplan, November 24, 1932.
111 Selma Kaplan to H. Kaplan, November 29, 1932.

112 M.M. Kaplan to H. Kaplan, December 11, 1932, transl. Joseph Benatov, 2015.
113 H. Kaplan to family, November 5, 1932, 13.
114 Stern, "He Walked through the Fields," 174.
115 H. Kaplan to family, October 23, 1932, 1.
116 H. Kaplan to family, November 28, 1932, 1.
117 H. Kaplan to family, November 28, 1932, 7.
118 H. Kaplan to family, December 6, 1932.
119 H. Kaplan to family, November 20, 1932.
120 H. Kaplan to family, December 6, 1932.
121 H. Kaplan to family, December 6, 1932, 1, 4; H. Kaplan to family, December 13, 1932, 1.
122 H. Kaplan to family, November 25, 1932.
123 H. Kaplan to family, November 28, 1932.
124 H. Kaplan to family, December 6, 1932, 4.
125 H. Kaplan to family, December 13, 1932.
126 H. Kaplan to family, December 13, 1932, 2.
127 Feuchtwanger, *Josephus*.
128 H. Kaplan to family, December 22, 1932, 1.
129 H. Kaplan to family, December 1, 1932.
130 H. Kaplan to L. Kaplan, December 7, 1932.
131 H. Kaplan to family, December 1, 1932.
132 H. Kaplan to M. Kaplan, n.d., trans. Joseph Benatov, 2015.
133 H. Kaplan to M. Kaplan, n.d.
134 L. Kaplan to H. Kaplan, December 25, 1932, 2–3.
135 Sophie Israeli to H. Kaplan, February 12, 1933, trans. Joseph Benatov, 2015.
136 Scult, *Judaism Faces the Twentieth Century*, 26, 351; S. Musher, "Reviving a 'Juniper in the Desert,'" 577.
137 Helman, *Coat of Many Colors*, 22–25, 40–41.
138 H. Kaplan to family, November 28, 1932; H. Kaplan to family, December 13, 1932; L. Kaplan to H. Kaplan, December 20, 1932; Helman, *Coat of Many Colors*, 22.
139 H. Kaplan to family, December 22, 1932, 2.
140 H. Kaplan to family, December 24, 1932, 6.
141 Helman, *Young Tel Aviv*, 59.
142 Spiegel, "Jewish Cultural Celebrations," 29.
143 Nahum Sokolow was an author and translator who succeeded Chaim Weizmann as the president of the World Zionist Organization from 1931 to 1935. See Holtzman, "Sokolow, Nahum."
144 H. Kaplan to family, December 25, 1932.
145 L. Kaplan to H. Kaplan, November 24, 1932.
146 L. Kaplan to H. Kaplan, November 21, 1932.

CHAPTER 5. FINDING HER WAY

1 H. Kaplan to family, n.d. (circa December 29, 1932). All Kaplan family correspondence from the author's personal collection.

2. Reid, *Contesting Antiquity in Egypt*, 146–147 (quote).
3. Byatt, introduction to *Arabian Nights*, xiv.
4. "Gisela Warburg Wyzanski, Zionist Leader, 79," obituary, *New York Times*, July 7, 1991, www.nytimes.com.
5. Gitre, *Acting Egyptian*, 5, 9–10, 15; Cormack, *Midnight in Cairo*, 7–9; Glauber-Zimra, "Summoning Spirits in Egypt," 25–38.
6. H. Kaplan to family, December 16, 1932; Read Henry to H. Kaplan, December 20, 1932, 3.
7. Reid, *Contesting Antiquity in Egypt*, 139, 169, 173.
8. On Western tourism in Egypt during the interwar period, see Hazbun, "East as an Exhibit"; and Reid, *Contesting Antiquity in Egypt*, 141–155.
9. Henry to H. Kaplan, December 20, 1932, 3.
10. L. Kaplan to H. Kaplan, January 12, 1933, 1.
11. Auerbach, *Print to Fit*, 24–25, 51–52; "Background," Levy (Joseph) Papers.
12. H. Kaplan to family, December 28, 1932, 3.
13. H. Kaplan to family, n.d. (circa December 29, 1932), 3.
14. L. Kaplan to H. Kaplan, January 12, 1933, 1.
15. H. Kaplan to family, January 11, 1933, 10.
16. L. Kaplan to H. Kaplan, January 12, 1933, 1.
17. L. Kaplan to H. Kaplan, January 12, 1933, 1.
18. H. Kaplan to family, January 4, 1933, 4; McLellan, "Golly, a Black Sherlock Holmes!," 13–14.
19. Vanderbilt, *Farewell to Fifth Avenue*, 221–227; C. G. Poore, "Cornelius Vanderbilt Jr.'s First Thirty-Five Years," review, *New York Times*, February 17, 1935, https://timesmachine.nytimes.com.
20. H. Kaplan to family, January 11, 1933, 3–4 (quote).
21. H. Kaplan to family, January 13, 1933, 7, 13 (quote).
22. Selma Kaplan to H. Kaplan, February 9, 1933.
23. L. Kaplan to H. Kaplan, January 1, 1933, 3.
24. L. Kaplan to H. Kaplan, January 31, 1933, 3.
25. L. Kaplan to H. Kaplan, January 11, 1933, 3.
26. The actual check amounted to $97. L. Kaplan to H. Kaplan, January 1, 1933, 4–5.
27. H. Kaplan to family, December 13, 1932; H. Kaplan to family, November 28, 1932, 8.
28. L. Kaplan to H. Kaplan, December 14, 1932.
29. L. Kaplan to H. Kaplan, January 4, 1933, 1.
30. L. Kaplan to H. Kaplan, January 12, 1933, 2.
31. L. Kaplan to H. Kaplan, January 12, 1933, 1–2.
32. L. Kaplan to H. Kaplan, January 31, 1933, 2.
33. L. Kaplan to H. Kaplan, February 7, 1933, 1–2.
34. N. Cohen, *Year after the Riots*, 56, 67, 99–100. For a longer discussion of non-Zionism, see Knee, "Jewish Non-Zionism."
35. L. Kaplan to H. Kaplan, January 24, 1933.

36 H. Kaplan to L. Kaplan, January 24, 1933.
37 L. Kaplan to H. Kaplan, February 14, 1933, 4–5.
38 L. Kaplan to H. Kaplan, February 14, 1933, 5.
39 H. Kaplan to L. Kaplan, February 13, 1933, 2.
40 "Ph.D. for Girl of 20," *New York Times*, August 16, 1932, https://timesmachine.nytimes.com.
41 Levine, *Allies and Rivals*, 207–208; Schafer, "W. E. B. Du Bois, German Social Thought, and the Racial Divide," 928–933.
42 Rennella and Walton, "Planned Serendipity," 372.
43 Review of Henry W. Simon's *What Is a Teacher?*
44 Selma Kaplan to H. Kaplan, February 9, 1933, 3.
45 Selma Kaplan to H. Kaplan, January 22, 1933.
46 Selma Kaplan to H. Kaplan, January 22, 1933.
47 Gruber, *Ahead of Time*, chap. 10.
48 L. Kaplan to H. Kaplan, February 22, 1933, 1.
49 Mordecai Kaplan, diary, May 17, 1933, in *Communings*, vol. 1, 503.
50 L. Kaplan to H. Kaplan, May 15, 1933, 3.
51 Judith Kaplan to H. Kaplan, March 20, 1933, 2.
52 Selma Kaplan to H. Kaplan, April 19, 1933, 5–6.
53 Rennella and Walton, "Planned Serendipity," 376.
54 Hadassah Kaplan, diary, "Ahad HaAm," n.d., personal collection.
55 H. Kaplan to family, March 1, 1933.
56 H. Kaplan to family, March 1, 1933; Judah Magnes, "Full Text Dr. Judah L. Magnes's Pamphlet 'Like All the Nations,'" *Daily News Bulletin* (Jewish Telegraphic Agency), January 24, 1930, www.jta.org.
57 Barak-Gorodetsky, *Judah Magnes*, 151–152, 184.
58 Magnes, "Like All the Nations," 5.
59 Magnes, 8.
60 Barak-Gorodetsky, *Judah Magnes*, 169 (quote).
61 H. Kaplan, diary, "J.L. Magnes, 'Like All the Nations,'" n.d.
62 Junior Hadassah, *Primer on Palestine*, 42, 44.
63 H. Kaplan to family, March 6, 1933.
64 H. Kaplan to family, March 7, 1933, 4.
65 M. Kaplan, diary, August 30, 1929, in *Communings*, vol. 1, 358–359.
66 Junior Hadassah, *Primer on Palestine*, 39, 46.
67 H. Kaplan to family, March 7, 1933, 4.
68 H. Kaplan to family, January 30, 1933.
69 H. Kaplan to family, January 30, 1933, 1–2.
70 Presumably Luke and Keith-Roach, *Handbook of Palestine*.
71 Magnes, "Like All the Nations," 7.
72 H. Kaplan to family, n.d. (circa February 20, 1933), 1.
73 H. Kaplan to L. Kaplan, February 13, 1933, 4–5.
74 H. Kaplan to L. Kaplan, February 14, 1933, 9.

75 Silber, "Why Did FDR's Bank Holiday Succeed?"
76 Naomi Kaplan to H. Kaplan, March 7, 1933, 1.
77 H. Kaplan to family, March 7, 1933, 1.
78 H. Kaplan to family, n.d.; H. Kaplan to family, March 25, 1933, trans. Joseph Benatov, 2015, 4.
79 H. Kaplan to L. Kaplan, February 13, 1933, 6.
80 Shoham, *Carnival in Tel Aviv*, 28, 36, 44.
81 H. Kaplan to family, n.d. (circa March 11, 1933).
82 Helman, *Young Tel Aviv*, 63, 65.
83 H. Kaplan to family, n.d. (circa March 11, 1933).
84 H. Kaplan to family, n.d. (circa March 11, 1933).
85 H. Kaplan to family, March 2, 1933; H. Kaplan to family, n.d. (circa March 11, 1933).
86 L. Kaplan to H. Kaplan, November 7, 1932, 3.
87 H. Kaplan to family, March 7, 1933, 4; H. Kaplan, diary, "Krutzoth" (colonies), n.d.
88 C. Waxman, *American Aliya*, 86.
89 L. Kaplan to H. Kaplan, February 22, 1933.
90 Gelber, *No Balm in Gilead*, 21, 23–24, 27–28.
91 M. Chazan, *Jewish Women and the Defense of Palestine*, 50–51, 79, 90.
92 Quoted in Lipsky, *Rise of Abe Cahan*, 152.
93 Waldinger, "Abraham Cahan and Palestine," 77–78, 87.
94 H. Kapan, diary, "Krutzoth" (colonies), n.d.
95 H. Kaplan to family, n.d. (circa March 1933).
96 Helman, *Coat of Many Colors*, 22–24.
97 Stern, "He Walked through the Fields," 161, 171, 177.
98 H. Kaplan to family, n.d. (circa March 16, 1933).
99 H. Kaplan to family, n.d. (circa March 1933).
100 H. Kaplan to family, March 27, 1933.
101 H. Kaplan to family, March 25, 1933, trans. Joseph Benatov, 2015; H. Kaplan diary, "Krutzoth" (colonies), n.d.
102 Divine, *Exiled in the Homeland*, 120–122.
103 Stern, "He Walked through the Fields," 171.
104 Danit, "With a Kvuzah of Shepherds," 39.
105 Lindheim, *Immortal Adventure*, 245.
106 H. Kaplan to family, March 27, 1933.
107 Fogiel-Bijaoui, "Kibbutz."
108 M. Chazan, *Jewish Women and the Defense of Palestine*, 51, 54 (quote), 58–59, 80 (quote).
109 H. Kaplan to family, November 21, 1932, 5.
110 H. Kaplan to family, March 27, 1933, 3.
111 H. Kaplan to family, March 27, 1933, 10.
112 Nadell, "'Long and Winding Road' to Women Rabbis," 33–34.
113 H. Kaplan to family, n.d. (circa March 16, 1933), 4; Judges 7:7, in Jewish Publication Society, *JPS Tanakh Gender Sensitive Edition*.

114 Lindheim, *Immortal Adventure*, 183–186.
115 Y. Katz, *Battle for the Land*, 338–339.
116 Karlinsky, *California Dreaming*, 5.
117 A. Shavit, *My Promised Land*, 26.
118 H. Kaplan to family, March 24, 1933, trans. Joseph Benatov, 2015.
119 K. Stein, *Land Question in Palestine*, 118, 127, 141, 163.
120 A. Shavit, *My Promised Land*, 26–47. Note that Shavit's work is journalistic rather than academic. Although he draws on interviews and Ein Harod's archives, he does not document his work. Also see Morris, *1948*, 96–97, 248, 299–308.
121 H. Kaplan to family, n.d. (circa March 16, 1933), 5.
122 H. Kaplan to family, March 24, 1933, trans. Joseph Benatov, 2015.
123 Gelber, *No Balm in Gilead*, 21.
124 H. Kaplan to family, n.d. (circa March 1933).
125 M. Kaplan to H. Kaplan, April 9, 1933. He also did not comment on the protest in his diary.
126 M. Kaplan, diary, March 24 and 28, 1933, 76–81, 81 (quote), 82, Mordecai M. Kaplan Diaries, 1933, January to March.
127 H. Kaplan to family, April 4, 1933, 2–3.
128 H. Kaplan to family, April 18, 1933.
129 H. Kaplan to family, April 18, 1933.
130 H. Kaplan to family, March 7, 1933, 3–4.
131 Harry Joffe to H. Kaplan, March 17, 1933.
132 Jack Wilner Sundelson to H. Kaplan ("Elsa"), March 20, 1933.
133 Milton I. Levine to H. Kaplan, March 30, 1933, 4.
134 Naomi Kaplan to H. Kaplan, March 20, 1933, 7–8.
135 Albert "Al" Addelston to H. Kaplan, April 5, 1933, 1.
136 Pruszynski, *Palestine for the Third Time*, 83.
137 Vandenberg-Daves, *Modern Motherhood*, 135.
138 H. Kaplan to L. Kaplan, cable, April 9, 1933.
139 H. Kaplan to family, April 4, 1933, 6.
140 H. Kaplan to family, April 12, 1933.
141 H. Kaplan to family, September 23, 1922, 13, 2.
142 H. Kaplan to family, June 2, 1933.

CHAPTER 6. RETURNING HOME
1 Krasner, *Benderly Boys*, 89.
2 Ingall, "Three Cheers for Anna!"
3 Dushkin, *Living Bridges*, 141; Krasner, *Benderly Boys*, 89; Pool, "Julia and Alexander Dushkin."
4 Gelber, *No Balm in Gilead*; Brown, "Sylva Gelber"; Krasner, *Benderly Boys*, 87; Dushkin, *Living Bridges*, 71.
5 L. Kaplan to H. Kaplan, April 4, 1933, 4. All Kaplan family correspondence from the author's personal collection.

6   M. Kaplan to H. Kaplan, April 9, 1933, 1–2.
7   M. Kaplan to H. Kaplan, April 9, 1933.
8   Scult, *Judaism Faces the Twentieth Century*, 339.
9   Scult, 338–340; L. Kaplan to H. Kaplan, July 4, 1933. Mordecai Kaplan, diary, February 5, 1933, in *Communings*, vol. 1, 491.
10 M. Kaplan to H. Kaplan, December 11, 1932, trans. Joseph Benatov, 2015.
11 H. Kaplan to M. Kaplan, n.d. (circa February 1933), trans. Joseph Benatov, 2015.
12 H. Kapan to M. Kaplan, n.d., trans. Joseph Benatov, 2015.
13 H. Kaplan to M. Kaplan, n.d., trans. Joseph Benatov, 2015.
14 Gelber, *No Balm in Gilead*, 16–17; H. Kaplan to M. Kaplan, n.d., trans. Joseph Benatov, 2015.
15 H. Kaplan to M. Kaplan, February 7, 1933, trans. Joseph Benatov, 2015.
16 H. Kaplan to M. Kaplan, April 1933, trans. Joseph Benatov, 2015, 1–3.
17 Naomi Kaplan to H. Kaplan, March 7, 1933; Judith (Kaplan) Addelston to H. Kaplan, March 20, 1933.
18 J. Addelston to H. Kaplan, March 20, 1933.
19 Albert Addelston to H. Kaplan, April 5, 1933.
20 H. Kaplan to family, March 7, 1933.
21 H. Kaplan to family, March 7, 1933.
22 H. Kaplan to family, April 4, 1933, 6.
23 H. Kaplan to family, April 12, 1933.
24 H. Kaplan to family, March 7, 1933.
25 L. Kaplan to H. Kaplan, March 20, 1933, 2–3.
26 L. Kaplan to H. Kaplan, April 4, 1933, 2–3.
27 M. Kaplan to H. Kaplan, April 9, 1933.
28 H. Kaplan to family, May 7, 1933.
29 H. Kaplan to family, April 18, 1933.
30 H. Kaplan to M. Kaplan, April, 1933, trans. Joseph Benatov, 2015.
31 Scult, *Judaism Faces the Twentieth Century*, 113.
32 M. Kaplan to H. Kaplan, May 16, 1933, trans. Joseph Benatov, 2015, 1.
33 L. Kaplan to H. Kaplan, April 20, 1933.
34 L. Kaplan to H. Kaplan, telegram, May 5, 1933.
35 L. Kaplan to H. Kaplan, May 9, 1933.
36 L. Kaplan to H. Kaplan, May 6, 1933.
37 M. Kaplan to H. Kaplan, May 16, 1933, trans. Joseph Benatov, 2015, 1–2.
38 Susman, *Culture as History*, 154.
39 Helman, *Young Tel Aviv*, 112.
40 Mintz, *Sanctuary in the Wilderness*, 274–277.
41 H. Kaplan to family, May 7, 1933.
42 L. Kaplan to H. Kaplan, May 15, 1933.
43 L. Kaplan to H. Kaplan, May 25, 1933; L. Kaplan to H. Kaplan, May 29, 1933.
44 L. Kaplan to H. Kaplan, April 27, 1933, 1.
45 L. Kaplan to H. Kaplan, April 27, 1933, 3.

46 Scult, *Judaism Faces the Twentieth Century*, 348; L. Kaplan to H. Kaplan, May 15, 1933, 1.
47 L. Kaplan to H. Kaplan, June 5, 1933.
48 Scult, *Judaism Faces the Twentieth Century*, 339.
49 L. Kaplan to H. Kaplan, July 4, 1933.
50 L. Kaplan to H. Kaplan, June 5, 1933, 1–2; H. Kaplan to family, May 24, 1933.
51 H. Kaplan to family, June 17, 1933.
52 Amkraut, *Between Home and Homeland*, 43–46; Hacohen, *To Repair a Broken World*, 265.
53 Penkower, *Twentieth Century Jews*, 261–267, 284–286, 295.
54 Gelber, *No Balm in Gilead*, 35.
55 Soyer, "Revisiting the Old World," 17, 20–23.
56 Quoted in Hacohen, *To Repair a Broken World*, 124.
57 H. Kaplan to family, July 8, 1933.
58 L. Kaplan to H. Kaplan, May 25, 1933.
59 L. Kaplan to H. Kaplan, July 7, 1933.
60 L. Kaplan to H. Kaplan, July 10, 1933.
61 L. Kaplan to H. Kaplan, July 21, 1933.
62 H. Kaplan to L. Kaplan, July 19, 1933.
63 Lipstadt, *Beyond Belief*, 34.
64 H. Kaplan to family, July 14, 1933, 4–5.
65 Hill, "Nazi Attack," 9, 12–13.
66 Rose, introduction to *Holocaust and the Book*, 1.
67 Lipstadt, *Beyond Belief*, 16, 18–19; Hill, "Nazi Attack," 13.
68 Lipstadt, *Beyond Belief*, 14, 18; Associated Press, "German Students Burn Books," 32; "Germany: Students Exult as 'Un-German' Books Burn," 14–15; Drake, "Manipulating the News," 15, 25, 38–39. For a more general discussion of how the *New York Times* reported but downplayed the story of Jewish discrimination, deportation, and destruction during the Holocaust, see Leff, *Buried by "The Times,"* 2–16.
69 "Miss Helen Keller's Warning," *Palestine Post*, June 13, 1933, 6.
70 Hill, "Nazi Attack," 16.
71 Munich Documentation Centre for the History of National Socialism, "Book Burnings in Germany and in Munich" (quote); "German Students Burn Thousands of Banned Books," *Christian Science Monitor*, May 12, 1933, 4, ProQuest Historical Newspapers; Ritchie, "Nazi Book Burning," 640.
72 H. Kaplan to family, July 14, 1933.
73 H. Kaplan and Selma Kaplan to family, cable, August 2, 1933.
74 Selma Kaplan to H. Kaplan, August 10, 1933.
75 For more on passing, see Itzkovitz, "Passing Like Me"; Morton, *I Am a Woman, and a Jew*.
76 Judith Addelston to H. Kaplan and Selma Kaplan, July 28, 1933.
77 L. Kaplan to H. Kaplan and Selma Kaplan, July 31, 1933, 2.
78 Judith (Kaplan) Addelston to H. Kaplan, October 17, 1932.

79 Special Collections and University Archives, University of Nevada, Reno Libraries, "Reno Divorce History"; Paine, "As We See It in Reno," 726; Grant, "How Reno Became 'the Divorce Capital of the World.'"
80 Judith (Kaplan) Addelston to H. Kaplan, October 6, 1932; L. Kaplan to H. Kaplan, October 11, 1932.
81 L. Kaplan to H. Kaplan, November 14, 1932.
82 Miriam Eisenstein interview.
83 L. Kaplan to H. Kaplan, July 27, 1933, 2.
84 L. Kaplan to H. Kaplan, July 21, 1933, 2.
85 L. Kaplan to H. Kaplan and Selma Kaplan, July 31, 1933, 3–4.
86 Selma Kaplan to H. Kaplan, August 10, 1933, September 4, 1933, and September 18, 1933.
87 List of US citizens, Southampton to New York, August 12, 1933, ship manifest, Statue of Liberty–Ellis Island Foundation, https://heritage.statueofliberty.org.
88 H. Kaplan to family, n.d. (circa August 10, 1933).
89 H. Kaplan to Judith (Kaplan) Addelston, n.d. (circa August 30, 1933).
90 Scult, *Judaism Faces the Twentieth Century*, 105, 111.
91 Henrietta Szold to H. Kaplan, October 9, 1933.
92 Hacohen, *To Repair a Broken World*, 263, 265; Shapira, *Israel*, 104; Lavsky, *Creation of the German-Jewish Diaspora*, 100–101, 106.
93 Lavsky, *Creation of the German-Jewish Diaspora*, 101, 107; Hacohen, *To Repair a Broken World*, 266.
94 Federal Writers' Project, *WPA Guide to New York City*, 259, 262.
95 Eddie Aspinall, Parent Association invitation, n.d., personal collection.
96 Federal Writers' Project, *WPA Guide to NYC*, 260–262.
97 H. Kaplan to Judith (Kaplan) Addelston, n.d. (circa August 30, 1933).
98 Selma Kaplan to H. Kaplan, September 4, 1933, 3.
99 Federal Writers' Project, *WPA Guide to NYC*, 352; Tavern on the Green, "History and Renovation."
100 For more on the Manischewitz family, see Alpern, *Manischewitz*.
101 Hadassah Kaplan Musher interview (author).
102 "Hadassah Kaplan to Wed," *New York Times*, December 3, 1934, 20, https://timesmachine.nytimes.com.
103 "Kaplan, Hadassah (Substitute)," Principals Report on Teaching Service, January 1934, personal collection; "Kaplan, Hadassah (Substitute)," Principals Report on Teaching Service, June 30, 1934, personal collection.
104 J. C. Gluck to H. Kaplan, December 5, 1934.
105 "Substitute Teacher Service Record," October 2, 1933, to December 7, 1934, Board of Education of the City of New York, teaching documents, personal collection.
106 J. C. Gluck to H. Kaplan, n.d., teaching documents.
107 J. C. Gluck to H. Kaplan, n.d., teaching documents.
108 J. C. Gluck to H. Kaplan, n.d., teaching documents.
109 J. C. Gluck and H. Kaplan, notes, n.d., teaching documents.

110 Markowitz, *My Daughter*, 55, 132.
111 Quoted in L. Cohen, *Making a New Deal*, 188.
112 Wenger, "Budgets, Boycotts, and Babies," 186–187; "Miss. Kaplan Bride of Sidney Musher," *New York Times*, January 8, 1935, 25, https://nyti.ms/3JOXHgI.
113 H. K. Musher interview (author).
114 Hadassah Kaplan Musher interview (Price).
115 H. K. Musher interview (Price).

CONCLUSION

1 Reinharz and Raider, introduction to *American Jewish Women*, xxii.
2 Reinharz and Raider, xxiv; Kaplan, *New Zionism*, 172.
3 See, for example, E. Katz, *Bringing Zion Home*, 1–18; Brautbar, *From Fashion to Politics*, 2–12.
4 Kaplan, *New Zionism*, 26.
5 Kaplan, "What the American Jewish Woman Can Do," 140 (quote), 145 (quote).
6 Quoted in Raider, "Girded for the Superhuman Task," 306–307 (quote).
7 Ingall, introduction to *Women Who Reconstructed American Jewish Education*, 1–2; Raider, "Girded for the Superhuman Task," 324–325, 342–343.
8 J. Eisenstein, *Festival Songs*; J. Eisenstein, *Gateway to Jewish Song*; J. Eisenstein, *Heritage of Music*; J. Eisenstein, *Shir ha-Shahar*; J. Eisenstein with Prensky, *Songs of Childhood*.
9 Kling, "Temima Gezari."
10 Waxman and Norden, "Challenge of Implementing Reconstructionism," 205–206, 215–218; Backenroth, "Temima Gezari," 167–171.
11 Waxman and Norden, "Challenge of Implementing Reconstructionism," 195–199.
12 See Ingall, "Three Cheers for Anna!,'" 143; Bennett, "Libbie L. Braverman," 82.
13 Dinin, *Zionist Education in the United States*, 6, 7, 34, 40, 95.
14 B. Chazan, "Palestine in American Jewish Education," 242.
15 Raider, "Girded for the Superhuman Task," 304, 310, 342–343.
16 Miriam Eisenstein interview.
17 Dushkin, *Living Bridges*, 28.
18 Scult, *Radical American Judaism*, 101.
19 Kaplan, "Status of the Jewish Woman," 12. This work was later lightly revised and reprinted in *The Reconstructionist Papers*, 130, 134–136.
20 Mordecai Kaplan, diary, December 2, 1950, in *Communings*, vol. 3, 374.
21 Hyman and Balin, "Bat Mitzvah"; Waxman, "Lady Sometimes Blows the Shofar," 87.
22 M. Kaplan, diary, December 2, 1950, in *Communings*, vol. 3, 374.
23 M. Kaplan, diary, May 16, 1951, in *Communings*, vol. 3, 390.
24 Waxman, "Lady Sometimes Blows the Shofar," 94, 97.
25 Waxman, 87, 92.
26 For an excellent study of the individual women and collective feminist groups that helped to transform Judaism during second-wave feminism, see Antler, *Jewish Radicalism*, 205–361.

27 Sidney Musher and Hadassah Musher correspondence, 1935–1939, personal collection; "Sidney Musher, 85, Inventor, Executive and Philanthropist," *New York Times*, November 22, 1990, https://nyti.ms/3lgEc6A.
28 Hadassah K. Musher, Substitute License, Board of Education of the City of New York, August 26, 1943, and November 17, 1947, personal collection; Hadassah K. Musher, certificate, Henry George School of Social Science, Board of Regents, SAJ, New York, June 16, 1938, personal collection; Joan Hollinghurst to H. K. Musher, letter of admission, Hunter College, New York, June 3, 1957, personal collection.
29 Peter Steinfels, "Judith Eisenstein, 86, Author and Composer," *New York Times*, February 15, 1996, https://nyti.ms/3HPpwTM. Note that this obituary omits significant parts of Judith's life, including her first marriage and, more significantly, her son, Ethan Eisenstein (1936–2012), who survived her death but had been institutionalized at Willowbrook State School in Staten Island since he was five years old.
30 "Dr. Naomi Kaplan a Bride," *New York Times*, November 11, 1944, 17, https://nyti.ms/3JP4ebt. Note that Mordecai was ambivalent about Naomi going to medical school and especially pursuing psychiatry. See Naomi and Seymour Wenner interview.
31 Selma Goldman, oral history.
32 Hadassah Kaplan Musher, oral history; "Lauds Advances in Israel," *New York Post*, May 12, 1955, personal collection.
33 Hadassah Kaplan Musher interview (Price).
34 Mordecai M. Kaplan, diary, March 24, 1951, 123, Mordecai M. Kaplan Diaries, 1951—Jan.-Mar.
35 Sidney Musher, oral history; Goodman, *66 Years of Benevolence*, 158.
36 Goodman, *66 Years of Benevolence*, 2–3; Judy Siegel, "PEF Never Solicits, but Gave $1.5M. This Year," *Jerusalem Post*, December 12, 1965, personal collection.
37 Berman, *American Jewish Philanthropic Complex*, 93–96.
38 "Musher, Hadassah K," paid notice: deaths, *New York Times*, March 13, 2013, https://archive.nytimes.com.
39 Marsha Pomerantz, "Giving to Israel Wisely: Concerned Hold on the Purse Strings," *Jerusalem Post*, April 26, 1977, 5, personal collection.
40 Selma Goldman, "Song for Hadassah," January 8, 1992, personal collection.
41 There are some overlaps between *Hadassah* the organization and PEF, inasmuch as several PEF trustees, including Zip Falk Szold, Rose Jacobs, Judith Epstein, and Etta Lasker Rosensohn, were or had also been *Hadassah* presidents. Note that Rose was one of Hadassah's mentors in Palestine, and Judith was the daughter of Sarah and Edward Epstein, other family friends in Palestine when Hadassah was there. Goodman, *66 Years of Benevolence*, 54.
42 Kaplan, *Future of the American Jew*, 359, 361.
43 Kaplan, *New Zionism*, 26, 174.

44 I. Eisenstein, *Creative Judaism*, preface, 99–100. This book represents an effort by Eisenstein to popularize and make more accessible to the "average reader" ideas articulated in Kaplan's more expansive and dense *Judaism as a Civilization*.
45 Hacohen, *To Repair a Broken World*, 286, 290.
46 L. Kaplan to Selma Kaplan, H. Kaplan, and Naomi Kaplan, July 24, 1938, 2–3. All Kaplan family correspondence from the author's personal collection.
47 Kaplan, *New Zionism*, 180.
48 Gelber, *No Balm in Gilead*, 274; Brown, "Sylva Gelber."
49 M. Kaplan, diary, March 24, 1951, 123, Mordecai M. Kaplan Diaries, 1951—Jan.-Mar.
50 Sylva directed the Women's Bureau of the Canada Department of Labor from 1968 to 1975 and represented Canada in the UN Commission on the Status of Women. For details, see Brown, "Sylva Gelber."
51 Berkson, "Libbie Suchoff Berkson"; Dinin et al., "Mrs. Isaac B. Berkson"; Krasner, *Benderly Boys*, 87.
52 Campbell Robertson, Michael Wines, and Zach Montague, "Jewish Groups Rally for Israel on National Mall," *New York Times*, November 14, 2023, www.nytimes.com.
53 Dov Waxman, *Trouble in the Tribe*; Alterman, *We Are Not One*.
54 Kaplan and Cohen, *If Not Now, When?*, 120.
55 Kaplan, *Questions Jews Ask*, 402.

BIBLIOGRAPHY

Almog, Shmuel, Jehuda Reinharz, and Anita Shapira. *Zionism and Religion.* Hanover, NH: Brandeis University Press, 1994.
Alpern, Laura Manischewitz. *Manischewitz: The Matzo Family: The Making of an American Jewish Icon.* New York: KTAV, 2008.
Alterman, Eric. *We Are Not One: A History of America's Fight over Israel.* New York: Basic Books, 2022.
Amkraut, Brian. *Between Home and Homeland: Youth Aliyah from Nazi Germany.* Tuscaloosa: University of Alabama Press, 2006.
Anderson, Charles W. "State Formation from Below and the Great Revolt in Palestine." *Journal of Palestine Studies* 47, no. 1 (185) (2017): 39–55. www.jstor.org/stable/26378726.
Antler, Joyce. *Jewish Radicalism: Voices from the Women's Liberation Movement.* New York: New York University, 2018.
———. *The Journey Home: Jewish Women and the American Century.* New York: Free Press, 1997.
———. "Zion in Our Hearts: Henrietta Szold and the American Jewish Women's Movement." In Nadell, *American Jewish Women's History,* 129–149.
Associated Press. "German Students Burn Books of Noted American Authors." *(Boise) Idaho Daily Statesman,* May 11, 1933. In *Americans and the Holocaust: A Reader,* edited by Daniel Greene and Edward Phillips, 32. New Brunswick, NJ: Rutgers University Press, 2021.
Auerbach, Jerold. *Print to Fit: The New York Times, Zionism and Israel, 1896–2016.* Boston: Academic Studies, 2019.
Backenroth, Ofra Arieli. "Temima Gezari: An Art Education Pioneer." In Ingall, *Women Who Reconstructed American Jewish Education,* 165–187.
Baker, Paul, and Jo Stanley. *Hello Sailor: The Hidden History of Gay Life at Sea.* New York: Routledge, 2003.
Baker, Paula Eisenstein. "Judith Kaplan Eisenstein." In *Shalvi/Hyman Encyclopedia of Jewish Women,* edited by Jewish Women's Archive, March 1, 2009. https://jwa.org.
Barak-Gorodetsky, David. *Judah Magnes: The Prophetic Politics of a Religious Binationalist.* Translated by Merav Datan. Philadelphia: Jewish Publication Society, 2021.
Bar-David, Molly Lyons. *My Promised Land.* New York: Putnam, 1958.
Bennett, Alan D. "Libbie L. Braverman: A Woman for All Seasons, 1900–1990." In Ingall, *Women Who Reconstructed American Jewish Education,* 75–96.

Berkson, Gershon. "Libbie Suchoff Berkson." In *Shalvi/Hyman Encyclopedia of Jewish Women*, edited by Jewish Women's Archive, December 31, 1999. https://jwa.org.
Berlovitz, Yaffah. "Hemdah Ben-Yehuda." In *Shalvi/Hyman Encyclopedia of Jewish Women*, edited by Jewish Women's Archive, December 31, 1999. https://jwa.org.
Brown, Michael. "Sylva Gelber." In *Shalvi/Hyman Encyclopedia of Jewish Women*, edited by Jewish Women's Archive, December 31, 1999. https://jwa.org.
Byatt, A. S. Introduction to *The Arabian Nights: Tales from a Thousand and One Nights*, translated by Richard Burton, xiii–xx. New York: Modern Library Edition, 2001.
Bentwich, Margery. *Lillian Ruth Friedlander: A Biography*. Jerusalem: Rubin Mass, 1957.
Berkowitz, Michael. *Western Jewry and the Zionist Project*. Cambridge: Cambridge University Press, 2003.
Berkowitz, Michael, Susan L. Tananbaum, and Sam W. Bloom, eds. *Forging Modern Jewish Identities: Public and Private Struggles*. London: Valentine Mitchell, 2003.
Berman, Lila Corwin. *The American Jewish Philanthropic Complex: The History of a Multibillion-Dollar Institution*. Princeton, NJ: Princeton University Press, 2020.
Bernstein, Deborah, ed. *Pioneers and Homemakers: Jewish Women in Pre-State Israel*. New York: State University of New York Press, 1992.
Brautbar, Shirli. *From Fashion to Politics: Hadassah and Jewish American Women in the Post World War II Era*. Boston: Academic Studies, 2013.
Carr, Jessica L. *The Hebrew Orient: Palestine in Jewish American Visual Culture, 1901–1938* Albany: State University of New York Press, 2020.
Case Western Reserve University. "Ezra Zelig Shapiro." In *Encyclopedia of Cleveland History*. Cleveland, OH: Case Western Reserve University, 2022. https://case.edu.
Central Conference of American Rabbis (Reform Movement). "Declaration of Principles: The Pittsburgh Platform." 1885. www.ccarnet.org.
———. "The Guiding Principles of Reform Judaism." 1937. www.ccarnet.org.
Chazan, Barry. "Palestine in American Jewish Education in the Pre-State Period." *Jewish Social Studies* 42, nos. 3–4 (Summer–Autumn 1980): 229–248.
Chazan, Meir. *Jewish Women and the Defense of Palestine: The Modest Revolution, 1907–1945*. Albany: State University of New York Press, 2022.
Clark, John Maurice, and J. W. Sundelson. *Economics of Planning Public Works*. Washington, DC: US Government Publication Office, 1935.
Cohen, Hillel. *Year Zero of the Arab-Israeli Conflict 1929*. Translated by Haim Watzmann. Waltham, MA: Brandeis University Press, 2015.
Cohen, J. X. *Jews, Jobs and Discrimination: A Report on Jewish Non-employment*. New York: American Jewish Congress, 1937.
Cohen, Lizabeth. *Making a New Deal: Industrial Workers in Chicago, 1919–1939*. Cambridge: Cambridge University Press, 1990.
Cohen, Naomi Wiener. *The Year after the Riots: American Responses to the Palestine Crisis of 1929–1930*. Detroit: Wayne State University Press, 1988.
Coons, Lorraine, and Alexander Varias. *Steamship Travel in the Interwar Years: Tourist Third Cabin*. Stroud, UK: Amberley, 2016.

Cormack, Raphael. *Midnight in Cairo: The Divas of Egypt's Roaring '20s*. New York: Norton, 2021.

Currell, Susan. *The March of Spare Time: The Problem and Promise of Leisure in the Great Depression*. Philadelphia: University of Pennsylvania Press, 2005.

Danit, Rivkah. "With a Kvuzah of Shepherds." In Katznelson-Shazar, *Plough Woman*, 38–40.

Dauben, Joseph Warren. *Abraham Robinson: The Creation of Nonstandard Analysis, A Personal and Mathematical Odyssey*. Princeton, NJ: Princeton University Press, 1995.

Davidson, Lawrence. *America's Palestine: Popular and Official Perceptions from Balfour to Israeli Statehood*. Gainesville: University Press of Florida, 2001.

Di Nepi, Serena, and Arturo Marzano, eds. "Travels to the 'Holy Land': Perceptions, Representations, and Narratives." *Issues in Contemporary Jewish History*, no. 6 (December 2013).

Diner, Hasia, Shira Kohn, and Rachel Kranson, eds. *A Jewish Feminine Mystique? Jewish Women in Postwar America*. New Brunswick, NJ: Rutgers University Press, 2010.

Dinin, Samuel. *Zionist Education in the United States: A Survey*. New York: Zionist Organization of America, 1944.

Dinin, Samuel, Max M. Furer, Isaac Toubin, and Alexander M. Dushkin. "Mrs. Isaac B. Berkson (Libbie Suchoff): In Memoriam." *Jewish Education* 40, no. 3 (1970): 5–8. https://doi.org/10.1080/0021642700400302.

Divine, Donna Robinson. *Exiled in the Homeland: Zionism and the Return to Mandate Palestine*. Austin: University of Texas Press, 2009.

Drake, Robert George. "Manipulating the News: The U.S. Press and the Holocaust, 1933–1945." PhD diss., University of Albany, 2003. ProQuest Historical Dissertations.

Dushkin, Alexander M. *Living Bridges: Memoirs of an Educator*. Jerusalem: Keter, 1975.

———. "Sanity in the Teaching of Palestine." *Jewish Education* 2, no. 2 (June 1930): 65–67.

Eisen, Arnold. "Mordecai Kaplan's 'Judaism as a Civilization' at 70: Setting the Stage for Reappraisal." *Jewish Social Studies*, n.s., 12, no. 2 (2006): 1–16. www.jstor.org/stable/4467729.

Eisenstein, Ira. *Creative Judaism*. New York: Behrman's Jewish Book House, 1936.

———. Oral history. Tape 1. December 28, 1999. Reconstructionist Rabbinical College (RRC) Oral History Project. RRC. Wyncote, PA.

Eisenstein, Judith Kaplan. *Festival Songs*. New York: Bloch, 1943.

———. *Gateway to Jewish Song*. New York: Behrman House, 1939.

———. *Heritage of Music: The Music of the Jewish People*. New York: Union of American Hebrew Congregations, 1972.

———. "Judith Kaplan Eisenstein Becomes the First Bat Mitzvah, 1921 [sic]." In *Eyewitness to Jewish History: The American Jew, 1915–1969*, edited by Azriel Eisenberg, 29–32. New York: Union of American Hebrew Congregation, 1982. www.ritualwell.org.

———. *Shir ha-Shahar* [Song of the Dawn]. New York: Transcontinental Music Publications, 1974.

Eisenstein, Judith Kaplan, and Ira Eisenstein. Interviewed by Mel Scult. Transcribed by Jane Susswein. N.d. (circa 1970s). Personal collection.
Eisenstein, Judith Kaplan, with Frieda Prensky. *Songs of Childhood*. New York: United Synagogue of America, 1955.
Eisenstein, Miriam. Interviewed by author. Zoom. July 8, 2021. Personal collection.
Engst, Elaine D. *Jewish Life at Cornell, 1865–2005*. Ithaca, NY: Cornell University Library, 2006. https://ecommons.cornell.edu.
Federal Writers' Project (FWP). *The WPA Guide to New York City*. 1939. Reprint, New York: Random House, 1982.
Feingold, Henry L. *A Time for Searching: Entering the Mainstream, 1920–45*. Vol. 4. Baltimore: Johns Hopkins University Press, 1995.
Fermaglich, Kirsten. "'Too Long, Too Foreign . . . Too Jewish': Jews, Name Changing, and Family Mobility in New York City, 1917–1942." *Journal of American Ethnic History* 34, no. 3 (2015): 34–57. https://doi.org/10.5406/jamerethnhist.34.3.0034.
Feuchtwanger, Lion. *Josephus*. London: Martin Secker, 1932.
Fiell, Charlotte. *1930s Fashion Sourcebook*. London: Welbeck, 2021.
Fogiel-Bijaoui, Sylvie. "Kibbutz." In *Shalvi/Hyman Encyclopedia of Jewish Women*, edited by Jewish Women's Archive, June 23, 2021. https://jwa.org.
Fox, Sandra. *The Jews of Summer: Summer Camp and Jewish Culture in Postwar America*. Stanford, CA: Stanford University Press, 2023.
Gal, Allon. "The Zionist Vision of Henrietta Szold." In Reinharz and Raider, *American Jewish Women and the Zionist Enterprise*, 25–43.
Gelber, Sylva M. *No Balm in Gilead: A Personal Retrospective of Mandate Days in Palestine*. Ottawa: Carleton University Press, 1989.
Geni. "Fred J. Isaacson." Last modified April 28, 2022. www.geni.com.
"Germany: Students Exult as 'Un-German' Books Burn." *Newsweek* 1, no. 14 (May 20, 1933): 14–15.
Gitre, Carmen M. K. *Acting Egyptian: Theater, Identity, and Political Culture in Cairo, 1869–1930*. Austin: University of Texas Press, 2019.
Glass, Joseph B. "American Olim and the Transfer of Innovation to Palestine, 1917–1939." In Lederhendler and Sarna, *America and Zion*, 201–232.
———. *From New Zion to Old Zion: American Jewish Immigration and Settlement in Palestine 1917–1939*. Detroit: Wayne State University Press, 2002.
———. "Settling the Old-New Homeland: The Decisions of American Jewish Women during the Interwar Years." In Reinharz and Raider, *American Jewish Women and the Zionist Enterprise*, 192–215.
Glauber-Zimra, Samuel. "Summoning Spirits in Egypt: Jewish Women and Spiritualism in Early Twentieth Century Cairo." *Nashim* 38 (Spring 2021): 25–38.
Goldman, Selma. Interviewed by author. April 17, 2006. New York. Personal collection.
———. Oral history. May 13, 2002. Tapes 2–3. Reconstructionist Rabbinical College (RRC) Oral History Project. RRC. Wyncote, PA.

Goodman, Philip. *66 Years of Benevolence: The Story of PEF Israel Endowment Funds.* New York: PEF Israel Endowment Funds, 1989.
Goren, Arthur. "Celebrating Zion in America." In Shandler and Wenger, *Encounters with the "Holy Land,"* 41–59.
———. *The Politics and Public Culture of American Jews.* Bloomington: Indiana University Press, 1999.
Goren, Tamir. "Developing Jaffa's Port, 1920–1936." *Israel Affairs* 22, no. 1 (January 2016): 172–188. https://doi.org/10.1080/13537121.2015.1111634.
———. "Relations between Tel Aviv and Jaffa 1921–1936: A Reassessment." *Journal of Israeli History* 36, no. 1 (2017): 1–21. https://doi.org/0.1080/13531042.2017.1415285.
———. "The Struggle to Save the National Symbol: Jaffa Port from the Arab Revolt until the Twilight of the British Mandate." *Middle Eastern Studies* 51, no. 6 (November 2015): 863–882. https://doi.org/10.1080/00263206.2015.1018186.
Grant, Sofia. "How Reno Became 'the Divorce Capital of the World'—and Why That Reputation Faded." *Time,* February 13, 2020. https://time.com.
Green, Nancy L. *Ready-to-Wear and Ready-to-Work: A Century of Industry and Immigration in Paris and New York.* Durham, NC: Duke University Press, 1997.
Greenberg, Michael, and Seymour Zenchelsky. "Private Bias and Public Responsibility: Anti-Semitism at Rutgers in the 1920s and 1930s." *History of Education Quarterly* 33, no. 3 (1993): 295–319. https://doi.org/10.2307/368195.
Gruber, Ruth. *Ahead of Time: My Early Years as a Foreign Correspondent.* New York: Basic Books, 2002.
Grunfeld, Katharina Kroo. "Hunter College." In *Shalvi/Hyman Encyclopedia of Jewish Women,* edited by Jewish Women's Archive, December 31, 1999. https://jwa.org.
Gurock, Jeffrey S. *Jews in Gotham: New York Jews in a Changing City, 1920–2010.* New York: New York University Press, 2012.
Gurock, Jeffrey S., and Jacob J. Schacter. *A Modern Heretic and a Traditional Community: Mordecai M. Kaplan, Orthodoxy and American Judaism.* New York: Columbia University Press, 1997.
Hacohen, Dvora. *To Repair a Broken World: The Life of Henrietta Szold, Founder of Hadassah.* Cambridge, MA: Harvard University Press, 2021.
Halperin, Liora R. *Babel in Zion: Jews, Nationalism, and Language Diversity in Palestine, 1920–1948.* New Haven, CT: Yale University Press, 2014.
———. *The Oldest Guard: Forging the Zionist Settler Past.* Stanford, CA: Stanford University Press, 2021.
Halpern, Ben. "The Americanization of Zionism, 1880–1930." *American Jewish History* 69, no. 1 (September 1979): 15–33.
Hazbun, Waleed. "The East as an Exhibit: Thomas Cook & Son and the Origins of the International Tourism Industry in Egypt." In Scranton and Davidson, *Business of Tourism,* 3–33.
Helman, Anat. *A Coat of Many Colors: Dress Culture in the Young State of Israel.* Boston: Academic Studies, 2011.

236 | BIBLIOGRAPHY

———. *Young Tel Aviv: A Tale of Two Cities*. Translated by Haim Watzman. Waltham, MA: Brandeis University Press, 2010.
Henry, Winston P. to University of Chicago Alumni, Tulsa, Oklahoma. "The Letter Box." *University of Chicago Magazine* 17, no. 6 (April 1925): 241. www.google.com.
Hill, Leonidas E. "The Nazi Attack on 'Un-German' Literature, 1933–1945." In Rose, *Holocaust and the Book*, 9–46.
Holtzman, Avner. "Sokolow, Nahum." Translated by David Fachler. In *YIVO Encyclopedia of Jews in Eastern Europe*. https://yivoencyclopedia.org.
Hyman, Paula E., and Carole B. Balin. "Bat Mitzvah: American Jewish Women." In *Shalvi/Hyman Encyclopedia of Jewish Women*, edited by Jewish Women's Archive, June 23, 2021. https://jwa.org.
Imhoff, Sarah. *The Lives of Jessie Sampter*. Durham, NC: Duke University Press, 2022.
Ingall, Carol K. Introduction to *Women Who Reconstructed American Jewish Education*, 1–23.
———. "'Three Cheers for Anna!' Anna G. Sherman, Adult Jewish Educator." In Ingall, *Women Who Reconstructed American Jewish Education*, 142–164.
———, ed. *The Women Who Reconstructed American Jewish Education, 1910–1965*. Lebanon, NH: University Press of New England, 2010.
International Holocaust Remembrance Alliance. "Working Definition of Antisemitism." 2015, https://holocaustremembrance.com.
Israel & Antisemitism. "The Nexus Document." 2021. https://israelandantisemitism.com.
Itzkovitz, Daniel. "Passing Like Me: Jewish Chameleonism and the Politics of Race." In *Passing: Identity and Interpretation in Sexuality, Race, and Religion*, edited by Maria C. Sanchez and Linda Schlossberg, 38–63. New York: New York University Press, 2001.
Jerusalem Declaration on Antisemitism. Home page. 2021. https://jerusalemdeclaration.org.
Jewish Publication Society. *The JPS Tanakh Gender Sensitive Edition*. Lincoln, NE: Jewish Publication Society, 2023.
Jewish Women's Archive, ed. *Shalvi/Hyman Encyclopedia of Jewish Women*. December 31, 1999. https://jwa.org.
Joselit, Jenna Weissman. *The Wonders of America: Reinventing Jewish Culture, 1880–1950*. New York: Holt, 1994.
Joselit, Jenna Weissman, and Karen S. Mittleman, eds. *A Worthy Use of Summer: Jewish Summer Camping in America*. Philadelphia: National Museum of American Jewish History, 1993.
Junior Hadassah. *A Primer on Palestine*. New York: Junior Hadassah, 1932.
Kaplan, Mordecai M. *Communings of the Spirit: The Journals of Mordecai M. Kaplan*. Vol. 1, *1913–1934*. Edited by Mel Scult. Detroit: Wayne State University Press and the Reconstructionist Press, 2001.
———. *Communings of the Spirit: The Journals of Mordecai M. Kaplan*. Vol. 2, *1934–1941*. Edited by Mel Scult. Detroit: Wayne State University Press and the Reconstructionist Press, 2016.

———. *Communings of the Spirit: The Journals of Mordecai M. Kaplan.* Vol. 3, *1942–1951*. Edited by Mel Scult. Detroit: Wayne State University Press and the Reconstructionist Press, 2020.

———. Mordecai M. Kaplan Diaries. Archival Documents Collection. Jewish Theological Seminary, NY. https://digitalcollections.jtsa.edu.

———. *The Future of the American Jew.* New York: Macmillan, 1948.

———. *Judaism as a Civilization.* New York: Reconstructionist Press, 1957.

———. *A New Zionism.* 1955. Reprint, New York: Herzl Press and Jewish Reconstructionist Press, 1959.

———. *Questions Jews Ask: Reconstructionist Answers.* New York: Reconstructionist Press, 1956.

———. "The Status of the Jewish Woman." *The Reconstructionist* 2, no. 1 (February 21, 1936): 7–14.

———. "The Truth about Reconstructionism." *Commentary*, December 1945. www.commentary.org.

———. "What the American Jewish Woman Can Do for Jewish Education." *Jewish Education* 4, no. 3 (Fall 1932): 139–147.

Kaplan, Mordecai M., and Arthur A. Cohen. *If Not Now, When? Toward a Reconstitution of the Jewish People.* New York: Schocken Books, 1973.

Kark, Ruth. "From Pilgrimage to Budding Tourism: The Role of Thomas Cook in the Rediscovery of the Holy Land in the Nineteenth Century." In Searight and Wagstaff, *Travellers in the Levant*, 155–174.

Kark, Ruth, Margalit Shilo, and Galit Hasan-Rokem, eds. *Jewish Women in Pre-State Israel: Life History, Politics, and Culture.* Waltham, MA: Brandeis University Press, 2008.

Karlinsky, Nahum. *California Dreaming: Ideology, Society, and Technology in the Citrus Industry of Palestine, 1890–1930.* Translated by Naftali Greenwood. Albany: State University of New York Press, 2005.

Katsburg-Yungman, Mirah. *Hadassah: American Women Zionists and the Rebirth of Israel.* Liverpool: Liverpool University Press, 2012.

Katz, Emily Alice. *Bringing Zion Home: Israel in American Jewish Culture, 1948–1967.* Albany: State University of New York Press, 2015.

Katz, Yossi. *The Battle for the Land: The History of the Jewish National Fund (KKL) before the Establishment of the State of Israel.* Jerusalem: Hebrew University Press, 2005.

Kessler-Harris, Alice. *In Pursuit of Equity: Women, Men, and the Quest for Economic Citizenship in 20th-Century America.* Oxford: Oxford University Press, 2003.

Kessner, Carole S. *Marie Syrkin: Values Beyond the Self.* Waltham, MA: Brandeis University Press, 2021.

Klapper, Melissa R. "The Great Adventure of 1929: The Impact of Travel Abroad on American Jewish Women's Identity." *American Jewish History* 102, no. 1 (2018): 85–107. https://doi.org/10.1353/ajh.2018.0005.

Kling, Suzanne. "Temima Gezari." In *Shalvi/Hyman Encyclopedia of Jewish Women*, edited by Jewish Women's Archive, December 31, 1999. https://jwa.org.

Knee, Stuart E. *The Concept of Zionist Dissent in the American Mind, 1917–1941*. New York: R. Speller, 1979.

———. "Jewish Non-Zionism in America and Palestine Commitment 1917–1941." *Jewish Social Studies*, 39, no. 3 (Summer 1977): 209–226.

Kobrin, Rebecca. "Teaching Profession in the United States." In *Jewish Women: A Comprehensive Historical Encyclopedia*, edited by Jewish Women's Archive, March 20, 2009. https://jwa.org.

Kotzin, Daniel P. "An Attempt to Americanize the Yishuv: Judah L. Magnes in Mandatory Palestine." *Israel Studies* 5, no. 1, "The Americanization of Israel" (Spring 2000): 1–23. www.jstor.org/stable/30245527.

Krasner, Jonathan B. *The Benderly Boys and American Jewish Education*. Waltham, MA: Brandeis University Press, 2011.

Kupferschmidt, Uri M. "Who Needed Department Stores in Egypt? From Orosdi-Back to Omar Effendi." *Middle Eastern Studies* 43, no. 2 (March 2007): 175–192.

Kuzar, Ron. *Hebrew and Zionism: A Discourse Analytic Cultural Study*. Berlin: De Gruyter, 2001.

Lahav, Penina. *The Only Woman in the Room: Golda Meir and Her Path to Power*. Princeton, NJ: Princeton University Press, 2022.

Lavsky, Hagit Hadassa. *The Creation of the German-Jewish Diaspora: Interwar German-Jewish Immigration to Palestine, the USA, and England*. Boston: Walter de Gruyter, 2017.

Lederhendler, Eli, and Jonathan D. Sarna, eds. *America and Zion: Essays and Papers in Memory of Moshe Davis*. Detroit: Wayne State University Press, 2002.

Leff, Laurel. *Buried by The Times: The Holocaust and America's Most Important Newspaper*. Cambridge: Cambridge University Press, 2005.

Levine, Emily Jane. *Allies and Rivals: German-American Exchange and the Rise of the Modern Research University*. Chicago: University of Chicago Press, 2021.

LeVine, Mark. *Overthrowing Geography: Jaffa, Tel Aviv, and the Struggle for Palestine, 1880–1948*. Berkeley: University of California Press, 2005.

Levy, Joseph. Papers. Online Archive of California. https://oac.cdlib.org.

Lindheim, Irma. *The Immortal Adventure*. New York: Macaulay, 1928.

Lipsky, Seth. *The Rise of Abe Cahan*. New York: Schocken Books, 2013.

Lipstadt, Deborah. *Beyond Belief*. New York: Free Press, 1986.

Luke, Harry Charles, and Edward Keith-Roach, eds. *Handbook of Palestine*. London: Macmillan, 1922.

Magnes, Beatrice Lowenstein. *Episodes: A Memoir*. Berkeley, CA: Judah L. Magnes Memorial Museum, 1977.

Magnes Collection Database. University of California, Berkeley. https://magnes.berkeley.edu.

Maritime Timetable Images. Collection of Björn Larsson. www.timetableimages.com.

Markowitz, Ruth Jacknow. *My Daughter, the Teacher: Jewish Teachers in the New York City Schools*. New Brunswick, NJ: Rutgers University Press, 1993.

Marzano, Arturo. "Visiting British Palestine: Zionist Travelers to Eretz Israel." In Di Nepi and Marzano, "Travels to the 'Holy Land,'" 174–200.

Mattar, Philip. "Al-Haram al-Sharif." In *Encyclopedia of the Palestinians*, edited by Michael R. Fischbach, 3rd ed. New York: Facts on File, 2017. Credo Reference.
McCaughey, Robert. *Stand, Columbia: A History of Columbia University*. New York: Columbia University Press, 2003.
McLellan, Ann K. "Golly, a Black Sherlock Holmes! Race, Cross-Promotion, and Robertson's Golliwog." *Journal of Popular Culture* 53, no. 1 (March 2020): 10–33.
Melman, Billie. *Women's Orients: English Women and the Middle East, 1718–1918*. Ann Arbor: University of Michigan Press, 1992.
Mickenberg, Julia L. *American Girls in Red Russia: Chasing the Soviet Dream*. Chicago: University of Chicago Press, 2017.
Mintz, Alan. *Sanctuary in the Wilderness: A Critical Introduction to American Hebrew Poetry*. Stanford, CA: Stanford University Press, 2011.
Monerescu, Daniel, and Haim Hazan. *Twilight Nationalism: Politics of Existence at Life's End*. Stanford, CA: Stanford University Press, 2018.
Moore, Deborah Dash. Foreword to Gurock, *Jews in Gotham*, xi–xxiii.
——. "Judaism as a Gendered Civilization: The Legacy of Mordecai Kaplan's Magnum Opus." *Jewish Social Studies* 12, no. 2 (Winter 2006): 172–186.
——. *Urban Origins of American Judaism*. Athens: University of Georgia Press, 2014.
Moore, Deborah Dash, Jeffrey S. Gurock, Annie Polland, Howard B. Rock, and Daniel Soyer. *Jewish New York: The Remarkable Story of a City and a People*. New York: New York University Press, 2017.
Morris, Benny. *1948: A History of the First Arab-Israeli War*. New Haven, CT: Yale University Press, 2008.
Morton, Leah. *I Am a Woman, and a Jew*. New York : J. H. Sears, 1926.
Munich Documentation Centre for the History of National Socialism. "The Book Burnings in Germany and in Munich." Accessed June 30, 2022. www.ns-dokuzentrum-muenchen.de.
Musher, David. Interviewed by author. July 26, 2018. New York. Personal collection.
Musher, Deborah Ann. "Reconstructionist Judaism in the Mind of Mordecai Kaplan: The Transformation from a Philosophy into a Religious Denomination." *American Jewish History* 86, no. 4 (December 1998): 397–417.
Musher, Hadassah Kaplan. Interviewed by author. September 1, 1994. Fairfield, CT. Personal collection.
——. Interviewed by Marilyn Price. August 19, 2002. New York. Personal collection.
——. Oral history. Tape 1. September 19, 2002. Reconstructionist Rabbinical College (RRC) Oral History Project. RRC. Wyncote, PA.
Musher, Sharon Ann. "Reviving a 'Juniper in the Desert': A Hebrew Exchange between Mordecai Kaplan and His Daughter Hadassah, 1932–1933." *Jewish Quarterly Review* 110, no. 3 (2020): 575–590.
Musher, Sidney. Oral history. June 1990. Personal collection.
Mykoff, Nancy. "Summer Camping in the United States." In *Jewish Women: A Comprehensive Historical Encyclopedia*, edited by Jewish Women's Archive, March 20, 2009 https://jwa.org.

Nadell, Pamela S., ed. *American Jewish Women's History: A Reader.* New York: New York University Press, 2003.

———. "'The Long and Winding Road' to Women Rabbis." In Schorr and Graf, *Sacred Calling*, 31–43.

Nadell, Pamela S., and Jonathan Sarna, eds. *Women and American Judaism: Historical Perspectives.* Hanover, NH: Brandeis University Press, 2001.

Near, Henry. *The Kibbutz Movement: A History.* Vol. 1. New York: Oxford University Press, 1992.

Nelson Glueck School of Biblical Archeology. "The NGSBA Mission." Accessed July 3, 2024. http://ngsba.org.

Newhouse, Alana. "Marjorie Morningstar: The Conservative Novel That Liberal Feminists Love." *Slate*, September 14, 2005. https://slate.com.

Newton, Frances E. *Fifty Years in Palestine.* London: Coldharbour, 1948.

———. *Palestine: Britain's Honour at Stake.* London: Britons, 1947.

———. *Searchlight on Palestine: Fair-Play or Terrorist Methods? Some Personal Investigations.* London: Arab Centre, 1938. www.loc.gov.

Nilsson, Arne. "Cruising the Seas: Male Homosexual Life on the Swedish American Line, 1950–1975." *Society of Queer Studies*, no. 71 (January 2006): 71–85.

Oppenheimer, Mark. "Columbia and Its Forgotten Jewish Campus." *Gatecrashers* (podcast), September 1, 2022. www.tabletmag.com.

Paine, Swift. "As We See It in Reno." *North American Review* 229, no. 6 (June 1930): 720–726.

Panitz, Michael. "Jewish Theological Seminary." In *Encyclopaedia Judaica*, edited by Michael Berenbaum and Fred Skolnik, 2nd ed., vol. 11, 328–331. New York: Macmillan Reference USA, 2007.

Penkower, Monty Noam. *Twentieth Century Jews: Forging Identity in the Land of Promise and in the Promised Land.* Boston: Academic Studies, 2010.

Pianko, Noam. *Jewish Peoplehood: An American Innovation.* New Brunswick, NJ: Rutgers University Press, 2015.

———. "Reconstructing Judaism, Reconstructing America: The Sources and Functions of Mordecai Kaplan's 'Civilization.'" *Jewish Social Studies*, n.s., 12, no. 2 (2006): 39–55. www.jstor.org/stable/4467732.

———. *Zionism and the Roads Not Taken: Rawidowicz, Kaplan, Kohn.* Bloomington: Indiana University Press, 2010.

"Pogroms in Palestine, The." *Forverts*, August 27, 1929. In *Jewish Radicals: A Documentary Reader*, edited by Tony Michels, 298–300. New York: New York University Press, 2012.

Pool, Tamar de Sola. "Julia and Alexander Dushkin in the History of Hadassah." *Jewish Education* 41, nos. 1–2 (June 1, 1971): 59–65.

Pratt, Mary Louise. *Imperial Eyes: Travel Writing and Transculturation.* 2nd ed. New York: Routledge, 2007.

Pratt, Norma Fain. "Transitions in Judaism: The Jewish American Woman through the 1930s." *American Quarterly* 30, no. 5 (1978): 681–702.

Prell, Riv-Ellen. "Antisemitism without Quotas at the University of Minnesota in the 1930s and 1940s: Anticommunist Politics, the Surveillance of Jewish Students, and American Antisemitism." *American Jewish History* 105, nos. 1–2 (January 2021): 157–188.

———. *Fighting to Become Americans: Assimilation and the Trouble between Jewish Women and Jewish Men*. Boston: Beacon, 1999.

Pruszynski, Ksawery. *Palestine for the Third Time*. Translated by Wiesiek Powaga. Boston: Academic Studies, 2020.

Raider, Mark A. "'Girded for the Superhuman Task': American Jews and the Trope of the Zionist Pioneer, 1925–1956." *American Jewish History* 103, no. 3 (July 2019): 303–343. https://doi.org/10.1353/ajh.2019.0032.

Raider, Mark A., and Miriam B. Raider-Roth, eds. *The Plough Woman: Records of the Pioneer Women of Palestine*. Critical ed. Hanover, NH: Brandeis University Press, 2002.

Reconstructionist Papers, The. Vol. 1. New York: Behrman's Jewish Book House, 1936.

Reid, Donald Malcolm. *Contesting Antiquity in Egypt: Archaeologies, Museums and the Struggle for Identities from World War I to Nasser*. New York: American University in Cairo Press, 2015.

Reinharz, Jehuda. "The Conflict between Zionism and Traditionalism before World War I." *Jewish History* 7, no. 2 (1993): 59–78.

Reinharz, Shulamit, and Mark A. Raider. Introduction to *American Jewish Women and the Zionist Enterprise*, xix–xxvii.

———. Introduction to "*Em Leemahot*: The Public Health Contributions of Sara Bodek Paltiel to the Yishuv and Israel, 1932–1993," by Peri Rosenfeld. In *American Jewish Women and the Zionist Enterprise*, 216–218.

———, eds. *American Jewish Women and the Zionist Enterprise*. Waltham, MA: Brandeis University Press; Hanover, NH: University Press of New England, 2005.

Rennella, Mark, and Whitney Walton. "Planned Serendipity: American Travelers and the Transatlantic Voyage in the Nineteenth and Twentieth Centuries." *Journal of Social History* 38, no. 2 (Winter 2004): 365–383.

Review of Henry W. Simon's *What Is a Teacher?* (New York: Collier Books, 1966). *Peabody Journal of Education* 45, no. 3 (November 1967): 186–188.

"Revolt of the Oppressed Arab Masses, A." *Di Morgn Frayhayt*, August 28, 1929. In *Jewish Radicals: A Documentary Reader*, edited by Tony Michels, 301–303. New York: New York University Press, 2012.

Rischin, Moses. *The Promised City: New York's Jews, 1870–1914*. Cambridge, MA: Harvard University Press, 1962.

Ritchie, J. M. "The Nazi Book Burning." *Modern Language Review* 83, no. 3 (1988): 627–643.

Roberts, Byrony. "Reba Rottenberg (1912–2002)." In *The Eye of the Collector: The Jewish Vision of Sigmund R. Balka*, edited by Jean Bloch Rosensaft, 152. New York: Hebrew Union College-Jewish Institute of Religion, 2006. http://huc.edu.

Rose, Jonathan, ed. *The Holocaust and the Book: Destruction and Preservation*. Amherst: University of Massachusetts Press, 2001.

―――. Introduction to Rose, *Holocaust and the Book*, 1–6.
Rosen, Gladys. "Bertha Singer Schoolman." In *Shalvi/Hyman Encyclopedia of Jewish Women*, edited by Jewish Women's Archive, 1999. https://jwa.org.
Rosenberg, Rosalind. *Changing the Subject: How the Women of Columbia Shaped the Way We Think about Sex and Politics*. New York: Columbia University Press, 2004.
Ryann, Donna F. *The Holocaust and the Jews of Marseille: The Enforcement of Anti-Semitic Policies in Vichy France*. Urbana: University of Illinois Press, 1996.
Sarna, Jonathan D. "Converts to Zionism in the American Reform Movement." In Almog, Reinharz, and Shapira, *Zionism and Religion*, 188–203.
Schafer, Axel R. "W. E. B. Du Bois, German Social Thought, and the Racial Divide in American Progressivism, 1892–1909." *Journal of American History* 88, no. 3 (December 2001): 925–949.
Schmidt, Sarah. "Deborah Kallen and the Palestinian Yishuv: The Personal Tragedy of an Educational Pioneer." *Nashim: A Journal of Jewish Women's Studies & Gender Issues*, no. 4 (Fall 2001): 197–232. www.jstor.org/stable/40326540.
Schorr, Rebecca Einstein, and Alysa Mendelson Graf, eds. *The Sacred Calling: Four Decades of Women in the Rabbinate*. New York: Central Conference of American Rabbis Press, 2016.
Schwartz, Shuly Rubin. "Rebecca Aaronson Brickner: Benderly Boy? 1894–1988." In Ingall, *Women Who Reconstructed American Jewish Education*, 63–74.
Scott, Joan Wallach. *Feminism and History*. Oxford: Oxford University Press, 2008.
Scranton, Philip, and Janet F. Davidson, eds. *The Business of Tourism: Place, Faith, and History*. Philadelphia: University of Pennsylvania Press, 2006.
Scult, Mel. *Judaism Faces the Twentieth Century: A Biography of Mordecai M. Kaplan*. 1993. Reprint, Detroit: Wayne State University Press, 2014.
―――. *The Radical American Judaism of Mordecai M. Kaplan*. Bloomington: Indiana University Press, 2013.
Searight, Sarah, and Malcolm Wagstaff, eds. *Travellers in the Levant: Voyagers and Visionaries*. London: Astene, 2001.
Segev, Tom. *One Palestine, Complete*. Translated by Haim Watzman. New York: Metropolitan Books, 2000.
Segev, Zohar. "From Philanthropy to Shaping a State: Hadassah and Ben-Gurion, 1937–1947." In special section, "Roundtable on the Status of Israeli Women Today." *Israel Studies* 18, no. 3 (Fall 2013): 133–157. https://doi.org/10.2979/israelstudies.18.3.133.
Shandler, Jeffrey, and Beth Wenger, eds. *Encounters with the "Holy Land": Place, Past and Future in American Jewish Culture*. Lebanon: University Press of New England, 1997.
―――. "'The Site of Paradise': The Holy Land in American Jewish Imagination." In Shandler and Wenger, *Encounters with the "Holy Land,"* 11–40.
Shapira, Anita. *Israel: A History*. Waltham, MA: Brandeis University Press, 2012.
Shavit, Ari. *My Promised Land: The Triumph and Tragedy of Israel*. New York: Random House, 2013.
Shavit, Zohar. "What Did Hebrew Children Speak." *Israel* 29 (2021): 7–30.

Shoham, Hizky. *Carnival in Tel Aviv: Purim and the Celebration of Urban Zionism.* Boston: Academic Studies, 2020.
Short, Emma. Introduction to "Women Writing Travel, 1890–1939." Special issue, *International Journal of Travel and Travel Writing* 16, no. 1 (Summer 2015): 1–7.
Silber, William L. "Why Did FDR's Bank Holiday Succeed?" *Economic Policy Review* 15, no. 1 (July 2009). www.newyorkfed.org.
Simmons, Erica B. "Playgrounds and Penny Lunches in Palestine: American Social Welfare in the Yishuv." *American Jewish History* 92, no. 3 (2004): 263–297.
Sinkoff, Nancy. *From Left to Right: Lucy S. Dawidowicz, the New York Intellectuals, and the Politics of Jewish History.* Detroit: Wayne State University Press, 2020.
Smith, Bonnie. *The Gender of History: Men, Women, and Historical Practice.* Cambridge, MA: Harvard University Press, 2000.
Snider, Marika Dalley. "Entropy and Exclusivity: Gender and Change in the Retail Environment, Alexandria, Egypt (1970–2011)." PhD diss., University of Utah, 2012.
Soyer, Daniel. "Revisiting the Old World: American-Jewish Tourists in Inter-War Eastern Europe." In Berkowitz, Tananbaum, and Bloom, *Forging Modern Jewish Identities,* 16–38.
Special Collections and University Archives, University of Nevada, Reno Libraries. "Reno Divorce History." 2014. http://renodivorcehistory.org.
Spiegel, Nina S. "Jewish Cultural Celebrations and Competitions in Mandatory Palestine, 1920–1947: Body, Beauty, and the Search for Authenticity." PhD diss., Stanford University, 2001.
Spurlock, John C. *Youth and Sexuality in the Twentieth-Century in the United States.* New York: Routledge, 2015.
Steadman, Jennifer Bernhardt. *Traveling Economies: American Women's Travel Writing.* Columbus: Ohio State University Press, 2007.
Stein, Kenneth W. *The Land Question in Palestine, 1917–1939.* Chapel Hill: University of North Carolina Press, 1984.
Stein, Regina. "The Road to Bat Mitzvah in America." In Nadell and Sarna, *Women and American Judaism,* 223–234.
Stern, Bat-Sheva Margalit. "'He Walked through the Fields,' but What Did She Do? The 'Hebrew Woman' in Her Own Eyes and in the Eyes of Her Contemporaries." *Journal of Israeli History* 30, no. 2 (September 1, 2011): 161–187.
Sundelson, Jacob Wilner. "Budgetary Methods in National and State Governments." PhD diss., Columbia University. Albany, NY: P. B. Lyon, 1938.
Susman, Warren. *Culture as History: The Transformation of American Society in the Twentieth Century.* Washington, DC: Smithsonian Books, 2003.
Swiggum, S., and M. Kohli. "The Fleets." The Ships List, last updated January 24, 2007. www.theshipslist.com.
Tavern on the Green. "History and Renovation." Accessed July 3, 2024. www.tavernonthegreen.com.
Tolkowsky, Samuel. *The Gateway of Palestine: A History of Jaffa.* New York: Albert and Charles Boni, 1925.

———. "The Jewish Colonisation in Palestine." Zionist Organization, London Bureau, 1918.
Townshend, Charles. "Going to the Wall: The Failure of British Rule in Palestine, 1928–1931." *Journal of Imperial and Commonwealth History* 30, no. 2 (May 2002): 25–52. https://doi.org/10.1080/03086530208583140.
Ulrich, Laurel Thatcher. *A Midwife's Tale: The Life of Martha Ballard, Based on Her Diary, 1785–1812*. New York: Vintage Books, 1991.
US Holocaust Memorial Museum. "Jewish Population of Europe in 1933: Population Data by Country." Accessed July 3, 2024. https://encyclopedia.ushmm.org.
Vandenberg-Daves, Jodi. *Modern Motherhood: An American History*. New Brunswick, NJ: Rutgers University Press, 2014.
Vanderbilt, Cornelius, Jr. *Farewell to Fifth Avenue*. New York: Simon and Schuster, 1935.
Wadleigh High School Collection, 1938–2007. Archives and Manuscripts. New York Public Library. https://archives.nypl.org.
Waldinger, Albert. "Abraham Cahan and Palestine." *Jewish Social Studies* 39, nos. 1–2 (Winter–Spring 1977): 75–92. www.jstor.org/stable/4466950.
Waxman, Chaim I. *American Aliya: Portrait of an Innovative Migration Movement*. Detroit: Wayne State University Press, 1989.
Waxman, Deborah. "From the First Bat Mitzvah to Religious Equality: The Emergence of Egalitarianism and the Status of Women at the Society for the Advancement of Judaism, 1922–1950." Paper presented at the Association for Jewish Studies Conference, Los Angeles, CA, December 18, 2002.
———. "A Lady Sometimes Blows the Shofar." In Diner, Kohn, and Kranson, *Jewish Feminine Mystique?*, 87–104.
Waxman, Deborah, and Joyce Galpern Norden. "The Challenge of Implementing Reconstructionism: Art, Ideology, and the Society for the Advancement of Judaism's Sanctuary Mural." *American Jewish History* 95, no. 3 (2009): 195–224. www.jstor.org/stable/23887931.
Waxman, Dov. *Trouble in the Tribe: The American Jewish Conflict Over Israel*. Princeton, NJ: Princeton University Press, 2016.
Weinberg, Sydney Stahl. "Longing to Learn: The Education of Jewish Immigrant Women in New York City, 1900–1934." *Journal of American Ethnic History* 8, no. 2 (1989): 108–126. www.jstor.org/stable/27500683.
Weller, Edith. "The Unattached Woman." *Jewish Social Service Quarterly* 10, no. 1 (September 1933): 53–56.
Wenger, Beth S. "Budgets, Boycotts, and Babies: Jewish Women in the Great Depression." In Nadell, *American Jewish Women's History*, 185–200.
———. *Uncertain Promise: New York Jews and the Great Depression*. New Haven, CT: Yale University Press, 1996.
Wenner, Mark. Interviewed by author. Zoom. Kensington, MD. June 5, 2023. Personal collection.
Wenner, Naomi, and Seymour Wenner. Interviewed by Mel Scult. Transcribed by Jane Susswein. N.d. (circa 1970s). Personal collection.
White, Cyrille. Interviewed by author. Gwynedd, PA. June 15, 2020. Personal collection.

Witmire, Ethelene. "Experience 1930s Europe through the Words of Two African American Women." *Smithsonian Magazine*, March 2, 2020. www.smithsonianmag.com.
Wouk, Herman. *Marjorie Morningstar*. Garden City, NY: Doubleday, 1955.
Zeitz, Joshua. *Flapper: A Madcap Story of Sex, Style, Celebrity, and the Women Who Made America Modern*. New York: Crown, 2009.

INDEX

Page numbers in *italics* indicate photos

Abyssinian Baptist Church, 176
accountant, Kaplan, L., as, 207n104
activists, Jewish female, 50, 51, 227n26
Addelston, Albert, 33, 41, 148, 149, 156, 172; and Kaplan, J., 173
Adler, Felix, 39
AECP. *See* American Economic Committee for Palestine
affording, Palestine, 35–40
African Americans, 25, 27, 38, 86, 177
agencies, teaching placement, 31
agricultural communities, in Palestine, 12, 93, 109, 139–40, *142*, *143*; citrus industry in, 97
agricultural settlement *(kvuzoth)*, 108, 109, 127, 138, 144–45, 156; Weizmann and, 147
Agronsky, Gershon, 112, 167
AJC. *See* American Jewish Congress
Aleichem, Sholem, 113
Alexander, Pop, 129, 130
aliya (ascent), 163, 186
Almansor (Heine), 169
Alteneuland (Herzl), 91
Amcha (folk or common person), 113–14
American dream, 160
American Economic Committee for Palestine (AECP), 189
American Export Lines, 48, 66
American Jewish Committee, 146
American Jewish Congress (AJC), 31, 32–33
American Jewish institutions, 13

American Jewish women, 2, 4–5, 9, 12, 66, 88–89; cohort of, 35, 42, 47, 50–51, 54, 181; community of, 13, 196; constraints on, 18; migration of, 30, 48–54; modern, 100–101; opportunities for, 62–63, 101; in Palestine, 10, 11, 42, 180; reform efforts by, 50–51, 58; as teachers, 29–30, 179; Torah and, 186; Zionism and, 181, 182–83, 202n27
American Jewry, 10, 13–14, 32–33, 40, 46, 185; assimilation of, 6, 51, 54, 57, 58; community of, 1, 6, 41, 42, 47, 62; fate of, 158; Great Depression effecting, 56, 62; music and, 183
American Judaism, 5, 45, 182–83
American School of Oriental Research (ASOR), 103–4
anniversary, of Kaplan, L. and Kaplan, M., 161–62
annual report, of Jewish Agency (1931), 108
antisemitism, 5–6, 9, 10, 13, 14, 33, 46; in Germany, 168–70, 193; Kaplan, L., concerns about, 60, 167; problem of, 56, 57; in Tel Aviv carnival, 137; tropes of, 80; in US, 40, 146, 156, 195
anti-Zionism, 9, 127
apartment, in New York City, for Kaplan family, 174, 177
applicants, for Jewish teacher position, 29–30
Arabian headdress *(keffiyeh)*, 106
Arabian Nights (1932), 118

247

Arab Palestinians, 11, 42, 46, 60, 62, 71; discontent of, 133; employment of, 107–8; in Jezreel Valley, 145; Magnes, J., on, 131–32; at port in Jaffa, 90; refugees, 193
Arab Revolt (1936), 192–93, 194, 211n93
Arabs, 85, 86, 87–88, 92, 93, 99; colonial framework about, 91; nationalism of, 19, 211n93
archives, of underrepresented people, 3; Musher, H., 10, 11
Arlosoroff, Chaim, 163–64, 165
art, Jewish, 6, 184
'arus al-bahr (bride of the sea), 90
'arus falastin (bride of Palestine), 90
ascent *(aliya)*, 163
Ashkenazi, 7, 24, 94
ASOR. *See* American School of Oriental Research
assassination, of Rabin, 12
assimilation, of Jewish people into America, 6, 51, 54, 57, 58
Associated Press, 168–69
Association of American Orthodox Hebrew Congregations, 16
attack and war, October 7, 2023 in Gaza, 13, 14, 59, 195
attention, Musher, H., receiving, 122
attitudes, Arabs receiving, 86–88, 99
authorities, British, 95, 96

Baedeker (publisher), 118, 166
Balfour Declaration (1917), 47, 55–56, 61
Bank Holiday, 135
Bank of the United States, 38
bans: on employment of married women, 33–34, 178–79; of religious ceremonies at Kotel, 95
bar mitzvah (male rite of passage), 23, 24, 73, 77
Barnard College, 39
barriers, in cultural backgrounds, 85–86
Bassewitz, Lilia, 142

Bastille Day, 167
bat mitzvah (female rite of passage): adult, 186; first, ix, 1, 7, 22–23, 186, 204n30; of Kaplan, H., 24
Bedouin camp, 145–46
Beirut, Lebanon, 4, 78, 103, 162–63, 164
Benderly, Sansom, 47, 154
Ben-Gurion, David, 214n40
Berkson, Libbie Suchoff, 43, 194
biases and equality, gender, 23, 31, 32, 94, 140–42, 186
Bible, Hebrew, 19, 44, 109, 131, 134, 135; stories from, 144
biblical sites, in Palestine, 109
biblical studies, of Musher, H., 104, 131
A Bill of Divorcement (film), 172
binationalism, 60–61, 73, 105–6, 131
b'nei mitzvah. *See* bat mitzvah and bar mitzvah
Board of Education, 136, 187
Board of Examiners, New York City, 30
Board of Trustees, SAJ, 22, 36
boat traveling, rates for, 67–68
Bodenheimer, Friedrich Simon, 104
book burnings, 10, 93, 130, 168, 169, 225n71
boycott, of Jewish businesses, 130, 146
Braverman, Libbie, 184
Brickner, Rebecca Aaronson, 50
bride of Palestine *('arus falastin)*, 90
bride of the sea *('arus al-bahr)*, 90
B'rith Shalom, 132
British authorities, 95, 96
British Government, Jewish-Arab relations and, 132, 145
British Mandate Palestine, 8, 10, 11, 71, 90
Brookings Institute, 35
burning, of books, 10, 93, 130, 168, 169, 225n71
businesses, Jewish, 130, 146

Cahan, Abraham, 139
Cairo, Egypt, 84, 85, 86–87, 99, 118, 119; Musher, H., in, 127

INDEX | 249

Callner, Esther, 52, 118, 119, 120–21, *121*
camel riding, Musher, H., *122*
Camp Cejwin, 43, 44, 208n7
Camp Modin, 42–48, 61, 208n7
Canaan, Maine, 43
carnival, in Tel Aviv, 136–37, 189
Central Hotel, Egypt, 120, 121
Central Park, NY, 15, 18, 26, 28, 177
chaperones, for Musher, H., 43, 70, 72, 99
Chazan, Barry, 184
Chelouche, Zadoc, 162–63, 164, *164*, 165
children, of Musher, H., and Musher, S., 187
children parade, for Hanukkah, 116
Chumash, of Hebrew Bible, 19, 22
citrus industry, in Palestine, 97
civilization, Jewish, 7, 23, 51, 54–63, 104, 180
Cleopatra Baths, 88, *89*
clothing, as form of expression, 64–65
Cohen, George M., 21
Cohen, Samuel S., 183
cohort, of American Jewish women, 35, 42, 47, 50–51, 54, 181
collectives *(kibbutzim)*, 109, 138–39, 142–43
"College Report," Hunter College (1938), 27
colonial framework, Arabs and, 87–88, 91
colonialism, 11, 13, 60, 87, 88, 91; hierarchies in, 86, 89
colonies *(moshavot)*, 109
Columbia University, 16, 26, 29, 34, 38; New College, 129; Teachers College, 73, 129, 188
commandment *(mitzvah)*, 100; bar mitzvah, 23, 24, 73, 77; bat mitzvah, ix, 1, 7, 22–23, 186, 204n30; Mordecai Kaplan on, 54–55
Commission on Economic Problems (AJC), 31, 32–33
communal consciousness, in Judaism, 55

communal groups *(kvutzot)*, 109–10, 136, 143
community, American Jewish, 1, 6, 41, 42, 47, 62; Kehillah, 105; in Marseille, 83; in New York, 55; summer camp, 43; women in, 13, 196
companionship, of Kaplan, J., and Kaplan, M., 25–26
concerns, of Kaplan, L., 99, 102, 117, 125, 127, 167
conditions, in profession of education, 29, 30
conflict, of Jews in Palestine, 165
congregants, of Kaplan, M., 21, 36, 43; gender disparities in, 186
connection, of American Jews with culture, 192
constraints, on American Jewish women, 18
Cornell University, 74
Council of the League of Nations, 8
Creative Judaism (Eisenstein), 229n44
1929 Crises, 59–60, 86, 95, 133, 155, 211n93
criticism of Musher, H., 109, 124–25
Crossley, Robin, 170, *171*
Crusaders, 135
cultural backgrounds, barriers in, 85–86
"cultural hyphenism," 57
culture, Jewish, 5, 6, 51, 57, 98, 180; connection of American Jews with, 192; Hebrew, 50

Danit, Rivkah, 141
datebooks, of Musher, H., 1, 2, 3, 4, 201n5
death camp, Nazi, 83
demonstrations, at Kotel, 92–93, 95
depression, in Palestine, 107–8
description, of daughters in Kaplan family, 19–21
devaluation, of Polish currency, 107
Dewey, John, 51, 54, 152
diaries: of Kaplan, J., 25, 204n18; of Kaplan, M., 130, 146, 201n2, 201n7, 204n30, 211n92; of Musher, H., 24, 84, 85, 87, 201n11, 214n58

diaspora, 6, 7, 9, 11, 56–57, 94; Jewish, 183, 195–96
Dillingham Immigration Restriction Action (1921), 49
Di Morgn Frayhayt (Yiddish Communist newspaper), 60
Dinin, Samuel, 160–61, 165, 167, 184, 185
discontent, of Arab Palestinians, 10, 11, 59–62, 92–93, 133, 145, 192–93
discrimination, 6, 30, 31, 32, 56, 80; Jewish, 194; of married women employment, 33–34
division, of Jews in Israel, 195–96
divorce, 69, 70, 75, 172–73, 185
Douglass, Mabel Smith, 29
Dushkin, Alexander and Julia Aaronson, 43–44, 48, 61–62, 72, 74, 203n32; advising Musher, H., 103; in Palestine, 185

Eckhardt, Carl Conrad, 168, 169
economic crises, in US, 107, 135–36, 146
economic status, of Kaplan family, 37, 125–26
editorial work, of Musher, H., 112
education, Jewish, 9, 27, 43, 48, 63, 184; of Kaplan family, 188, 204n24, 206n62, 228n30; study abroad as, 181
educational style, of Dewey, 51, 54
Egypt, 118–20, *121*, 122, 123, 127, 220n8; Alexandria, 79, 84, 85, 88, *89*, 99; Cairo, 84, 85, 86–87, 99; Luxor, 88, 124
Egyptology, 119
Ein Harod (Kibbutz), 139–40, 142, *143*, 144, 145 *142*
Eisenstein, Ethan (nephew), 228n29
Eisenstein, Ira (brother-in-law), 25, 36, 185, 186, 202n17, 207n99; *Creative Judaism*, 229n44; Kaplan, J., and, 228n29
Eisenstein, Judith (Kaplan). *See* Kaplan, Judith
Eisenstein, Miriam (niece), 173, 186
EL. *See* elevated train
Elements of Palestine (Nimtzowitz), 183–84

elevated train (El), 25, 28
emancipation, of Jewish people, 6, 185
employment: of Arab Palestinians, 107–8; of Jewish women, 31–32, 33–34
end of life, Musher, H., 191–92
English-language guidebook of Egypt (Baedeker), 118
entertainment, causing juvenile delinquency, 32
Epstein, Edward and Sarah, 101
Eretz, Israel, 154–55
Esther (biblical character), 136, 137, 189
ethical-liberal, Jewish nation, 61
ethnonationalism, 59, 62
Europe, 2, 10, 15, 91, 147, 157; immigrants from, 74, 175; Musher, H., in, 170, *171*
exchange, international student, 128–29, 130
Exochorda (ship), 2, 52, 65, 76, 90, 212n10; passengers on, 68–69; traveling on board, 64–89
expenses for travels, to Palestine, 39–40, 125–26
expression, clothing as form of, 64–65

faculty, JTS, 17
Fairfield, Connecticut, 2
family history, of Kaplan family, 1–14
Family Law Act (1969), 173
fashion, of Musher, H., 64–65, 115
fate, of American Jewry, 158
FDR. *See* Roosevelt, Franklin Delano
feminism, 10, 22, 119, 142, 187, 192; Jewish activists in, 50, 51, 227n26
Feuchtwanger, Lion, 112
financial means, of Kaplan family, 38, 125–26, 127, 135, 157, 161–62; frugality of, 173–74
first-class travelers, on *Exochorda*, 66
Flotilla (ship), 63
folk or common person (*Amcha*), 113–14
"Four Aces," American Export Lines, 66, 67

France, 82–84, 85, 165, 166
friction, among Jews, political, 164–65
Friedlander, Lillian, 152
fundraising, for Kol Nidre, 98

Gaza Strip, 12, 13, 14, 195
Gelber, Sylva, 44, 45, 52–53, 67, 139, *163*; *Hadassah* organization and, 153; idealism of, 165; *No Balm in Gilead*, 194; on *Vulcania*, 212n14
gender, equality and biases, 23, 31, 32, 94, 140–42, 186; inclusivity services for, 95
gender disparities, in congregation of Kaplan, M., 186
"gender-inclusive services," 95
Gentile, 82, 88
German Jews, 168–69; in Palestine, 175–76
Germany, 10, 17, 128, 129–30, 137, 163; Jews leaving, 175–76; Munich, 168, 169, 193, 225n71; refugees in, 202n22; violence and antisemitism in, 168–70, 193
Geva, 140, 141
Gezira Island, 120, *121*
Gideon (biblical character), 144
Glass, Joseph, 53
Gluck, J. C., 178, 179
Glueck, Nelson, 104
Goldman, Selma (sister). *See* Kaplan, Selma
Goldsmit House, 91–92, 93, 102, 103
graduation, Hunter College, 29
Grand Synagogue, 83
Great Depression, 15, 18, 32, 33, 35, 36; American Jews during, 40, 56, 62; economic hardship during, 37, 124; as Hollywood Golden Age, 64
Great Migration, of African Americans, 25
Gruber, Ruth, 10, 128, 129

Ha'am, Ahad, 7, 57, 61, 130
Habima (theater company), 113, 114
Hadassah (myrtle), 18

Hadassah organization, 18, 43, 49, 63, 133–34, 228n41; aid for minority groups, 59; Gelber and, 153; Jacobs, R., as president of, 72–73; model society by, 51; Study Circle, 17, 52, 73, 105; women of, 58, 72–75
Haifa, Palestine, 90, 91, 110, *150*
Halkin, Abraham, 45, 56
Halkin, Simon, 160
halutzim/haluzim (Zionist pioneers), 182–84
Hamas militants, in Palestine, 12–13, 59, 195
Hanukkah (Jewish holiday), 115–16
happiness, of Kaplan, M., 153–56
hardships, Great Depression economic, 37, 124
Harlem, NY, 16, 24, 25
Harry, Myriam, 46
Hashomer Hatzair (The Young Guard), 46, 47, 138, 149
Hatzafon Kvutzah (settlement of the Socialist Zionist youth group), 149
Hebrew, 1, 2, 4, 5, 6, 7; Bible, 19, 44, 109, 131, 134, 135; *Chumash* of, 19, 22; culture, 50; Kaplan, M., and, 158; language of, 44, 110–12, 113, 202n19; letters, from Musher, H., in, 112–13, 114, 155; literature, 54, 61, 93, 111, 114, 130–31; modern, 8, 9, 44, 50; school, 8, 19, 21, 37; teacher of, 74, 103, 111, 115, 160
Hebrew Language Committee, 8
Hebrew Teacher Seminary, in Jerusalem, 74, 103
Hebrew University, 1, 40, 43, 50, 54, 72; Magnes, J., at, 105, 133; professors from, 104
Heine, Heinrich, 169
Helovan, SS, 162, *163*, *164*, 170
Henry, Alvan (Read), 78–79, 80, 82, 84, 88; in Cleopatra Baths, *89*; in Egypt, 119, 120
Henry, Elaine and Robert (Pat), 78
Herzl, Theodor, 56, 90–91

hierarchies, in colonialism, 86, 89
Hitler, Adolf, 10, 71, 80, 129, 137, 146;
   Youth members of, 169
Hollywood Golden Age, 64
Holy Land, tourism to, 47–48, 53, 91, 134
homeland, Jewish, 5, 40, 46, 55, 61, 116;
   Kaplan, M., on, 192; Magnes, J., and B.,
   on, 132
homeless shelters, Jewish, 35
Hoover, Herbert, 107, 123–24
Hoover, Lou, 66–67
hostility, in Jewish-Arab relations, 95
houseboat, on Gezira Island, 120, *121*
households, Jewish, 8, 35, 36
Hunter College, 2, 24, 25, 26, 27, 28; graduation from, 29; master's program at, 187
al-Husseini, Haj Amin, 93

ICJ. *See* International Court of Justice
iconography, Zionist, 47
idealism, of Gelber, 165
idealization, of Palestine, 61–62, 155
identities, Jewish, 5, 6, 22, 196
identity, travel as vehicle to forge, 66
IDF. *See* Israeli Defense Force
Ihud association (Unity), 105–6
immigrants, 4, 25, 27, 38, 46, 49; from
   Europe, 74, 175; from Germany, 163,
   175–76; Glass on, 53; to Palestine, 91, 193;
   representation of mothers as, 100–101
The Immortal Adventure (Lindheim), 46
importance, of American Jewish women
   community, 196
incomes, Jewish family, 35–36
Institute of Musical Art. *See* Julliard School
institutions, American Jewish, 13
intergenerational bridge, Musher, H.,
   story as, 14, 182
international: exchange of students,
   128–29, 130; travel, 35, 209n36
International Court of Justice (ICJ), 13
interwar period, 8–9, 10, 128–29, 165, 182,
   220n8

Isaacson, Fred, 72
Isaacson, Lena, 71
Isaacson, Reba, 52, 70, 71–72, 75, *76*, 77; in
   Cairo, 86–87; in New York, 152; Yellin
   and, 103; YWHA and, 118
Israel, 5, 8, 12–14, 16, 145, 154–55; Jewish women influence on, 182, 194–95;
   organizations in, 195; PEF and UJA
   support in, 190; State of, 47, 182,
   193–94; Unterberg, 39–40
Israeli Defense Force (IDF), 13
Ivrit b'Ivrit (learning Hebrew by speaking
   Hebrew), 8, 47

Jabotinsky, Vladimir, 164
Jacobs, Joshua, 73–74
Jacobs, Rose Gell, 72–73, 80, 101, 118, 208n4
Jacobs, Ruth, 73
Jaffa, Palestine, 2, 63, 90–91, *163*
jealousy, of Kaplan, L., 110
Jerusalem, 1, 2, 10, 53–54, 59–60, 71; Hebrew
   Teacher Seminary in, 74, 103; Musher,
   H., in, 91–92, 93, 97–98, 111, 124, 149–51;
   Yishuv Welfare Bureau in, 153
Jew-Gentile, 82, 88
Jewish Agency, annual report (1931), 108;
   Arlosoroff as leader of, 163
Jewish-Arab relations, 10, 11, 60, 61, 62,
   73; British Government and, 132, 145;
   hostility within, 95
Jewish camp, 42–48, 61, 145–46, 208n7
Jewish Center, 19, 21, 36, 37, 39, 45
Jewish Day School (Jewish Center), 21
Jewish education, 9, 27, 43, 48, 63, 184
Jewish holidays, 25; Hanukkah, 115–16;
   Lag B'Omer, 149; in Palestine, 92–95,
   115–16, 136–38, 149–51, *150*; Passover,
   136, 137–38, 143–44, 149–50; Purim,
   136, 137, 138, 188–89; Rosh Hashanah, 82, 83, 115; Shavuot, 149–51, *150*,
   161; Simchat Torah, 94; Sukkot, 98;
   Tu B'shvat, 136; Yom Kippur, 91–95, 98
Jewish Institute of Religion (JIR), 144

Jewish migration, 30, 48–54
Jewish National Fund (JNF), 144, 145
Jewishness, 29, 32, 42, 61, 96, 170
Jewish New Year. *See* Rosh Hashana
Jewish Palestinians, 46, 99, 110–11, 115
Jewish peoplehood, 18, 55, 57, 104, 114, 210n61
Jewish pioneers *(halutzim)*, 184
"Jewish Problem," 5–6
Jewish Reconstructionist Federation, 3
Jewish Second Temple, 92
Jewish Theological Center, 18
Jewish Theological Seminary (JTS), 1, 6, 16, 17, 36, 37, 45; Halkin and, 45; Kaplan, M. and, 18–19, 29, 43; Szold and, 57; Teachers' Institute, 6, 8, 21, 26, 33, 43; Unterberg and, 39–40
Jezreel Valley, 145
JIR. *See* Jewish Institute of Religion
JNF. *See* Jewish National Fund
Joffe, Harry, 96, 97, 103, 109, 147, 153
Joseph, Jacob, 16
Josephus, Flavius, 112, 134
journey, of Musher, H., 12, 13, 34, 38, 40, 42; meaning of, 196
joy *(nachas)*, 100
JTS. *See* Jewish Theological Seminary
Judaism, 6, 7, 9, 12, 39, 44; American, 5, 45, 182–83; communal consciousness in, 55; Kaplan, M., on, 54–63, 104, 146; revitalization of, 40, 57; role of women in, 11–12, 58, 94, 95, 181
"Judaism and Nationality" (Kaplan, M.), 57
Judaism as a Civilization (Kaplan, M.), 54–63, 154, 162
Julliard School, 19
Junior Hadassah, 131, 132, 133
juvenile delinquency, entertainment causing, 32

Kail, Milton, 34
Kallen, Deborah, 54
Kaplan, Anna (Grandma), 100

Kaplan, Hadassah, *4*, 5, 6, 7, 9, 23–24; archives of, 10, 11; attention given to, 122; attitude toward Arabs, 86–88; biblical studies of, 104, 131; in Cairo, 127; Camp Modin, Zionism and, 42–48; chaperones for, 43, 70, 72, 99; Chelouche and, 162–63, 164, *164*, 165; children of, 187; criticism by Kaplan, L., of, 108–9, 124–25; datebooks of, 1, 2, 3, 4, 201n5; diaries of, 24, 84, 85, 87, 201n11, 214n58; Dushkin advising, 103; editorial work of, 112; in Egypt, 118–20, *121*; at Ein Harod, 139–40, 142, *142*, *143*, 144, 145; end of life, 191–92; in Europe, 170, *171*; on the *Exochorda*, 64–89, *65*, *76*; fashion of, 64–65, 115; Gelber and, 52; at Geva, 140, 141; on Gezira Island, 120, *121*; Gluck and, 178, *179*; *Hadassah* organization and, 133–34; Hebrew studies of, 110–12, 113; in Jerusalem, 91–92, 97–98, 111, 124, 149–51; journey of, 12, 13, 34, 38, 40, 42; Kaplan, M., and, 26, 41–42; knowledge and skills of, 180; leaving Palestine, 152, 156–57, 159–60, 162–63; life path of, 160; Magnes D., and, 106, 132; maturation of, 179, 181–82; mentors of, 101, 102, 103, 152; Musher, S., and, 34–35, 177, 179, 187, 189, 190; in New York, 174–80; Palestine and, 41, 43, 50–52, 63, 128, *150*; personal letters of, 44–45, 88, 94, 101–2, 109, 177; in Petra, 103, 104, *105*; reading list of, 131; at religious sites, 134–35; riding camels, 122; send-off picture of, 64–65, *65*; Sherman and, 102; story as intergenerational bridge, 14, 182; as substitute teacher, 28, 29, 136, 187, 206n62; Szold and, 174–75, 176; teaching, 30–31, 176, 183; in Tel Aviv, 90–91, 158, 160; tone in letters by, 113; traveling expenses of, 37–38, 39–40, 125–26; in Venice, 165, 166, *166*; weight of, 37, 78, 207n109; as a widow, 190–91; in Willy's Knight, 205n56

Kaplan, Judith (sister), 1, 9, 12, 18, 19, 20; Addelston and, 33, 173; at Barnard College, 39; bat mitzvah accounts from, 22–23; diaries of, 25, 204n18; divorce of, 172–73; education of, 188, 204n24, 206n62; Eisenstein and, 185, 228n29; Hunter College accounts by, 25; Kaplan, M., and, 25–26, 41–42, 201n7; marriage of, 116, 172; Palestine and, 26; teaching, 183; tutors of, 204n15

Kaplan, Lena (mother), 1, 12, 17, 36, 37, 51; as accountant, 207n104; anniversary to Kaplan, M., 161–62; attitude toward Arabs, 86; concerns of, 99, 102, 117, 125, 127, 167; criticism of Musher, H., 108–9, 124–25; financial means of, 125–26, 127, 128, 157, 161–62; jealous of Musher, H., 110; on Kaplan, S., 116–17; letters to Musher, H., 77–78, 99–100, 106, 108–9, 125–26; on Palestine, 159–60; send-off picture of, 65

Kaplan, Mordecai (father), 1, 2, 6–7, 8, 11–12; American Jewish community and, 41; American Judaism and, 45; Bank of the United States, 38; bat mitzvah ceremony and, 22–23, 24; congregants of, 21, 36, 43; diaries of, 130, 146, 201n2, 201n7, 204n30, 211n92; happiness of, 153–56; Hebrew and, 158; influence on Kaplan daughters, 26, 41–42; on Jewish homeland, 192; on Judaism, 54–63, 104, 146; "Judaism and Nationality," 57; on *Judaism as a Civilization* and Zionism, 54–63, 154; Kaplan, J., and, 25–26, 201n7; letters to Musher, H., 78, 98, 154–55, 157–58, 207n109; in New York (1889), 16–17; on Palestine, 159–60; on Reconstructionism, 202n7, 227n19; in Rosenwald competition, 154, 162; sabbatical of, 129, 138, 153–54, 157, 161, 185; SAJ and, 154; Scottsboro Trials and, 86; send-off picture of, 65; social justice seminar and, 153–54; Szold and, 155–56; and Teachers' Institute, 18–19, 29, 43; "What the American Jewish Woman Can Do for Jewish Education," 58; on Zionism, 54–63, 185, 192

Kaplan, Naomi (sister), 9, 12, 18, 19, 20, 37; education of, 188, 228n30; Kaplan, M., and, 41–42; letter to Musher, H., 77, 148; at New York Society for Ethical Culture and, 39

Kaplan, Selma (sister), 3, 9, 12, 18, 19, 20; education of, 188, 206n62; in England, 170, *171*; Kaplan, L., letter about, 116–17; Kaplan, M., and, 41–42; letter to Musher, H., 76–77; at New York Society for Ethical Culture and, 39; songs by, 191; traveling to Germany, 129, 130; *When We Were Very Young*, 20

Kaplan, Sophie (Great-Aunt), 100, 114–15

kashrut (religious laws preparing food for consumption), 16, 55

Katznelson, 111

keffiyeh (Arabian headdress), 106

Kehillah (Jewish Community), 105

Kehillat Jeshurun synagogue (KJ), 17, 18, 21

Keller, Helen, 169

kibbutz (agricultural community), 12, 93, 109, 110, 111, 138–40, *142*, 142–43; Musher, H., on, *143*

King David Hotel, 96, 103, 106, 134

KJ. *See* Kehillat Jeshurun

Klausner, Joseph, 54, 93, 160

knowledge, of Musher, H., 180

Knox, William Van, 78, 80, 81, 84, 85, 86–87; in Egypt, 120

Koestler, Arthur, 98

Kol Nidre services, 92, 93, 98

Kotel (Western Wall), 92–93, 95–96

Kramer, Stanley, 189

Kronick, Miriam, 90

kvutzot (communal groups), 109–10, 136

kvutzot/kvuzoth (agricultural communal settlements), 108–10, 127, 136, 138, 144–45, 156

Lag B'Omer (Jewish holiday), 149
La Guardia, Fiorello, 178–79
land, as central to Jewish nationalism, 96
language, Hebrew, 44, 47, 110–12, 113, 202n19; Musher, H., working on, 110–12; reclamation of, 8; renewal of, 114, 115, 130; Zionism and, 44
law, Jewish, 41, 42
learning Hebrew by speaking Hebrew (Ivrit b'Ivrit), 8, 47
Lenox, "Negro Harlem," 176
Levine, Milton, 147
Levinthal, Helen, 144
Levy, Esther and Joseph, 120–22, 123, 124, 127, 135
liberation, for Jewish women, traveling as, 50, 66, 88–89, 181–82
libraries, in *kibbutzim*, 143
Lichtman, Sydney, 107
Lieberman, Ralph, 34, 106–7, 177
life path, of Musher, H., 160
"Like All the Nations?" (Magnes, J.), 131, 133
Lindheim, Irma, 46, 138, 141, 142–43, 152
Lipstadt, Deborah, 225n68
literature, Hebrew, 54, 61, 93, 111, 114, 130–31
Livny, 111
London, England, 170, *171*
Lower East Side, NY, 15, 16, 17, 25, 27, 68

Magnes, Beatrice Lowenstein and Judah Leon, 104–7, 131–32, 133, 134, 147
Magnes, David, 104–5, 106
Malcolm, Douglas, 68
Malkin, Minnie, 160
Manhattan, NY, 7, 15, 18, 35, 176
manual labor, 140–41, 142, 146, 179
Marjorie Morningstar (Wouk), 28, 205n52
marriage, of Kaplan, J., 116, 172
married women, employment bans of, 33–34, 178–79
Marseille, France, 82–83, 85

Marseille, Jewish communities in, 83
Marshall, Louis, 57, 105
masters program, at Hunter College, 187
maturation of, Musher, H., 179, 181–82
Mediterranean Sea, 59, 66, 68, 83
Megillah (scroll), 189
Mein Kampf (Hitler), 80
Menorah (1915), 58
Menorah Society, 27, 43
mentors, of Musher, H., 101, 102, 103, 152
Middle East, 1
migration, of American Jewish women, 30, 91; promised land tourism and, 48–54
Miller, William, 70
minority groups, *Hadassah* organization aid for, 59
missionary families, on board the *Exochorda*, 70
mitzvah and *mitzvot* (commandments), 23, 100
Mixed Court, 78
Mizrachi, Zionist movement, 47, 56, 181, 202n23
model society, by *Hadassah* organization, 51
modern, American Jewish women, 100–101
modern Hebrew, 8, 9, 44, 50
Moore, Deborah Dash, 23
Morgenstern, Marjorie (fictional character), 28
moshavot (colonies or family-based settlements), 109
mother-daughter relationships, Jewish, 100, 117
mother of the stranger *(umm al-gharib)*, 90
movement, Zionist, 47, 49, 56, 184
Muhammad, 92
Munich, Germany, 168, 169, 193, 225n71
Murray, Martin, 70
Musher, Daniel (son), 187

Musher, Hadassah. *See* Kaplan, Hadassah
Musher, Jeremy (son), 187
Musher, Sidney (husband), 34–35, 177, 179, 187, 189–90
music, American Jewry and, 183
myrtle (*Hadassah*), 18

nachas (joy), 100
Naples, France, 83–84, 85, 165, 166
nation, ethical-liberal Jewish, 61
nationalism, Jewish, 52, 54, 55, 56, 57, 58–59; and Arab, 92, 193, 211n93; land as central to, 96; relationship to peoplehood, 210n61
national marriage rate, 35
Nazis, 10, 71, 83, 129, 146, 168–70
"Negro Harlem," Lenox Street, NY, 176
neighborhoods, "Yekke" German Jewish, 175
Nevada, 172–73
New College, at Columbia University, 129
New Hebrew Woman, 140–41
New Jew, 115, 139–40
Newton, Francis, 70–71, 213n31, 213n32
New York (NY), 20, 36, 55, 127, 152, 174–80; Board of Examiners in, 30; Central Park, 15, 18, 26, 28, 177; *Exochorda* docked in, 64, 65; Harlem, 16, 24, 25; Jewish homeless shelters in, 35; Lower East Side, 15, 16, 17, 25, 27, 68; private schools, public *versus*, 38, 39; public college in, 27, 28, 39; Upper East Side, 17, 18, 24, 26, 27; Upper West Side, 7, 15, 18, 21, 35, 40
New York Society for Ethical Culture, 39
New York Sun, 30
New York Times, 68, 119, 120, 128, 177, 225n68
Nimtzowitz, Temima, 183–84
Nineteenth Amendment, 21–22
No Balm in Gilead (Gelber), 194
non-Zionist, 55, 60, 93, 118–19, 127
NY. *See* New York

October 7, 2023, attack and war in Gaza, 13, 14, 59, 195
Olympic (ship), 130
opportunities, for American Jewish women, 62–63, 101
orange groves, in Palestine, 97, 109
orchards (*pardes*), 141
organizations, of American Jews, 46; in Israel, 195
Orientalist stereotypes, of Arabs, 11, 86, 123, 164
Orthodox Jews, 9, 16, 17, 21, 202n23
Oslo Accords, 12–13
Ottoman Empire, 8, 92, 95

Palestine, 1, 4, 5, 6, 7, 35–40; affording, 35–40; agricultural communities in, 12, 93, 109, 139–40, *142*, *143*; American Jewish women in, 10, 11, 42, 180; American Jewry and, 185; biblical sites in, 109; British Mandate over, 8, 10, 11, 71, 90; challenges in, 155; depression in, 107–8; German Jews in, 175–76; Haifa, 90, 91, 110, *150*; Hamas militants in, 12–13, 59, 195; idealization of, 61–62, 155; immigration to, 91, 193; Jaffa, 2, 63, 90–91, *163*; Jewish conflict in, 165; Jewish holidays in, 92–95, 115–16, 136–38, 149–51, *150*; Jewish migrants to, 91, 193; Kaplan, J., and, 26; leaving, 152, 156–57, 159–60, 162–63; Musher, H., and, 41, 43, 50–52, 63, 128, *150*; orange groves in, 97, 109; pilgrimages to, 47–48; prosperity of, 107–8; religion in, 94–95; tourism in, 47–54, 91, 134; traveling to, 9, 18, 40, 41, 64–89, 184; violence in, 193–95, 211n93; Yishuv (Jewish population in Palestine), 91, 115, 116
Palestine Endowment Fund (PEF), 189–90, 228n41
Palestine Liberation Organization (PLO), 12
Palestine Post, 112, 136, 169

Palestinians, 214n39; Arab, 11, 42, 46, 60, 62, 71; Jewish, 46, 99, 110–11, 115
pardes (orchards), 141
Parker, Hugh, 79–81, 83–84, 85, 88, 95, 120; poem by, 214n62
parties, Musher, H., at, 24, 96, 116, 122, 123, 129; anniversary of Kaplan, L. and Kaplan, M., 161–62; Purim, 137, 138
passengers, on the *Exochorda*, 68–69
passing, Jewish, 82, 170
Passover (Jewish holiday), 136, 137–38, 143–44, 149–50
Pat. *See* Henry, Robert
PEF. *See* Palestine Endowment Fund
peoplehood, Jewish, 18, 55, 57, 104, 114, 210n61
performance *(shpiel)*, 137
period, interwar, 8–9, 10, 128–29, 165, 182, 220n8
personality, of Kaplan daughters, 19–21
personal letters, of Musher, H., 44–45, 88, 94, 101–2, 109, 177; in Hebrew, 112–13, 114, 155; to Kaplan family, 212n11, 212n14
Petra, Jordan, 103, 104, *105*
pharaonic past, of Egypt, 119
Pianko, Noam, 210n72
Pickford, Lucy W., 69–70
pilgrimages, for Jewish revitalization, 47–48
pioneers, Jewish women as, 181–82
PLO. *See* Palestine Liberation Organization
poem, by Parker, 214n62
Polish currency, devaluation of, 107
political friction, among Jews, 164–65
popularization, of Zionism, 51
population, of Jewish New Yorkers, 15
port, in Jaffa, 90
Powell, Adam Clayton, 176
Pratt, Mary Louise, 85–86
Prell, Riv-Ellen, 100
premarital relations, 81–82, 148–49
preparations, for bat mitzvah, 22

president, of *Hadassah* (organization), 72–73
Primer on Palestine (Junior Hadassah), 131, 132, 133
principles, Jewish, 132
private schools, in New York, public *versus*, 38, 39
privilege, 29, 38, 71
problem, of antisemitism, 13, 14, 33, 56, 57
profession of education, conditions in, 29, 30
professors, from Hebrew University, 104
promised lands. *See specific topics*
propaganda, Nazi, 168
prosperity, of Palestine, 107–8
protest, of 1929 Crises, 133
Pro-Wailing Wall Committee (Klausner), 93
Pruszynski, Ksawery, 107–8
public college, educating women in, 27, 28
pulpit, 6, 18, 21, 29, 36–37
Purim (Jewish holiday), 136, 137, 138, 188–89

Quaker Oats, 187

rabbi, 6, 12, 16, 19, 144
Rabin, Yitzhak, 12
racism, 86, 99, 123, 195
Raider, Mark, 181
rams horn (shofar), 95, 96, 97
Rashi. *See* Yitzhaki, Shlomo
rate, national marriage, 35
rates, for boat traveling, 67–68
Read. *See* Henry, Alvan
reading list, of Musher, H., 131
Reagan, Ronald, 173
reclamation, of Hebrew language, 8
reconstruction, of American Jewry, 154–55
Reconstructionism, 1, 7, 11, 41, 55, 187; Kaplan, M., on, 202n7, 227n19
Reconstructionist Rabbinical College (RRC), 1

reformers, Jewish, 47, 50–51, 58
Reform Movement, 52–53, 58, 144
refugees: Arab Palestinian, 193; German, 202n22
Reines, Isaac Jacob, 56
Reinharz, Shulamit, 181
relations, Jewish-Arab, 10, 11, 60, 61, 62, 73; British Government and, 132, 145
relationship: of American Jewish women and Palestine, 10–11; of Jewish nationalism to peoplehood, 210n61; mother-daughter, 100, 117; between Musher, H., and Gluck, 178, 179; between Musher, H., and Parker, 81–82
religion, 134–35; in Palestine, 94–95; PS 89 communities and, 176–77
religious laws preparing food for consumption (kashrut), 16, 55
renewal, of Hebrew language, 114, 115, 130
representations, of immigrant mothers, 100–101
Revisionists, Zionist, 92, 164, 165
revitalization, of Judaism, 40, 57; pilgrimages for, 47–48
rites, of passage: bar mitzvah (male rite of passage), 23, 24, 73, 77; bat mitzvah (female rite of passage), 1, 7, 22–24, 186, 204n30
roles, of women in Judaism, 11–12, 58, 94, 95; traveling as liberation for, 50, 66, 88–87, 181–82
Roosevelt, Eleanor, 188
Roosevelt, Franklin Delano (FDR), 18, 38, 106–7, 135
Rosenblatt, Zvi, 164
Rosenwald competition, Kaplan, M., in, 154, 162
Rosh Hashanah (Jewish holiday), 82, 83, 115
RRC. *See* Reconstructionist Rabbinical College
Rubin, Dorothy (cousin), 2
Rubin, Isadore (uncle), 39

Rubin, Naomi (cousin), 2
Ruppin, Arthur, 93
Russell Sage Foundation, 31
Russian Revolution, impacting immigrants, 49

Sabbath, 2, 41, 53, 55, 96, 97; in Tel Aviv, 98
sabbatical, of Kaplan, M., 129, 138, 153–54, 161, 185
SAJ. *See* Society for the Advancement of Judaism
Sampter, Jessie, 94–95, 155–56
Schechter, Mathilde and Solomon, 57, 58, 203n32
school, Hebrew, 8, 19, 21, 37
Schoolman, Albert and Bertha Singer, 43, 44, 72, 74–75, 103, 208n7
Schwartz, Helen, 90, 118, 165, 167
Scottsboro Trials, 86
scroll (*Megillah*), 189
Scult, Mel, 37, 158, 203n31, 207n104
Second Intifada, 12
send-off, of Musher, H., 64–65, 65
Sephardim, 7, 83, 92, 93
services, Kol Nidre, 92, 93
Seth Low Junior College, 38–39
settlements, family-based (*moshavot*), 109
Shapiro, Ezra, 97
Shapiro, Zelda, 96
Shavit, Ari, 223n120
Shavuot (Jewish holiday), 149–51, 150, 161
Sherman, Anna Grossman, 101–2, 103, 184
shofar (rams horn), 95, 96, 97
Shoham, Hizky, 137
shpiel (performance), 137
Simchat Torah (Jewish holiday), 94
Simon, Jack, 85, 92, 96, 102–3, 147, 214n58
Six-Day War (1967), 13
social clubs, in New York, 26
social justice seminar, Kaplan, M., 153–54
social life, in Tel Aviv, 98, 160–61
social status, of Jewish people, 33

INDEX | 259

Society for the Advancement of Judaism (SAJ), 2–3, 21, 45, 70, 94, 186; bat mitzvah oath for, 23–24; Board of Trustees, 22, 36; Great Depression effecting, 36; Kaplan, M., frustrations with, 154; pulpit salary at, 36–37; synagogue of, 154, 183; Women Division at, 188
Sokolow, Nahum, 113–14, 219n143
songs, by Kaplan, S., 191
Soyer, Daniel, 49
spiritual center, Palestine as, 94
Springtide in Palestine (Harry), 46
State of Israel, 5, 13, 47, 182, 193–94
Stavsky, Avraham, 164
stereotypes, Orientalist, 11, 86, 123, 164
studies, of Musher, H., 104, 131
study, Brookings Institute, 35
study abroad, 12, 130, 153, 161, 179–80, 181
Study Circle, *Hadassah*, 17, 52, 73, 105
substitute teacher, Musher, H., as, 28, 29, 136, 187, 206n62
Sukkot (Jewish holiday), 98
summer camp, Jewish community at, 43
Sundelsohn, John (Jack), 34, 147
supplemental programs, at Jewish Center and Society for the Advancement of Judaism, 45
Susman, Warren, 160
synagogues, 6, 15, 18–19, 36, 46, 56; Grand, 83; SAJ, 154, 183; Sephardic, 93
Szold, Henrietta, 17, 51, 57, 72, 73, 74; Gelber and, 153; *Hadassah* organization founded by, 18, 43, 49, 63, 133–34, 228n41; Kaplan, M., and, 155–56; Musher, H., and, 174–75, 176

Tavern on the Green, Central Park, NY, 177
Tchernichovsky, Shaul, 54, 160
teachers: Hebrew language, 74, 103, 111, 115, 160; Jewish women as, 29–30, 179; Musher, H., as, 30–31, 176, 183

Teachers College, at Columbia University, 26, 38, 129, 188
Teachers' Institute of the Jewish Theological Society, 6, 8, 21, 26, 33, 43; Kaplan, M., and, 18–19, 29, 43
teaching placement agencies, 31
Tel Aviv, 7–8, 37, 54, 76, 96–97, 116; carnival in, 136–37, 189; Musher, H., in, 90–91, 158, 160; social life in, 98, 160–61
Thomas Cook & Son, 49, 86
threats, to State of Israel, 193–94
tone, of Musher, H., letters, 113
Torah, 22, 24, 44, 47, 50, 94; Jewish women and, 186
tourism, in Palestine: Holy Land, 47–48, 53, 91, 134; migration of Jewish women and promised land, 48–54
Tower of David, 134
transatlantic travel, 10, 49, 66, 68
travel: international, 35, 209n36; as vehicle to forge identity, 66
traveling, to Palestine, 2–3, 4–5, 9, 19, 47–48, 184; on *Exochorda*, 64–89, 65, 76; expenses for, 37–38, 39–40, 125–26; as liberation for Jewish women, 50, 66, 88–89, 181–82
Tripoli, 161, 162, 165
tropes, antisemitic, 80
"Truth from the Land of Israel" (Ha'am), 61
Tu'B'shvat (Jewish holiday), 136
Tutankhamun, 87, 119
tutors, of Kaplan, J., 204n15

UJA. *See* United Jewish Appeal
umm al-gharib (mother of the stranger), 90
underrepresented people, archives of, 3
United Jewish Appeal organization (UJA), 190
United Nations, 13
United States (US), 6, 9, 11, 27, 30, 33; antisemitism in, 40, 146, 156, 195; Bank of, 38; economic crises in, 107, 135–36, 146

Unity (Ihud association), 105–6
Unterberg, Israel, 39–40
Untermyer, Samuel, 130
Upper East Side, NY, 17, 18, 24, 26, 27
Upper West Side, NY, 7, 15, 18, 21, 35, 40 "uptown Jews," 15
uptown life, of Kaplan family, 18–28
US. *See* United States

Vagabond Mediterranean Cruises, 68
Valley of the Tombs of the Kings, 119
Van Camp Co., 34
Vanderbilt, Cornelius, Jr., 122, 123–24
Varner, Carmen, 191
Venice, Italy, 165, 166, *166*
violence: in demonstrations at Kotel, 93; in Germany, 168–70, 193; in Palestine, 193–95, 211n93
voices, of women and underrepresented people, 3
volunteers, Kaplan H., and Musher as, 190
Voorhis, John, 207n109
voyagers, on the *Exochorda*, 65–66
Vulcania (ship), 212n14

Wadleigh, Lydia, 24
Wadleigh High School for Girls, 24, 25, 26
war and attack, in Gaza Strip, 12, 13, 14, 195
Warburg, Felix and Frieda Schiff, 57, 102, 119, *122*, 126, 127
Warburg, Gisela, 119, *122*
weight, of Musher, H., 37, 78, 207n109
Weizmann, Chaim, 147
Wenner, Naomi (sister). *See* Kaplan, Naomi
Wenner, Seymour (brother-in-law), 37
West Bank, 12, 13
Westernland (ship), 174
Western Wall. *See* Kotel
"What the American Jewish Woman Can Do for Jewish Education" (Kaplan, M.), 58

When We Were Very Young (Kaplan, S.), 20
Wide-Open Gambling Act (1931), 172–73
widow, Musher, H., as, 190–91
Willy's Knight (automobile), Musher, H., in, 205n56
Wise, Stephen Samuel, 144, 146, 160, 189
Wolfe, Thomas, 65
women, American Jewish, 2, 4–5, 9, 10, 11, 12; community of, 13; emancipation of, 185; employment of, 31–32, 33–34, 178–79; of *Hadassah* organization, 58, 72–75; history of, 3; influence on Isreal, 182, 194–95; manual labor of, 140–41, 142; migration and, 48–54; participation in SAJ, 186; as pioneers, 181–82; public college for, 27, 28; Reconstructionism and, 187
Women's Division, at SAJ, 188
World War I, 8, 78, 104, 164
World War II, 5, 15, 47, 182, 192
Wouk, Herman, 28, 205n52

Ben-Yehuda, Eliezer, 8, 202n20
"Yekke," German Jewish neighborhoods, 175
Yellin, David, 103
Yiddish, 7, 8, 9. *See also* Hebrew
Yishuv (Jewish population in Palestine), 91, 115, 116
Yishuv Welfare Bureau, Jerusalem, 153
Yitzhaki, Shlomo (Rashi), 19
YMCA. *See* Young Men's Christian Association
Yom Kippur (Jewish holiday), 91–95, 98
The Young Guard (Hashomer Hatzair), 46, 47, 138, 149
Young Men's Christian Association (YMCA), 134
Young Women's Hebrew Association (YWHA), 118, 134
Youth Aliya, 163
youth groups, 46–47, 50, 55–56, 138, 149

Youth members, Hitler, 169
YWHA. *See* Young Women's Hebrew Association

Zionism, 5–6, 7, 8, 9, 17, 42; American Jewish women and, 181, 182–83, 202n27; at Camp Cejwin, 208n7; Hebrew language and, 44; iconography of, 47; *Judaism as a Civilization* and, 54–63, 154; Kaplan, M., on, 54–63, 185, 192; Mizrachi movement in, 47, 56, 181, 202n23; mother-daughter relationships and, 100; movement in, 47, 49, 56, 184; Musher, H., Camp Modin and, 42–48; popularization of, 51; Revisionists, 92, 164, 165; youth groups within, 46–47, 55–56, 138, 149; "Zum Gali Gali," 40

Zionist Organization of America, 72

Zionist pioneers *(haluzim)*, 182–83

Zoological Gardens, 87

"Zum Gali Gali" (poem), 40

ABOUT THE AUTHOR

SHARON ANN MUSHER is Professor of History at Stockton University and author of *Democratic Art: The New Deal's Influence on American Culture*. She is a granddaughter of Hadassah Kaplan Musher and a great-granddaughter of Mordecai Kaplan.